An Introduction to the Philosophy of Art

In this book Richard Eldridge presents a clear and compact survey of
philosophical theories of the nature and significance of art. Drawing on
materials from classical and contemporary philosophy as well as from
literary theory and art criticism, he explores the representational,
expressive, and formal dimensions of art, and he argues that works of
art present their subject matter in ways that are of enduring cognitive,
moral, and social interest. His discussion, illustrated with a wealth of
examples, ranges over topics such as beauty, originality, imagination,
imitation, the ways in which we respond emotionally to art, and why we
argue about which works are good. His accessible study will be
invaluable to students and to all readers who are interested in the
relation between thought and art.

RICHARD ELDRIDGE is Professor of Philosophy at Swarthmore College,
Pennsylvania. His previous publications include *Beyond Representation:
Philosophy and Poetic Imagination* (1996), *The Persistence of Romanticism* (2001),
Stanley Cavell (2003), and many journal articles.

An Introduction to the Philosophy of Art

RICHARD ELDRIDGE
Swarthmore College, Pennsylvania

CAMBRIDGE
UNIVERSITY PRESS

CAMBRIDGE UNIVERSITY PRESS
Cambridge, New York, Melbourne, Madrid, Cape Town, Singapore,
São Paulo, Delhi, Dubai, Tokyo

Cambridge University Press
The Edinburgh Building, Cambridge CB2 8RU, UK

Published in the United States of America by Cambridge University Press, New York

www.cambridge.org
Information on this title: www.cambridge.org/9780521805216

First published 2003
Fourth printing 2006

A catalogue record for this publication is available from the British Library

Library of Congress Cataloguing in Publication data
Eldridge, Richard Thomas, 1953–
An introduction to the philosophy of art / Richard Eldridge.
    p.   cm.
Includes bibliographical references and index.
ISBN 0 521 80135 4 – ISBN 0 521 80521 X (paperback)
1. Arts – Philosophy.   2. Aesthetics.   I. Title.
BH39.E535   2003
111′.85 – dc21   2003043501

ISBN 978-0-521-80135-5 Hardback
ISBN 978-0-521-80521-6 Paperback

Transferred to digital printing 2009

Contents

Acknowledgments

Hilary Gaskin suggested this book project to me. She secured insightful readers for my first proposal, and their comments and her suggestions helped me to find what is, I hope, a useful scheme of topics.

I have been fortunate to have had gifted teachers of philosophy in general and of the philosophy of art in particular. First among the philosophers of art who were my teachers, I thank Ted Cohen. I am grateful to have had his influence on the substance of my thinking about art and on my philosophical sensibility and style. This influence was evident to me continuously as I wrote, including but well beyond the direct discussions of his work in these pages.

Over the last twenty years I have had detailed conversations on every topic in this book with members of the American Society for Aesthetics. I am pleased to count its members as my colleagues and friends. It is a wonderful society, with members ready both to argue and to listen, always with genuine enthusiasm for both the practices of art and for philosophical understanding. The talks I have heard, the essays I have read, and the conversations I have enjoyed are far too numerous to detail, even if I could recall all the dates and names, as I cannot. Together with particular thanks to Stanley Bates (also once my teacher), who has heard and discussed so many ASA talks with me, I must let an expression of gratitude to the Society cover my manifold debts to all its members.

Alex Neill read a late draft of chapter 8 and provided detailed and acute comments that led to improvements; any errors that remain are mine, not his.

The philosophers who have through their writing especially influenced my thinking are discussed in the text and listed in its footnotes. Among them, however, I especially note here Monroe Beardsley, my predecessor as a teacher of the philosophy of art at Swarthmore College. Though I have sometimes disagreed with him, I found much more agreement than disagreement between my thoughts and his as I worked through the topics of this book. I am pleased to think of myself as connected with him not only by philosophical interests, but also in sharing a common extended audience in the students of Swarthmore College. I have worked out many of my thoughts in this book in the course of teaching the philosophy of art to them and in the conversations that have accompanied that teaching. I am grateful to the college that Beardsley helped to shape and to the students who have graced my classes within it.

Joan Vandegrift read every sentence of this manuscript as it came into being chapter by chapter. She served as a patient scrutinizer of both the accessibility of the prose and the plausibility of the thought, as well as acting as a constant source of encouragement and support. I also thank Hannah Eldridge, Sarah Eldridge, and Jonathan Eldridge, who are now to my delight old enough to ask at the dinner table what I have been writing all day, to take an interest in the answers, and to offer thoughts of their own. Together Joan, Hannah, Sarah, and Jonathan have been this book's daily and first audience, and I thank them for encouraging me in their responses to think that it might find a wider audience as well.

1 The situation and tasks of the philosophy of art

Who needs a theory of art?

For almost all people in almost all cultures, either the fact (as in dance) or the product (as in painting) of some commanding performance that is both somehow significant and yet absorbing in its own right (rather than as an immediate instrument of knowledge or work) has raised strong emotions. The dramatic rhapsode Ion, in Plato's dialogue, reports that when in performance he looks "down at [the audience] from the stage above, I see them, every time, weeping, casting terrible glances, stricken with amazement at the deeds recounted."[1] Richard Wagner finds nothing less than salvation in the experience of art.

> I believe in God, Mozart and Beethoven...I believe in the Holy Spirit
> and the truth of the one, indivisible Art...I believe that through this
> Art all men are saved, and therefore each may die of hunger for Her...
> I believe...that true disciples of high Art will be transfigured in a
> heavenly veil of sun-drenched fragrance and sweet sound, and united for
> eternity with the divine fount of all Harmony. May mine be the sentence
> of grace! Amen![2]

Yet such commanding performances, their products, and their effects in their audiences are puzzling. They often seem to come into being, so Socrates claims, "not by skill [techne] but by lot divine."[3] Mysteriously, poets and dancers and composers "are not in their senses" when they do their work and "reason is no longer in [them]."[4] Whatever considerable thought is involved in making art, it seems to be not exactly the same kind

---

[1] Plato, *Ion*, trans. Lane Cooper, in Plato, *The Collected Dialogues*, ed. Edith Hamilton and Huntingdon Cairns (Princeton, NJ: Princeton University Press, 1961), 535e, p. 221.
[2] Richard Wagner, "Ein Ende in Paris," *Sämtliche Schriften* 1:135, cited in Daniel K. L. Chua, *Absolute Music and the Construction of Meaning* (Cambridge: Cambridge University Press, 1999).
[3] *ibid.*, 536d, p. 222.   [4] *ibid.*, 534a, 534b, p. 220.

of thought that is involved in solving standard problems of trade, manufacture, or knowledge. Different audiences, moreover, respond to very different performances and works. The temple of Athena on the Acropolis, John Coltrane's *Giant Steps*, Jane Austen's *Pride and Prejudice*, and J. M. W. Turner's *Sunrise with a Boat between Headlands* do not, on the face of it, seem to have very much to do with one another. They were produced in strikingly different media, for different audiences, in different cultural circumstances. Do they or can they or should they all matter to larger audiences in the same or similar ways? What about such further efforts as the body-performance art of Karen Finley or art student Matthew Hand's flipping and catching of a beer coaster 129 times in a row, a "human installation" intended to explore "our perceptions of success and our desire to be recognized as achievers"?[5] What about woven baskets, video art, and sports? Is art then a matter centrally of more or less local interests and effects? Perhaps art is, as the English philosopher Stuart Hampshire once remarked, "gratuitous,"[6] in being connected with no central problems or interests that attach to humanity as such. And yet, again, works of art – products of human performance with powerfully absorbing effects – are there in all human cultures, and some of them have seemed to some of their audiences to be as important in life as anything can be.

In response to these facts, it is natural – for a variety of reasons – to wish for a theory of art, or at least for some kind of organizing account of the nature and value of artistic performances and products. Aristotle, in one of the earliest systematic accounts of the nature and value of works of art in different media, seems to have been motivated by curiosity about his own experience. His remarks on tragic drama in the *Poetics* are presented as an account, developed by abstracting from his own experience of plays, of how the trick of engaging and moving an audience is done and of its value. He suggests that similar accounts can be developed for the other media of art. In contrast, Plato in the *Republic* seems to be motivated centrally by a combination of fear and envy of the seductive power of the arts, together with a wish to displace the narrative art of Homer in the job of orienting

---

[5] Matthew Hand's work, "part of his final studies in contemporary art" at Nottingham Trent University in the United Kingdom, is reported in David Cohen, "Pop Art," *Chronicle of Higher Education* 47, 41 (June 22, 2001), p. A8.

[6] Stuart Hampshire, "Logic and Appreciation," *World Review* (October 1952), reprinted in *Art and Philosophy*, ed. W. E. Kennick, 2nd edn (New York: St. Martin's Press, 1979), p. 652.

fourth-century BCE Greek culture. Barnett Newman's famous quip that "Aesthetics is for the artist as ornithology is for the birds"[7] suggests that active artists have all too often found definitions of art in the Platonic style to be irrelevant and obtuse at best and envious and hostile at worst. It is true that some philosophers and theorists of art – perhaps preeminently Plato, in his pursuit of stability and order, both personal and cultural, above all other values – have been motivated by envy and fear of art's contingency, of the wayward creativity of artists, and of the powerful but unruly emotions that works of art can induce. Yet it is equally difficult for work in the arts simply to go "its own way," for what that way is or ought to be is desperately unclear. Artists typically find themselves sometimes wanting to say something general about the meanings and values of their works, so as to cast these works as of more than merely personal interest, thence falling themselves into theory.

One might further hope that an account of the nature and value of art would provide principles of criticism that we might use to identify, understand, and evaluate art. If we could establish that all centrally successful works of art necessarily possessed some valuable and significant defining feature F, then, it seems, the task of criticism and the justification of critical judgments would be clear. The critic would need only to determine the presence or absence of F in a given work and its status and significance would be settled. In talking about such things as significant form, artistic expressiveness, having a critical perspective on culture, or originality, critics (and artists) seem often to draw on some such conception of a defining feature of art.

Yet a dilemma troubles this hope. Either the defining feature that is proposed seems abstract and "metaphysical" (significant form; productive of the harmonious free play of the cognitive faculties; artistically expressive), so that it could, with just a bit of background elucidation, be discerned in nearly anything, or the defining feature seems clear and specific enough (sonata form in music; triangular composition in painting; the unities of time, place, and action in drama), but inflexible, parochial, and insensitive to the genuine varieties of art. As a result, the prospects for working criticism that is clearly guided by a settled definition of art do not

---

[7] Barnett Newman, August 23, 1952. As a speaker at the Woodstock Art Conference in Woodstock, New York, according to Barnett Newman Chronology, archived at www.philamuseum-newman.org/artist/chronology.shtml

seem bright. At worst, for example in Heidegger's talk of art as "the truth of beings setting itself to work,"[8] the proposed definition seems both metaphysical and parochial, here part of Heidegger's own efforts (like Plato's in a different direction) to urge on us quite specific forms of art and life at the expense of others.

Hence theories of art seem likely not to be of immediate use in criticism. They are sometimes motivated by fear, envy, and a wish for cultural mastery. They can seem strikingly irrelevant, and even hostile, to the specific work of both artists and critics. Yet they also arise out of natural curiosity about the nature of a powerful experience, and they seem unavoidable in attempting to say anything – to oneself or to others – about the nature and value of that experience. What, then, are we really doing when we are theorizing about art?

Philosophy as articulation

Instead of thinking of the philosophy of art as issuing in a settled theory – the job of definition done once and for all – we might think of various conceptions of art as successful partial articulations of the nature, meaning, and value of a certain kind of experience. These articulations, albeit that each of them may be in one way or another one-sided, may help us to become clearer about several things that we do in making and responding to art, and they may help us to connect these artistic doings with other fundamental human interests: for example, cognitive interests, moral interests, and interests in self-display and performance. Iris Murdoch, writing about goodness in general in many domains, offers a useful characterization of how a metaphysical conception of the Good, including the Good of Art, can be, as she puts it, "deep."

> Our emotions and desires are as good as their objects and are constantly being modified in relation to their objects...There is no unattached will as a prime source of value. There is only the working of the human spirit in the morass of existence in which it always and at every moment finds itself immersed. We live in an "intermediate" world...We experience the *distance* which separates us from perfection and are led to place our idea of it in a figurative sense outside the turmoil of existent being...The

---

[8] Martin Heidegger, "The Origin of the Work of Art," trans. Albert Hofstadter, in *Poetry, Language, Thought* (New York: Harper & Row, 1971), p. 36.

Form of the Good ... may be seen as enlightening particular scenes and setting the specialized moral virtues and insights into their required particular patterns. This is how the phenomena are saved and the particulars redeemed, in this *light* ... This is metaphysics, which sets up a picture which it then offers as an appeal to us all to see if we cannot find just this in our deepest experience. The word "deep," or some such metaphor, will come in here as part of the essence of the appeal.[9]

As we live within the morass of existence – surrounded by and caught up in various artistic and critical practices; uncertain of the proper direction for personal and cultural development; and in all this feeling ourselves distinctively, yet variously, moved by different works that seem inchoately to intimate a fuller value that they embody only in part – we might hope at least to become clearer and more articulate about our experiences and commitments: more deep. We might hope to see the many phenomena of art "in a certain light." Carried out in this hope, the philosophy of art will itself then be a kind of neighbor to the activity of art itself, in that it will seek (without clear end) – albeit more via abstract thought, explicit comparison, and discursive reasoning – both clarity *about* and further realization *of* our natural interest in what is good within the morass of existence.

Art as a natural social practice

In beginning to try to be articulate about what in various works of art distinctly moves us, it is important to remember that making and responding to works of art, in many media, are *social* practices. It is inconceivable that these practices are the invention of any distinct individual. Any intention on the part of an individual to make art would be empty, were there no already going practices of artistic production and response. If there are no shared criteria for artistic success, then the word *art* cannot be used objectively, as a descriptive term. If I have only myself to go on, then "whatever is going to seem right to me [to call art] is right. And that only means that here we can't talk about 'right.'"[10]

---

[9] Iris Murdoch, *Metaphysics as a Guide to Morals* (Harmondsworth: Penguin, 1991), p. 507.

[10] Ludwig Wittgenstein, *Philosophical Investigations*, 3rd edn, trans. G. E. M. Anscombe (New York: Macmillan, 1958), §258, p. 92e; interjection added.

In fact works of art – objects and performances singled out for special attention to their significances fused with their forms – are present in all cultures (and not clearly among other animals). Children typically delight in the activities of play, gesture, and imitation out of which art making emerges. Learning to recognize and make representations – to pretend, to imagine, to draw – goes together with learning to talk. Succeeding in representation, in forming and articulating one's experience, involves a sense of accomplishment and liberation, overcoming frustration and difficulty.

Without offering any scientific account of the material basis of their emergence, Nietzsche usefully speculates in *The Birth of Tragedy* on the motives and experiences that may have figured in some of the historically earliest distinctively artistic makings. Artistic making, Nietzsche proposes, stems from the interfusion of two tendencies. The Apollinian tendency is the tendency to delight in representations, appearances, preeminently dreams at first, *as* appearances, including "the sensation that [the dream] is *mere appearance*,"[11] something I entertain that, however intense, does not immediately threaten or touch me. I can delight in contemplating these appearances as mine. The Dionysian tendency is the tendency, affiliated with intoxication, to abandon one's individuality so as both to reaffirm "the union between man and man" and to "celebrate . . . reconciliation" with otherwise "alienated, hostile, or subjugated" nature.[12] These tendencies emerge at first "as artistic energies which burst forth from nature herself, *without the mediation of the human artist*,"[13] as people find themselves both dreaming, talking, and representing, on the one hand, and engaging in rituals (as forms of "intoxicated reality"[14]), on the other. When these two tendencies are somehow merged – when the Dionysian orgies are taken over by the Greeks, who in them are aware of themselves *as* performing and representing (and not simply and utterly abandoning individuality), then art exists and "the destruction of the *principium individuationis* for the first time becomes an artistic phenomenon."[15] Individually and collectively, human beings come to *represent* their world and experiences not simply for the sake of private fantasy, not simply for the sake of instrumental communication about immediate threats and problems,

---

[11] Friedrich Nietzsche, *The Birth of Tragedy and the Case of Wagner*, trans. Walter Kaufmann (New York: Random House, 1967), p. 34.
[12] *ibid.*, p. 37.   [13] *ibid.*, p. 38.   [14] *ibid.*   [15] *ibid.*, p. 40.

but *as* an expression of a common selfhood, "as the complement and con-summation of [the] existence"[16] of human subjectivity, "seducing one to a continuation of life"[17] as a subject.

Whatever their accuracy in detail, Nietzsche's speculations are surely apt in proposing the emergence of artistic making and responding as cultural rather than distinctly individual, as more or less coeval with the emergence of distinctively human culture and self-conscious subjectivity as such, as driven by deep, transpersonal needs and tendencies, and as serving a significant interest of subjectivity in its own articulate life. Their aptness is confirmed both in the presence of art in all cultures and in the ontogenetic development of children into full self-conscious subjectivity in and through play, imitation, representation, expression, and art.

Action, gesture, and expressive freedom

Both personal development and cultural development are freighted with frustration and difficulty. The German poet Friedrich Hölderlin suggested in an early essay, in a line of thought both latent in Judaeo-Christian primeval history and later developed by Freud among others, that we become distinctly aware of ourselves as subjects only through transgres-sion. Our first awareness of our responsibility as subjects for what we do, Hölderlin proposes, appears through the experience of punishment: through coming actively to understand that one has done one thing when one could and ought to have done something else. "The origin of all our virtue occurs in evil."[18] Likewise, it is scarcely possible that we would be aware of ourselves as having and participating in culture, as opposed to mere persistent and automatic routine, were there no experiences of an-tagonism and negotiation over what is to be done: over how to cook or hunt or build, or how to sing, decorate the body, or form kinship rela-tions. Any distinctly human cultural life has alternatives, antagonisms, and taboos everywhere woven through it.

Suppose, then, that one finds oneself caught up in a difficult and ob-scure course of personal and cultural development. One might well seek

---

[16] *ibid.*, p. 43.   [17] *ibid.*

[18] Friedrich Hölderlin, "On the Law of Freedom," in *Essays and Letters on Theory*, ed. and trans. Thomas Pfau (Albany, NY: State University of New York Press), pp. 33–34 at p. 34.

full investment in a worthwhile activity of performance or making. One might seek to have the performance or product that results from this activity be one's own – concretely infused with one's particular sense of embodiment, attitude, interest, sensibility, and personal history – and yet also be meaningful to others, rather than emptily idiosyncratic. In this way, one might hope to have achieved through this activity, and in its performance or product, a widely ratifiable exemplification of the possibilities of human subjectivity and action as such, thereby establishing for oneself a more secure place as a subject amidst transgressions and antagonisms.

In different but closely related ways, both John Dewey and Theodor Adorno pose this – the achievement of the most concrete and fullest possibilities of human communicative action as such – as the task of art. For Dewey, "Art is the living and concrete proof that man is capable of restoring consciously, and thus on the plane of meaning, the union of sense, need, impulse, and action characteristic of the live creature."[19] For Adorno, art is "the image of what is beyond exchange";[20] that is, the genuine work of art, unlike the fungible manufactured commodity, is specifically and concretely meaningful, as the result (whether as performance or product) of the activity of discovering, through the formative exploration of materials, what can be done with paint, sound, stone, the body, words, or light.

This idea of the concrete and specifically meaningful product or performance, formed through explorative activity, makes it clear that the antithesis that is sometimes posed – is art a (physical) product or thing, or is it an (experienced) idea or meaning? – is a false one. Dewey usefully observes that "the actual work of art is what the product [whether performance or physical object] does with and in experience."[21] That is, there must be a product, whether performance or physical object or document or text, but in order to function as art this product must matter specifically and concretely within human experience. Even found art, supposing it to be successful, is experienced as the result of the selecting activity of governing intentionality, put before us in order to *be* experienced. Dewey

---

[19] John Dewey, *Art as Experience* (New York: Penguin Putnam, 1934), p. 25.

[20] Theodor W. Adorno, *Aesthetic Theory*, ed. and trans. Robert Hullot-Kentor (Minneapolis, MN: University of Minnesota Press, 1997), p. 83.

[21] Dewey, *Art as Experience*, p. 3.

distinguishes between the art product (the vehicle *of* the artistic experience) and the work of art (the vehicle *as* it is actually experienced), and
he argues that product and work are essentially interrelated.[22] Perhaps
the importance of the product-of-activity-as-experienced is what Heidegger had in mind in speaking of "the work-being of the work"[23] and of
how "the happening of truth is at work"[24] in it.

Dewey goes on to note that the media in which art activity can successfully occur – in which concretely and specifically communicative artistic
products can be achieved – are not fixed. "If art is the quality of an activity,
we cannot divide and subdivide it. We can only follow the differentiation
of the activity into different modes as it impinges on different materials
and employs different media."[25] *Some* materials and media, and some art
products or vehicles (whether performances or texts or physical things)
achieved through formative activity exercised in relation to materials and
media, are necessary in order for there to be art. But there is no way of
fixing in advance of explorative activity which materials and media can
be successfully explored in which ways. There is, rather, what Dewey calls
"a continuum, a spectrum"[26] of an inexhaustible variety of available media running roughly from the "automatic" or performance-related arts,
using "the mind-body of the artist as their medium," to the "shaping"
arts, issuing in a distinctly formed physical product.[27] Along this rough
and variable spectrum, which successes are available in which media – in
basket making or whistling, in painting, in song, or in the movies – is not
predictable in advance of explorative activity and aptly attentive experience. To suppose otherwise is to attempt – as Plato attempted – vainly to
erect a regnant classicism to constrain the efforts of human subjects to
achieve concretely and specifically meaningful actions and vehicles (performances or products) in an exemplary way.

It is useful here to compare works of art with gestures (which may
themselves be both components of fine art and independent vehicles of social art). Gestures (such as attentively following a conversation, or making
an unexpected gift, or brushing a crumb from someone's shoulder) stem
from intelligence addressing a problem in context. They are "saturated"
with intentionality, which has both an individual aspect and a cultural
background always present as part of its content. They essentially involve

---

[22] *ibid.*, p. 162.   [23] Heidegger, "Origin of the Work of Art," p. 55.
[24] *ibid.*, p. 60.   [25] Dewey, *Art as Experience*, p. 214.   [26] *ibid.*, p. 227.   [27] *ibid.*

bodily activity or doing one among a great variety of possible things in a specific way. They involve the balancing or adjustment of social relations. They carry a message or significance, but often one that it is difficult wholly to "decode" or paraphrase, involving as it does specific bodily posture and ongoing nuances of relationship. They exist, in different forms, in all cultures.

Works of art may, however, be unlike gestures in the range and depth of the claims that they exert upon our attention. Anyone unable to follow and to produce a certain range of gestures appropriate to occasions within a specific culture would be a kind of social idiot. Yet we do not have practices of formal training in social gestures, as we instead leave such matters to elders, normal family life, and the occasional etiquette book. There is no curriculum in gestures anything like the one that runs in the arts from the music lessons and art classes of young childhood into conservatories and schools of art. Some ability to participate in or to follow intelligently the activities of making and understanding art, including forms of this activity outside one's immediate cultural context, and some interest in doing so are typically thought to be a mark of an educated person. One who lacked this ability and interest altogether would be thought to be a philistine or in some way not deep. The study and practice of painting or music or literature is thought to be a fit central occupation for some lives, whereas the study and practice of manners is a simple requirement of ordinary sociality. To be sure, these differences may not be sharp everywhere. A certain cosmopolitanism in manners may require certain forms of study, and there may be highly ritualized patterns of social gesture, such as Japanese tea ceremonies, which themselves verge on fine art. Yet broadly speaking these differences in range and depth of claim on us seem to be widely accepted. For all their importance, manners seem – it seems natural to say – in their specific patterns to be significantly relative to specific cultures.

In contrast, works of art, though they vary widely in specific form both across and within cultures, seem somehow more "objective" in the claims they make on us. If this is indeed so, then it must be because, as Richard Wollheim elegantly puts it, the making and understanding of art somehow involve "the realization of deep, indeed the very deepest, properties of human nature."[28] It is, however, desperately difficult to say, clearly and

---

[28] Richard Wollheim, *Art and its Objects*, 2nd edn (Cambridge: Cambridge University Press, 1980), p. 234.

convincingly, both what these deep properties or interests of human nature that are realized in art might be and how, specifically, different works achieve this realization. The variety of works of art must be faced. Perhaps there is no single central function or functions that different works of art variously fulfill, so that they are in the end thoroughly like gestures and manners in being relative to culture and individual taste. Further, many of the works that it seems reasonable to regard as art are not particularly successful: they are preparatory studies, or failed attempts, or children's first efforts to take up a region of practice. Not everything that it is reasonable to call art will clearly and distinctly fulfill a central function. Any function that works of art might be taken centrally to aim at fulfilling (with some of them actually fulfilling it in an exemplary way) must both accommodate present varieties of art and leave room for further innovative explorations of new media.

Despite these real difficulties, however, many works of art – and not always either from one's own culture or to one's individual immediate liking – seem to make a claim on us. We think it worthwhile to teach them formally, to train people formally in the activities of making and understanding such works, and to encourage further explorations of possibilities of artistic success. Those who achieve artistic success can sometimes strike us, as Stanley Cavell puts it in describing an ambition of philosophical writing, as having achieved "freedom of consciousness, the beginning of freedom . . . freedom of language, having the run of it, as if successfully claimed from it, as of a birthright."[29] It has already been suggested that such an achievement involves a widely ratifiable exemplification of the possibilities of human subjectivity and action as such, or the restoration of "the union of sense, need, impulse, and action characteristic of the live creature" (Dewey), or an embodiment of "the image of what is beyond exchange" (Adorno). A common theme in these summary formulas is that artistic activity aims at the achievement of *expressive freedom*:[30] originality blended with sense; unburdening and clarification blended with representation.

Whatever their interest, such summary formulas nonetheless raise considerable problems. Exactly what is meant by *expressive freedom* or

[29] Stanley Cavell, *This New yet Unapproachable America: Lectures after Emerson after Wittgenstein* (Albuquerque, NM: Living Batch Press, 1989), p. 55.
[30] For a partial elucidation of the notion of expressive freedom, see Richard Eldridge, *Leading a Human Life: Wittgenstein, Intentionality, and Romanticism* (Chicago, IL: University of Chicago Press, 1997), *passim* but especially pp. 6–7 and 32–33.

original sense[31] or *what is beyond exchange* or *unburdening* or *the union of sense, need, impulse, and action*? How are such ends achievable through different kinds of artistic formative activity? Why does the achievement of such ends matter? Is their achievement genuinely a deep human interest? Can such achievements be accomplished in ways that admit of and even command wide, perhaps universal, endorsement among attentive audiences? Or are they always to some degree partial and parochial?

These questions and related ones have been central to the most fruitful work in the philosophy of art. In treating them, the philosophy of art must draw all at once on the philosophy of mind, social theory, metaphysics, ethics, and the history and criticism of particular arts. Accounts of specific artistic achievements in specific styles must be interwoven with accounts of cultural developments, in order to show how specific achievements may advance deep and general human interests. Nor does work in the philosophy of art leave work in the philosophy of mind, social theory, metaphysics, ethics, and criticism unaltered. Given that engagements with some specific forms of art is a normal and significant human activity, theories of mind should take account of the powers and interests that are embodied in these engagements, just as the philosophy of art must take account of how human powers and interests are engaged in other domains.

Schiller on art, life, and modernity

Friedrich Schiller's philosophy of art offers a particularly clear illustration of the difficulties involved in addressing the problems of human powers and interests in art and in other regions of life. Schiller notoriously contradicts himself in *Letters on the Aesthetic Education of Man*. He argues first that engagement with artistic achievements is instrumental to the further ends of political freedom and individual moral autonomy. "If we are to solve [the] political problem [of freedom] in practice, [then] follow the path of aesthetics, since it is through Beauty that we arrive at freedom."[32] "There

---

[31] On original sense as Kant and Wordsworth theorized about it, see Timothy Gould, "The Audience of Originality: Kant and Wordsworth on the Reception of Genius," in *Essays in Kant's Aesthetics*, ed. Ted Cohen and Paul Guyer (Chicago, IL: University of Chicago Press, 1982), pp. 179–93.

[32] Friedrich Schiller, *On the Aesthetic Education of Man, in a Series of Letters*, trans. Reginald Snell (London: Routledge & Kegan Paul, 1954), second letter, p. 27.

is no other way to make the sensuous man rational than by first making him aesthetic."[33] But Schiller also argues, second, that artistic activity is an end itself, in both incorporating and transcending mere morality and politics.

> Beauty alone can confer on [Man] a *social character*. Taste alone brings harmony into society, because it establishes harmony in the individual. All other forms of perception divide a man, because they are exclusively based either on the sensuous or on the intellectual part of his being; only the perception of the Beautiful makes something whole of him, because both his [sensuous and rational–moral] natures must accord with it...Beauty alone makes all the world happy, and every being forgets its limitations as long as it experiences her enchantment.[34]

This contradiction is not a simple mistake on Schiller's part. Instead it displays the difficulty of establishing the usefulness and significance of art, in the relation of artistic activity to central, shared human problems, on the one hand, and of respecting the autonomy of art, including its ability to deepen and transform our conceptions of our problems and interests, on the other.

Schiller's sense of art's divided roles – as instrument for social–moral good and as end in itself – further embodies his wider sense of the nature of human culture, particularly of human culture in modernity. There is no human culture without some distinct social roles and some division of labor. Peoples in different places develop different customs and sets of social roles. Social roles and the division of labor develop as cognitive and technological mastery of nature increase, in ways that do not happen in other species. Human life becomes increasingly dominated by what is done within one or another cultural role, rather than by naked necessities of immediate survival. As this development takes place, those occupying distinct social roles can become more opaque to one another. Manufacturers and those predominantly bound up in immediate social reproduction (historically, typically women) can misunderstand and scorn one another, as can manual workers and intellectuals, farmers and warriors, traders and politicians. At the same time, however, as social roles increase in number, complexity, and opacity to one another, social boundaries also become to some extent more permeable. As the requirements for playing a

---

[33] *ibid.*, twenty-third letter, p. 108.   [34] *ibid.*, twenty-seventh letter, pp. 138–39.

distinct social role come to depend more on knowledge and less on immediate biological or familial inheritance, people come to be able to take up
new social roles somewhat more freely, though severe constraints stemming from inequalities in background social, economic, and cognitive
capital remain in place.

The result of all these developments, in Schiller's perception, is a combination of development toward civilization and what he calls *antagonism*:
a mixture of mutual opacity, envy, vanity, and contestation that pervades
the playing of developed social roles. Development and antagonism set for
us a problem to be solved, the problem of the free and fit, reharmonized
development of culture, so as to lift ourselves out of mere one-sidedness
and vanity.

> There was no other way of developing the manifold capacities of Man
> than by placing them in opposition to each other. This antagonism of
> powers is the great instrument of culture, but it is only the instrument;
> for as long as it persists, we are only on the way towards culture.
>
> ...Partiality in the exercise of powers, it is true, inevitably leads the
> individual into error, but the race to truth. Only by concentrating the
> whole energy of our spirit in one single focus, and drawing together our
> whole being into one single power, do we attach wings, so to say, to this
> individual power and lead it artificially beyond the bounds which Nature
> seems to have imposed upon it.[35]

Schiller imagines, almost certainly erroneously, that once upon a time
Greek life formed a beautiful whole in which religion, art, ethical life, politics, and economic life were all one. "At that time, in that lovely awakening
of the intellectual powers, the senses and the mind had still no strictly
separate individualities, for no dissension had yet constrained them to
make hostile partition with each other and determine their boundaries."[36]

---

[35] *ibid.*, sixth letter, pp. 43, 44. Schiller's remarks on antagonism as both the instrument of civilization and as a problem to be overcome are a transcription of Kant's
remarks on antagonism in his essay "Idea for a Universal History from a Cosmopolitan Point of View," in Immanuel Kant, *On History*, ed. Lewis White Beck (Indianapolis,
IN: Bobbs-Merrill, 1963), pp. 11–26, especially pp. 15–16. Compare also Schiller's "On
Naïve and Sentimental Poetry," trans. Daniel O. Dahlstrom, in Friedrich Schiller,
Essays, ed. Walter Hinderer and Daniel O. Dahlstrom (New York: Continuum, 1993),
pp. 179–260, especially pp. 249–50.

[36] *ibid.*, sixth letter, p. 38.

Abstract thought and sensation, art and religion, politics and farming were all, Schiller imagines, in harmony with one another. In work, in civic life, in religion, in science, and in art the Greeks could, Schiller supposes, exchange roles and understand one another.

Schiller's fantasy seems very likely to underestimate genuine divisions and antagonisms that were present in Greek life. Yet as a fantasy it has two further functions. First, it offers a diagnosis of our current situation, problems, and prospects. Selfhood within culture, in involving taking up one among a number of opposed, available social roles, is experienced as a problem. One comes to be unsure of the meaning or significance of what one does and who one is. One's actions feel motivated by coercion – either immediate or stemming from the necessity of instrumentally satisfying desires in oneself that are mysterious – rather than by expressive intelligence. Or, as Schiller describes modern life,

> That zoophyte character of the Greek states, where every individual
> enjoyed an independent life and, when need arose, could become a
> whole in himself, now gave place to an ingenious piece of machinery, in
> which out of the botching together of a vast number of lifeless parts a
> collective mechanical life results. State and Church, law and customs,
> were now torn asunder; enjoyment was separated from labour, means
> from ends, effort from reward. Eternally chained to only one single little
> fragment of the whole Man himself grew to be only a fragment; with
> the monotonous noise of the wheel he drives everlastingly in his ears, he
> never develops the harmony of his being, and instead of imprinting
> humanity upon his nature he becomes merely the imprint of his
> occupation, of his science.[37]

However it may have been with the Greeks, this diagnosis of the experience of selfhood and action in modern culture as an experience of fragmentariness, lack of harmony, and lack of evident significance is likely to resonate with many. Given the nature of modern divided labor, it is very difficult to see how this experience might be transformed.

Second, Schiller's fantasy of Greek life leads him to identify art – particularly art as manifested in Greek sculpture and epic, now to be taken up by us as a model, in relation to modern needs – as the proper

---

[37] ibid., p. 40.

instrument of the transformation of experience and the achievement of meaningfulness.

> We must be at liberty to restore by means of a higher Art this wholeness in our nature which Art has destroyed...Humanity has lost its dignity, but Art has rescued and preserved it in significant stone; Truth lives on in the midst of deception, and from the copy the original will once again be restored.[38]

This too may be a fantasy. Schiller is himself all too aware of the depth of the

> rather remarkable antagonism between people in a century in the process of civilizing itself. Because this antagonism is radical and is based on the internal form of the mind, it establishes a breach among people much worse than the occasional conflict of interests could ever produce. It is an antagonism that robs the artist and poet of any hope of pleasing and touching people generally, which remains, after all, his task.[39]

If there is deep and standing rather than occasional conflict of interest, arising out of divided social roles, and if the artist has no hope of pleasing universally, then perhaps art cannot do its job, and perhaps fully significant action and selfhood are not quite possible.

Schiller's fantasy about art nonetheless continues to be felt by many people in modern culture, though almost surely not by everyone. Though earlier cultures were perhaps more unified in certain respects than modern western culture, this fantasy may nonetheless have been distinctly felt by those who in those cultures devoted themselves to painting, drama, lyric, epic, or dance. They were surely aware of themselves as doing something quite different from what many or most people did in the courses of economic and social life. The idea or hope or fantasy that in and through artistic activity one might achieve fully significant action and selfhood – achieve a kind of restoration and wholeness of sensation, meaning, and activity in the face of present dividing antagonisms – has deep sociopsychological roots, ancient and modern, and it does not easily go away. Yet the social differences that provoke this idea and make it seem necessary

---

[38] *ibid.*, sixth letter, p. 45; ninth letter, p. 52.
[39] Schiller, "On Naïve and Sentimental Poetry," p. 249.

do not go away either. The hoped-for redemption never quite comes completely, and some remain untouched by or even hostile to each particular form of artistic activity.

Identification versus elucidation

In this situation the task of the philosophy of art involves balancing the *identification* of distinct works of art against the critical *elucidation* of the function and significance of art, as they are displayed in particular cases. Theories of art that focus preeminently on the task of *identification* include Hume's theory of expert taste, institutional theories of art such as that of George Dickie, and so-called historical theories of art such as that of Jerrold Levinson. Theories of this kind tend at bottom to have more empiricist and materialist epistemological and metaphysical commitments. The central task of theory is taken to be that of *picking out* from among the physical things in the universe the wide variety of things that count as art. Hume appeals to the judgment of expert critics to do this job;[40] Dickie invokes the institutions of art and the idea of presentation to an art world;[41] Levinson appeals to presentation of an object at time *t* under the intention that it be regarded "in any way (or ways) artworks existing prior to *t* are or were correctly (or standardly) regarded."[42]

These different but related definitions of art have considerable merits. They address the question of identification directly and sharply. They specify that things are works of art not, as it were, "in themselves," but rather only in relation to human sensibility and to historical human practices and institutions. They accommodate well the enormous variety of things that are commonly counted as art. Yet they also have an air of both circularity and disappointment. How can expert judges, relevant institutions, and appropriate manners of regard be specified without *first* specifying the nature of the works to which attention is to be directed? As Monroe Beardsley usefully objects to Levinson, if "correctly (or standardly)" in

---

[40] See David Hume, "Of the Standard of Taste," in *The Philosophy of Art: Readings Ancient and Modern*, ed. Alex Neill and Aaron Ridley (New York: McGraw-Hill, 1995), pp. 255–68. Hume's theory of taste will be discussed at length in chapter 7 below.

[41] See George Dickie, *Art and the Aesthetic* (Ithaca, NY: Cornell University Press, 1974) and his *The Art Circle* (New York: Haven Publications, 1984).

[42] Jerrold Levinson, "Defining Art Historically," *British Journal of Aesthetics* 19 (1979); reprinted in *Philosophy of Art*, ed. Neill and Ridley, pp. 223–39 at p. 230.

Levinson's definition is to mean more than merely "habitually" (since there may be bad habits of regard), then something more will have to be said about the values and functions that correct regard discerns.[43] If we cannot say how and why we are supposed to regard works in order correctly to discern their value, then reference to regarding-as-art will seem both circular and empty. Theories that highlight the variety of objects that are historically identified as art, without offering general accounts of the value and meaning of art, run risks of triviality and emptiness. Similar objections can be made against both Hume's and Dickie's theories of artistic identification.

Levinson is, however, well aware of these problems. For him, any critical elucidation of *the* functions and values of art will be both dogmatically inflexible, in the face of the legitimate varieties of art, and insensitive to the details of the historical evolution of artistic practices. Hence Levinson frankly concedes that his theory "does *not* explain the sense of 'artwork'";[44] that is, he offers only a theory of identification procedures, not a theory of *the* value and significance of works of art in general, for works of art have many, incommensurable values, significances, and historical modes of appearance. "There are," he rightly observes, "no clear limits to the sorts of things people may seriously intend us to regard-as-a-work-of-art."[45] This is not a purely sociological or "external" theory of art, since success and failure in presentation for such regarding *are* possible, but contrary to centrally functional theories of art there is no single account on offer of what all works of art should or must do, of what values or significances they should or must carry. Historically, art is too variable for that. Despite the airs of circularity and disappointment that they carry, it is impossible not to feel the force of such stances. Art *is* for us an evolving and unsettled matter.

Theories of art that focus preeminently on the task of *elucidation* include such widely differing theories as Aristotle's theory of artistic representation, Kant's theory of artistic value, and R. G. Collingwood's theory of expression. These theories all propose to tell us in some detail how and why art does and should matter for us. They undertake to specify a function for art in solving a fundamental human problem or in

---

[43] Monroe C. Beardsley, *Aesthetics: Problems in the Philosophy of Criticism*, 2nd edn (Indianapolis, IN: Hackett, 1981), p. xxii.
[44] Levinson, "Defining Art Historically," p. 236.   [45] *ibid.*, p. 239.

answering to a fundamental human interest. In thus focusing primarily on human problems and interests, described in terms that are not immediately physical, such theories tend at bottom to have more rationalist and functionalist epistemological and metaphysical commitments. For each of them, making and attending to art are centrally important to getting on well with human life: for example, to knowing what human life is like and to training the passions, to achieving a kind of felt harmony with one's natural and cultural worlds, and to overcoming repressiveness and rigidity of mind and action.

These different but more value- and function-oriented theories of art likewise have considerable merits. They offer articulate accounts of how and why art matters for us. Thus they immediately suggest why we do and should have formal practices of training in the arts and their criticism. They offer prospects of engaging in the practices of art and criticism with more alert critical awareness of what these enterprises are all about. Yet they too run considerable risks. They tend toward somewhat speculative, not clearly empirically verifiable, accounts of human interests. Not everyone will immediately feel the presence and force of the supposedly "deep" human problems that art is taken to address. When they attend to individual works of art at all, they tend to focus on a narrower range of centrally exemplary cases, ignoring the great variety of things that have been historically regarded as art. Hence in both their accounts of art's functions and in the identifications that flow from them, they tend toward one-sidedness and tendentiousness. Critical power is purchased at the cost of flexibility.

Kant and Collingwood, in particular, each have some awareness of this problem. Hence they seek to make their functional definitions of art abstract enough to accommodate significant differences in successful works, and they each resist limiting success in artistic making to any fixed media of art. As their definitions become more abstract and flexible, however, they tend sometimes to lose the very critical and elucidatory content that they were intended to provide. Moreover, the application of such definitions seems to require the very kind of creative, perceptive critical work that is carried out by the kinds of experts, representatives of institutions, and historical varieties of audiences that are highlighted in centrally identificatory theories of art. Yet despite their risks of one-sidedness and tendentiousness, it is impossible too not to feel the force of such stances. Art, and especially art as it is instanced in some central cases, does seem centrally to matter for us, in ways about which we might hope to become more articulate.

The tension between accounts of art that focus on identification of the varieties of art and those that focus on the critical elucidation of art's functions and values is a real one. It reflects the deeper tension in human life generally, and especially in modernity, between the idea that humanity has a function,[46] or at least a set of human interests to be fully realized in a "free" human cultural life that is richer and more self-conscious than are the lives of other animals, and the idea that human beings are nothing more than elements of a meaningless, functionless physical nature, wherein accommodation, coping, and compromise are the best outcomes for which they can hope. As Dewey penetratingly remarks,

> The opposition that now exists between the spiritual and ideal elements
> of our historic heritage [stemming from Greek teleology and medieval
> Christian theology] and the structure of physical nature that is disclosed
> by [modern, physical] science, is the ultimate source of the dualisms
> formulated by philosophy since Descartes and Locke. These formulations
> in turn reflect a conflict that is everywhere active in modern civilization.
> From one point of view the problem of recovering an organic place for
> art in civilization is like the problem of reorganizing our heritage from
> the past and the insights of present knowledge into a coherent and
> integrated imaginative union.[47]

Both art and the theory of art are everywhere contested within this pervasive opposition and conflict. What counts as artistic success is unclear. Human interests in general are not coherently and transparently realized in social life. New media can be explored in the attempt to fulfill the functions of art, and the functions of art can themselves be rearticulated, in the effort to bring them into clearer alignment and affiliation with the pursuit of other interests. Hence the philosophy of art – involving both its identification and the elucidation of art's function and value – is

---

[46] The classical locus for the ineliminability of the idea that human consciousness, including openness to the force of reasons, has the function of determining human life and culture as a free product in accordance with reason is Kant's discussion of the fact of reason in the *Critique of Practical Reason*. For a rehearsal of Kant's development of this idea, see Richard Eldridge, *The Persistence of Romanticism: Essays in Philosophy and Literature* (Cambridge: Cambridge University Press, 2001), pp. 13–19.

[47] Dewey, *Art as Experience*, p. 338.

likewise contested and unclear. While it is logically possible to have both agreement in the application of the term *art* but disagreement about the functions of art *and* agreement about functions but disagreement about application, in fact disagreements about both application (identification) and functions (meaning) are pervasive, and this is because of the background in (modern) social life of pervasive unclarity about and contestation of common human functions, problems, and interests in general.

What may we hope for from the philosophy of art?

This social situation of art and of the theory of art explains both the rise, fall, and yet continuing appeal of so-called antiessentialism about art and the current largely antagonistic relations between the normative philosophy of art and "advanced" (poststructuralist and materialist) critical theory and practice. Beginning in the late 1950s, inspired by a certain reading (arguably a misreading) of Wittgenstein,[48] Morris Weitz[49] and W. E. Kennick,[50] among others, argued that art has no essence, fulfills no single function, solves no single common problem. Yet we know perfectly well, they further claimed, which individual works count as art. Art and criticism have neither need of nor use for theory. ("Aesthetics is for the artist as ornithology is for the birds.") Maurice Mandelbaum replied that it might be possible to formulate an abstract, relational, functional generalization about the nature and value of art,[51] and Guy Sircello added that in proposing various defining functions for art theorists were – reasonably but contestably – expressing their particular senses of central human problems to which art might answer. Here the stance of Weitz and Kennick embodies a certain conservatism about high culture coupled with respect

---

[48] For a general survey of so-called Wittgensteinian antiessentialism, see Richard Eldridge, "Problems and Prospects of Wittgensteinian Aesthetics," *Journal of Aesthetics and Art Criticism* 45, 3 (spring 1987), pp. 251–61.

[49] See Morris Weitz, "The Role of Theory in Aesthetics," *Journal of Aesthetics and Art Criticism* 15 (1956); reprinted in *Philosophy of Art*, ed. Neill and Ridley, pp. 183–92.

[50] See W. E. Kennick, "Does Traditional Aesthetics Rest on a Mistake?," *Mind* 67, 267 (July 1958); reprinted in *Aesthetics Today*, ed. M. Philipson and P. J. Gudel (New York: New American Library, 1980), pp. 459–76.

[51] Maurice Mandelbaum, "Family Resemblances and Generalization Concerning the Arts," *American Philosophical Quarterly* 2, 3 (1965); reprinted in *Philosophy of Art*, ed. Neill and Ridley, pp. 193–201.

for art's diversities and suspicion of the tendentiousness of theory, while Mandelbaum and Sircello are attracted by functional explanations of art, yet tentative about asserting any one explanation definitely. In retrospect, we can now recognize this debate as a reflection of the social situation of art, against the background of unclarity about and contestation of functions in human life more generally.

Contemporary advanced "materialist" criticism of art and literature, stemming from such late Marxist figures as Louis Althusser, Pierre Macherey, Pierre Bourdieu, and Fredric Jameson, emphasizes that all so-called works of art are produced by people with certain material, social backgrounds (certain places in a network of economic and cultural capital) and for audiences with certain material, social backgrounds and consequent expectations about art.[52] Since the material social world is always saturated with multiple inequalities in economic and cultural capital (worker vs. owner; white collar vs. industrial worker; modern individualist vs. traditionalist, etc.), no work of art can "succeed" for everyone, and the efforts of traditional art theory to specify a central function for art in general for people in general are misbegotten. The best we can aspire to is "critical" self-consciousness about who produces what for whom. At some level of description, such accounts are surely illuminating. Against this kind of cultural materialist theory and criticism, more traditional, normative theorists object that there are unpredictable works that transcend standard class affiliations, transfiguring the experience and perception of significantly diverse audiences. In Tom Huhn's apt phrase, there is sometimes an "opacity of success"[53] in the arts – an unpredictable success in realizing artistic value in a way that holds diverse attentions – that cultural materialist theorists such as Bourdieu sometimes neglect or underarticulate. Why should we not theorize about that (including theorizing about cultural conditions under which various achievements of this kind are managed)? Here, too, we can recognize in this debate the social situation of art and its theory. Art seems both to have a function, sometimes exemplarily realized, in relation to deep human problems and interests, and it

---

[52] For a general survey of this kind of late or post-Marxist work, see Richard Eldridge, "Althusser and Ideological Criticism of the Arts," in *Explanation and Value in the Arts*, ed. Ivan Gaskell and Salim Kemal (Cambridge: Cambridge University Press, 1993), pp. 190–214; reprinted in Eldridge, *Persistence of Romanticism*, pp. 165–88.

[53] Tom Huhn, book review, *"The Field of Cultural Production: Essays on Art and Literature* by Pierre Bourdieu," *Journal of Aesthetics and Art Criticism* 54, 1 (winter 1996), p. 88B.

seems also in every particular case to be by and for particular makers and audiences, responding to problems and pressures that are not universal.

In this situation, reasonable argument about both the elucidatory definition of art and the identification of particular works remains possible. Yet argument here must remain motivated not by any methodological assurance of conclusiveness, but rather by the hope of agreement, to be achieved in and through arriving at a more transparent, shared culture, in which it is clearer than it is now which practices fulfill which functions and serve which reasonable interests. The hope of agreement is here supported by partial successes in the identification of particular works, in critical commentary on them, and in the elucidation of the nature of art. With regard to some particular works, there are deep, unpredictable and yet to some extent articulable resonances of response among widely varying audiences, and criticism and theory have managed in many cases to arrive at compelling articulations of artistic achievements, in particular and in general, even where disagreements also remain. A standing human interest in art, as that interest has been realized in some exemplary cases, has been given some articulate shape by criticism in conjunction with the theory of art.

Roger Scruton has suggested that our response to art involves the engagement of what he calls our sense of the appropriate. This sense can come into play throughout human life: in social relations, in games, in business, in sports, and in jokes, among many other places, as we are struck by the internal coherence of a performance and its aptness to an occasion. Scruton suggests that it is especially freely and powerfully engaged by art. "Our sense of the appropriate, once aroused, entirely penetrates our response to art, dominating not only our awareness of form, diction, structure, and harmony, but also our interest in action, character, and feeling."[54]

The most compelling and significant developed philosophies of art – the theories of imitation and representation, of form and artistic beauty, and of expression – that are the subjects of the next three chapters – can best be understood as focusing on various aspects of the artistic achievement of appropriateness. Representation, form, and expression are all, one might say, interrelated *aspects* of artistic achievement. (Note that Scruton claims that the sense of the appropriate includes awareness all at once of

---

[54] Roger Scruton, *Art and Imagination* (London: Routledge & Kegan Paul, 1982), p. 248.

what is represented [action and character], of form, and of what is expressed [feeling].) The major theorists of representation, form, and expression – Aristotle, Kant, and Collingwood, and their contemporary inheritors and revisers, such as Walton, Beardsley, and Goodman – each highlight for us a particular dimension of the artistic engagement of our sense of appropriateness, and, as we shall see, in doing so they further begin to acknowledge the interrelations of these dimensions of artistic success. Without representation and expression, in some sense, there is no artistic form, but only decoration; without artistic form, there is no artistic representation or artistic expression, but only declamation and psychic discharge. By following closely and critically major theories of artistic representation, artistic form, and artistic expression, and then by considering artistic originality, critical understanding, evaluation, emotional response, art and morality, and art and society in the light of these theories, we may hope to make some progress in becoming more articulate about the nature of art and its distinctive roles in human life. To recall Murdoch's picture of metaphysics, we might hope from within the morass of existence in which we find ourselves immersed to set up a picture of the nature and function of art as a kind of appeal – to ourselves above all, and without any assured termination – to see if we can find just *this* in our deepest experiences of art and of ourselves.

2 Representation, imitation, and resemblance

Representation and aboutness

Art products and performances seem in some rough sense to be *about* something. Even when they do not carry any explicitly statable single message, they nonetheless invite and focus thought. Marcel Duchamp's ready-mades, Sol Le Witt's constructions, Vito Acconci's performance pieces, and Louise Lawler's conceptual art are all put forward, in Duchamp's phrase, "at the service of the mind,"[1] in that they are intended to set up in an audience a line of thinking about a subject matter. Most literary works clearly undertake to describe an action, situation, or event. Works of dance typically have a narrative-developmental structure, and even works of architecture seem both to proceed from and to invite thoughts about how space is and ought to be experienced and used. Works of textless pure or absolute music have beginnings, middles, and ends that have seemed to many listeners to model or share shapes with broad patterns of human action.[2] The abstract painter Hans Hoffmann in teaching used to have his students begin by putting a blue brush stroke on a bare canvas and then asking them to think about its relations to the space "behind," "in front of," and around it, as though the mere stroke were already a means of

---

[1] Marcel Duchamp, "Interview with James Johnson Sweeney," in "Eleven Europeans in America," *Bulletin of the Museum of Modern Art* (New York) 12, 4–5 (1946), pp. 19–21; reprinted in *Theories of Modern Art*, ed. Herschel B. Chipp (Berkeley: University of California Press, 1968), p. 394.

[2] See for example Fred Everett Maus, "Music as Drama," in *Music and Meaning*, ed. Jenefer Robinson (Ithaca, NY: Cornell University Press, 1997), pp. 105–30, and Anthony Newcomb, "Action and Agency in Mahler's Ninth Symphony, Second Movement," in *Music and Meaning*, ed. J. Robinson, pp. 131–53. The fullest treatment of how music came historically to be understood as being "about" something, but indefinitely, is in Carl Dahlhaus, *The Idea of Absolute Music*, trans. Roger Lustig (Chicago, IL: University of Chicago Press, 1989).

incipiently presenting a three-dimensional world on a two-dimensional surface.

Yet these facts about presentation of a subject matter in the arts raise considerable problems. *How* is representation achieved in various media? Does representation centrally involve any likeness or resemblance (as seems to be the case in much visual depiction) between representer and represented, or does it involve centrally the manipulation of syntactically structured conventional codes (as in linguistic representation)? Is the same sense of "representation" (with different means of achieving it) involved in different media of art? Does the value of a work of art depend upon what it represents, and if so, how? Is representationality even necessary for art? Is it sufficient?

In any straightforward sense of "represents," representationality is clearly present in many regions of practice and is not a sufficient condition for art. A legislator represents constituents, and a bottle cap may represent the position of a player in a model of a play to be run in a game, yet neither the legislator nor the bottle cap is art. In the more restricted sense of "(visual) depiction," representationality is clearly not necessary for art. Salman Rushdie's *Midnight's Children* presents many events, but it does not visually depict them, in that one cannot see the events presented in the words on the page, nor do works of music make subject matter available to vision. Nonetheless, without "aboutness" of some kind, there seems to be no art, but only empty decorativeness.

Aristotle on imitation

Aristotle in the *Poetics* helps us to think about how and why this might be so. In developing his theory of the nature and value of tragic drama, Aristotle begins by distinguishing three forms of human, conceptually formed activity and their associated products. *Theoria*, the activity of theoretical knowing, has as its product knowledge (*episteme*), that is, the explicit presentation of general relations among kinds of things. For example, all triangles in Euclidean geometry are such that the sum of their angles is identical to a straight line. *Praxis*, the activity of doing, has as its product objects or alterations of objects in order to satisfy desires: for example, the building of a bridge or the managing of the affairs of a city. *Poesis*, the activity of nonoriginal or imitative making, has as its product *imitations* (*mimemata*) or presentations of the universal *in* the particular: for example, what it is like to recognize someone from the scar on his thigh (as Odysseus's nurse Euryclea feels it). Though these are all natural and conceptually informed intelligent human activities, they are carried out in pursuit of distinct ends. *Theoria* aims at knowledge or understanding (of the general), *praxis* aims at well-being (*eudaimonia*) as the satisfaction of reasonable desires, and *poesis* aims at the achievement of a felt sense or understanding of rational finitude: of what it is like to be an embodied rational creature, a human being, in this situation or that.

Imitations, Aristotle goes on to argue, may then "differ from one another in three ways, by using for the representation (i) different media, (ii) different objects [subject matter], or (iii) a manner [point of view] that is different and not the same."[3] Of these three differences, the third is important but has received little notice in the critical literature. Aristotle has in mind first of all the distinction already noted in Plato's *Republic* between narrative and dramatic (impersonative) presentation of an action. That is, one can describe (as either an omniscient narrator or a distinctly situated, specific first-person narrator) what people do, or one can simply present them, speaking their own words and doing their own doings, or one can mix narrative and dramatic presentation.[4] What is often not noticed, however, is that Aristotle's account of *manner* of presentation extends naturally to other media of art. A painting offers to an audience a point of view: apples on a table or a red patch hovering over a yellow one as seen from *just here*. Works of sculpture and architecture offer multiple points of view, as one moves around or through them. One follows a dance from a certain orienting vantage point toward the dancers' bodies and motions. Even in attending to a work of purely instrumental music, one must hear from a spatial point in relation to the sound source, and one must follow the development of statement, departure, tension, and return from that location. As Paul Woodruff usefully notes, a successful imitation for Aristotle must have "the power of engaging our attention and our emotions almost as if it were real."[5] That an imitation has and affords a point of view on its subject matter is crucial to its having this

---

[3] Aristotle, *Poetics*, trans. Richard Janko (Indianapolis, IN: Hackett, 1987), p. 1; interpolations added.

[4] *ibid.*, p. 3.

[5] Paul Woodruff, "Aristotle on Mimesis," in *Essays on Aristotle's Poetics*, ed. A. Rorty (Princeton, NJ: Princeton University Press, 1992), pp. 73–95 at p. 81.

power of engagement. The audience takes up the afforded point of view and so comes to be aware of the subject matter *as it is experienced* from it. This makes it clear that what is presented in a successful imitation is not just a subject matter "in itself," but a subject matter as it matters to and for an experiencing human intelligence.

The different traditional forms of fine art are then determined by differences in objects presented and in media. Either what is presented may be a physical thing or an appearance of a thing, as in painting and sculpture. Sculpture uses or may use as its means of presentation all three of color, line, and three-dimensional form. Painting uses or may use only color and line (with three-dimensional form limited to surface textural effects in presenting a three-dimensional image on a two-dimensional surface). Or what is presented may be an action or series of actions, using language, rhythm, and harmony as means. All three means are used in drama (as Aristotle knew it, which included song) and in opera. Language only (with at least less emphasis on rhythm) is used in the novel. Harmony and rhythm alone are used in pure instrumental music.[6]

It is common to object against Aristotle's account of art objects as imitations or presentations of a subject matter that many centrally successful works of art do not present a subject matter at all. Noël Carroll, for example, lists some abstract paintings, most orchestral music, and some abstract video and performance pieces as things that "stand for nothing, but are presented as occasions for concentrated perceptual experiences."[7] Anne Sheppard similarly notes that "there is nothing in the sensible world which an abstract painting, a lyric poem, or a piece of music demonstrably represents."[8] Though a theorist might then "fall back on the claim" that abstract paintings and works of music represent emotions or states of mind such as anger or grief, this move stretches the notions of *representation* and *imitation* beyond any reasonable limits, Sheppard argues, since for some works we can neither see the subject matter presented in the work (in the way we can see objects in representational paintings) nor see

---

[6] Aristotle, *Poetics*, pp. 1–2.

[7] Noël Carroll, *Philosophy of Art: A Contemporary Introduction* (London: Routledge, 1999), p. 26.

[8] Anne Sheppard, *Aesthetics: An Introduction to the Philosophy of Art* (Oxford: Oxford University Press, 1987), p. 16.

the work as resembling its subject matter. There is "non-representational art."[9]

These observations are surely correct. We do not see recognizable objects *in* many abstract paintings or hear them *in* works of music. But these observations are somewhat sideways to the wide sense of *imitation* (*mimesis*) in which Aristotle claims that works of art are *imitations* (*mimemata*). According to the wide sense of *imitation* that Aristotle has in mind, all that is required for being an imitation is presentation of a subject matter as a focus for thought, fused to perceptual experience of the work. It is for this reason that, as Paul Shorey notes, both Plato and Aristotle regard music as "the most imitative of the arts."[10] Works of pure instrumental music do not normally visually or audibly *depict* particular sensible objects, scenes, or even emotions, but they do invite us to think about *action*, in particular about abstract patterns of resistance, development, multiple attention, and closure that are present in actions, and they invite us to these thoughts in and through perceptual experience of the musical work itself. In inviting and sustaining thoughts, fused to the perceptual experience of the work, about (abstract patterns in) action, music, as Lawrence Kramer puts it, "participates actively in the construction of subjectivity"[11] in presenting abstractly a sense of its plights and possibilities. We do hear this kind of presentation *in* the work. It may have many different forms in different cultural contexts, but if it is entirely absent then there is no *work* of music, but only the empty decorativeness of a soundscape, mere background.

Similarly, Kendall Walton has argued that abstract paintings typically invite us to see shapes in front of and behind one another in a three-dimensional pictorial space. For example, Kasimir Malevich's *Suprematist Painting* (1915) invites us to see "a yellow rectangle in front of a green one." This is "a full-fledged illusion," since the painting is literally "a flat surface, with no part of it significantly in front of any other."[12] The

---

[9] *ibid.*, pp. 16–17.

[10] Paul Shorey, notes to Plato, *Republic I*, trans. Paul Shorey (London: Heinemann [Loeb Classical Library], 1930), p. 224, note c.

[11] Lawrence Kramer, *Classical Music and Postmodern Knowledge* (Berkeley: University of California Press, 1995), p. 21.

[12] Kendall Walton, *Mimesis as Make-Believe: On the Foundations of the Representational Arts* (Cambridge, MA: Harvard University Press, 1990), p. 56.

point of this illusion is the *presentation* in two dimensions of a three-dimensional pictorial space for visual exploration. This presentation invites us to think about the experience of exploring this abstract "world in the work," including encountering resistances, energies, balances, distractions, and so forth, as an abstract pattern of the experiences of living in our ordinary natural and social world. To be sure the presentation is indefinite. No distinct vase of flowers, say, is presented for visual recognition. But thought (about subjectivity's paths in its natural and social worlds) is abstractly invited and focused, fused to perceptual experience of the work.

The line between empty decorativeness (wallpaper, soundscapes) and art is fuzzy. Decorative elements are parts of many successful works. But the presentation of a subject matter – inviting thought about it, fused to the perceptual experience of the work – is *a* criterion of art. One might rank the various media of art on a very rough scale from those in which the emphasis lies more on the perceived formal elements to those in which a more definite thought is encoded as follows: abstract painting and photography; pure instrumental music; abstract dance; architecture; depictive painting and photography; sculpture; realistic narrative literature; movies. More useful perhaps are Dewey's identifications of the representational potentials of different media of art, that is, of the kinds of subject matters about which thought is most naturally invited by works in different media. As Dewey has it, architecture presents thoughts about human affairs; sculpture about movement arrested and about repose, balance, and peace; painting about spectacle, view, and the "look" of things (including abstract things); music about changes, events, effects, "stir, agitation, movement, the particulars and contingencies of existence"; literature about common life and vernacular culture.[13] These representational potentials are natural tendencies to present a certain kind of subject matter, not fixed absolutes. Their realizations are matters of degree. They can be overridden, in that there can be, for example, agitated sculpture or "abstract" literature (as in Robbe-Grillet or certain works of Samuel Beckett's). But the deep point underlying Dewey's identifications is that without some presentation of a subject matter as a focus for thought fused to perceptual experience the status of a work as art is reasonably subject to doubt.

---

[13] Dewey, *Art as Experience*, pp. 228–40; the passage cited about music is from p. 236.

This fact, however, does not yield a definition of art that fully enables either the identification of works or the elucidation of art's functions. It is only one criterion of art. Some linguistic and visual representations are largely "transparent," in that they serve principally to communicate information that might be put otherwise. The representation itself is not centrally part of the intended focus for attention. It is unclear exactly what the phrase "presentation of a subject matter as a focus for thought fused to perceptual experience" *means*. It is unclear how such presentations are achieved, and it is unclear how and why they matter, over and above the normal function of communicating information that is discharged by most representations. Why do we and should we, in the case of art, pay attention also to the representation itself and not only to what it presents as a focus for thought? How can artistic representations, which must involve something more than simply the conventional use of a fully arbitrary code, be achieved?

Visual depiction, resemblance, and game-playing

Answers to these questions seem most immediately available in the case of visual representation or *depiction*. Here debate has focused on *resemblance* versus *convention* as the central means of achieving visual representation. Dominic M. McIver Lopes nicely summarizes the competing intuitions that resemblance and convention theories of depiction each seek to accommodate. (i) We frequently understand which object *o* a given work *w* visually represents effortlessly, without explicit instruction; (ii) When *w* visually represents *o*, then we have visual experience that is "as of" *o*; yet (iii) there are wide varieties of styles of representation of roughly the same subject matter in different cultures ("Consider, for example, how a Cubist, a Haida printmaker, and a Byzantine icon painter would portray a face"[14]). Is it then necessary for a successful visual representation to look like what it depicts? Or is what *counts* as looking like and as the achievement of depiction settled by historically and locally variable conventional codes in use?

In Book X of the *Republic*, Plato seems to favor the first answer, as Socrates and Glaucon agree that a depictive painting must "imitate that

---

[14] Dominic M. McIver Lopes, "Representation: Depiction," in *Encyclopedia of Aesthetics*, ed. Michael Kelly (New York: Oxford University Press, 1998), vol. IV, pp. 139B–143B at p. 139B.

which appears as it appears."[15] This passage at least strongly suggests that a successful depiction must *have* the appearance of the object *o* that it depicts; it must itself look the way *o* looks from a certain angle. Alan Goldman usefully spells out this kind of resemblance theory as follows: "A painting represents a certain object if and only if its artist [successfully] intends by marking the canvas with paint to create visual experience in viewers that resembles the visual experience they would have of the object."[16]

Despite the naturalness of this suggestion and its immediate appeal in capturing intuitions (i) and (ii), it seems to be open to immediate objections. Nelson Goodman has detailed the most important of these objections in chapter 1 of *The Languages of Art*. Resemblance is obviously not sufficient for representation. Identical twins resemble one another to a high degree, but neither depicts the other.[17] "Nor," Goodman claims, "is resemblance necessary" for depiction.[18] Crucially, there are many things any given object is – for example, "the object before me is a man, a swarm of atoms, a complex of cells, a fiddler, a friend, a fool, and much more"[19] – and any object has many aspects. Even the idea that we are correctly to *reproduce* just one of an object's aspects is, Goodman claims, of no use. In undertaking to reproduce an aspect visually, we are *construing* an object, identifying its look not "in itself," but in relation to our purposes, habits, and interests. Hence "in representing an object [visually] we do not copy such a construal or interpretation – we *achieve* it."[20] Goodman adds that this is as much true for the camera as it is for the pen or brush. "The choice and handling of the instrument participate in the construal."[21] Hence, Goodman concludes, visual representation (like all object construal) is conventionalized through-and-through. Rather than resting on resemblance, depiction is a matter of the use of a certain kind of conventionalized scheme for achieving *denotation*.

In a painting or photograph there are no differentiable, repeatable characters (such as letters or words in linguistic representations); every

---

[15] Plato, *Republic*, trans. G. M. A. Grube, revised C. D. C. Reeve (Indianapolis, IN: Hackett, 1992), Book X, 598b, p. 268.

[16] Alan Goldman, "Representation: Conceptual and Historical Overview," in *Encyclopedia of Aesthetics*, ed. Kelly, vol. IV, pp. 137A–139B at p. 137A.

[17] Nelson Goodman, *The Languages of Art*, 2nd edn (Indianapolis, IN: Hackett, 1976), p. 4.

[18] *ibid.*, p. 5.   [19] *ibid.*, p. 6.   [20] *ibid.*, p. 9.   [21] *ibid.*, p. 9, n. 8.

small difference in marking can make a difference to what is represented (which aspect is presented); and every aspect of the mark itself matters. In Goodman's terminology, visual representation in painting and photography is a syntactically dense, semantically dense, and relatively replete way of denoting or referring to something.[22] That is, it is different from denoting by means of using language, which is syntactically and semantically discontinuous, in having differentiable and repeatable letters and words. But visual representation is nonetheless a conventionalized means of denoting, and it has the usual primarily cognitive interest of denotations generally. "Denotation is the core of representation and is independent of resemblance."[23] Visual representation as dense and relatively replete denotation is one way of achieving and communicating a construal of things.

Against Goodman and in favor of resemblance theory, Goldman has objected that Goodman's examples of resemblers that do not represent (identical twins; peas in a pod) do not touch the definition of visual representation in terms of resemblance, since these things were not made with the intention to create a visual experience in viewers.[24] But this objection against Goodman misses the mark, for – Goodman can argue – how can the intention to create a depictive visual experience arise and be realized except through the use of a conventionalized language of dense and relatively replete denotation? It is through the use of such a language that visual resemblance that is relevant to presenting an object is defined. Depiction-relevant resemblances between objects to be represented and surface configurations of marks are *not* lurking in the world to be noted and recorded independently of *our* construing-establishing of relevant resemblances within a language of depiction.

Flint Schier has also attempted to distinguish visual representation or depiction from linguistic representation, objecting, against Goodman, that (unlike linguistic representations) visual depictions are informed by no syntactic and semantic rules for recognizing the object that is represented.[25] This is true, but it again misses the mark, for it is just Goodman's point that depiction involves the use of a different *kind* of

---

[22] *ibid.*, pp. 226–30.   [23] *ibid.*, p. 5.

[24] Goldman, "Representation: Conceptual and Historical Overview," p. 137B.

[25] See Flint Schier, *Deeper into Pictures: An Essay on Pictorial Representation* (Cambridge: Cambridge University Press, 1986) and Goldman's discussion of Schier's work in *ibid.*, p. 139B.

language – syntactically and semantically dense and relatively replete – from verbal representation.

Kendall Walton has objected against Goodman that denotation is not the core of representation, since there could be a world in which people created representations – used them as props in games of the make-believe presentation of objects – without supposing the objects in question actually to exist. For example, it is possible for there to be a world in which people traffic in visual representations of unicorns only, without there actually being any unicorns. Hence visual representation cannot be understood as a function of the picking out, construal, or denotation of the actual.[26]

This objection too is not compelling. It is not clear in general which kinds of worlds are possible and which are not. It is not clear specifically that there could be people who use unicorn representations without also representing actual horses, birds, and deer. Representations may have an inherent connection with some bits of actuality. Furthermore, Goodman accounts in detail for the existence of depictions that depict nothing. A picture of a unicorn is best understood as a *kind of picture*: a *unicorn-presenting picture* with null denotation. There can come to be these kinds of pictures that present nonexistent objects only because pictures can also be used to denote actually existing objects. Unicorn-presenting pictures result from recombinations of denotative elements from staghorn-depicting pictures and horse-presenting pictures, some of which denote actual staghorns and horses.[27] Walton's objection underrates the extent to which world intake – denotation of the actual – is required for representation in general.

A second objection of Walton's proves more telling, and it begins to point the way toward combining and integrating elements of Goodman's conventionalism with classical resemblance theory. Walton notes that Goodman has difficulty explaining the greater realism of, for example, a painting by Vermeer compared with one by Braque.[28] In order to explain this difference, Walton argues, we must distinguish between *depiction* and *description* (referring by means of the use of language). *Contra* Goodman, depiction is not just a different *kind* of language for referring; it works differently. To depict an object *o* in a work *w* is to *prescribe* that

[26] Walton, *Mimesis as Make-Believe*, p. 125.
[27] Goodman, *Languages of Art*, pp. 21–26.
[28] Walton, *Mimesis as Make-Believe*, p. 299.

an audience, in looking at *w* is to *imagine* that it is looking at *o*. "A work depicts a particular actual object if in authorized games [of imagining or making-believe] it is fictional [i.e. part of the game] that that object is what the viewer sees."[29]

This account of depiction explains the varieties of successful visual representation and their connections with varying historical habits and conventions. Many quite different marked surfaces and three-dimensional objects are such that we can successfully imagine that in looking at them (literally) we are looking at a represented object. Suitably instructed, we can imagine that in looking at a bicycle seat and handlebars we are looking at a bull's head,[30] and we can imagine that in looking at 4-by-6 black and white photograph we are seeing a multihued circus carousel or a 6-foot tall man. Styles of visual representation together with instructions for seeing represented objects "in" them do change over time and place.

But Walton's analysis also explains both our sense of the visual immediacy of the represented object and the comparative realism of some representations. When we imagine seeing a represented object *o* in a work *w*, then this imagining suffuses our perceptual experience of *o*. "Suitably internalized, the principles of make-believe guide the imaginings that inform one's perceptual experience."[31] In thus pretending, we really do seem to ourselves to see *o* itself. A visual representation is then comparatively realistic *not* when it "directly resembles" what it represents: any black-and-white snapshot of a middle-sized object at a medium distance is much more like any other such snapshot than it is like the thing represented. Rather, a visual representation is comparatively realistic when it is possible from inside the game of imagining or pretending to explore the representer visually as a way of getting further information about the represented. That is, in looking at the representer continuously and with attention to different aspects of it, one takes oneself, in the game, to get more information about what is represented.[32] In looking at *w*, one sees that one object represented is behind another or one sees that a person on an occasion had just this expression. This kind of visual exploration of

---

[29] *ibid.*, p. 297.

[30] Picasso's *Bull's Head* (1943) appears on the cover of the paperback edition of Walton's book.

[31] *ibid.*, p. 302.

[32] See *ibid.*, pp. 328–31, and see also Scruton, *Art and Imagination*, p. 204.

the representer in order to get further information about the represented is not possible with nondepictive, verbal representation.

It is important to remember, however, that there is often little "direct resemblance" between representer and represented. Again, most snapshots are more like one another than they are like what they represent. At a distance one can readily confuse two distinct snapshots of a person, but it is much harder to mistake a person for a snapshot and vice versa. Instead, the resemblances that matter are between looking at an object o and imagining or pretending to look at o (by or in looking at w). The relevant resemblances are mediated by the visual-imaginative game.

This further explains why there is no *pure* or *absolute* realism. In painting or photography we must always choose between having a sharp focus on all objects represented throughout the visual field or presenting some objects in focus and some distant objects blurred. Either choice can work within a game of seeing objects "in" the representation. But neither corresponds perfectly to how we see. In actually looking at objects rather than visual representations of them, we can refocus our eyes on objects at different distances, thereby changing what is blurry and what is sharp. Visual representations do not permit this kind of change of focus. Any given object is presented in the representation either sharply or somewhat blurred.[33] Furthermore, it is often effective (in both visual and verbal representation) to be reminded of either the visual or verbal object as an artifact, say by leaving patches of canvas bare or by authorial aside. Such reminders both allow us to marvel at the representation as a constructed thing and to become aware that it embodies a point of view on what it represents.[34]

Walton's account of visual representation elegantly combines elements of resemblance theory and elements of conventionalism. In construing visual representation as a certain kind of imagining game – imagining that one is seeing o – that is played with certain kinds of two-dimensional objects (paintings, photographs, prints, etc.) and three-dimensional objects (sculpture), Walton is able to account for the historical varieties of representational styles, rooted in our decisions to play imagining games in certain ways, and he is able to account for the comparative realism of some visual representations. But how and why do games of visual representation come to be played? It is difficult to reject the intuition that the playing of these games rests not only and simply on decisions,

---

[33] *ibid.*, p. 328.   [34] *ibid.*, p. 275.

but also on noticings of resemblances between protorepresenter and represented.

Richard Wollheim develops a theory that articulates this intuition. He argues that visual representation arises out of *seeing-in*, for example, the kind of seeing of a bear in a cloud that anyone, even a child, might manage. For human beings, some visual experiences of objects in nature – clouds, stains on the walls of caves, reflections on the surfaces of ponds, patterns of grain in wood or rock – have what Wollheim calls "twofoldness,"[35] in that we are aware of both the surface looked at *and* some presented something that seems to stand out from or in or behind the surface. This seeing-in is a natural human visual experience, and it is, Wollheim argues, "prior...logically and historically"[36] to visual representation and the playing of any games of make-believe. It is prior logically, "in that I can see something in surfaces that neither are nor are believed by me to be representations."[37] Clouds, for example, are not symbols or denoters of anything; they just are, and yet we can see things in them. It is prior historically in that the likeliest route of emergence of visual representation involves someone – aware of natural seeing-in in relation to clouds, plays of shadow on rock, and so forth – undertaking to "mark... a surface with the intention of getting others around him to see some definite thing in it: say, a bison."[38] In this way, the practice or game of visual representation arises out of and builds on natural seeing-in, natural awareness of resemblances.

Against Wollheim's account, Walton objects that the twofoldness of seeing-in needs explanation. How and why, Walton asks, are we aware of *both* the marked surface and the object that we seem to see in it? The answer, Walton argues, is that we are aware of ourselves as *imagining* seeing the object represented rather than literally seeing it – that is, aware of ourselves as using the cloud or cave wall as a prop for *our* pretending – and so we are returned to the theory of representation as make-believe.[39]

Representing as natural, human, world-responsive activity

It seems unlikely that this dispute between Wollheim and Walton – which comes first: our doing something, playing a game, or resemblances there

---

[35] Richard Wollheim, *Painting as an Art* (Princeton, NJ: Princeton University Press, 1987), p. 46.

[36] *ibid.*, p. 47.   [37] *ibid.*   [38] *ibid.*, p. 48.

[39] Walton, *Mimesis as Make-Believe*, p. 301.

to be noted by imaginative perception? – either can or should be resolved. Depicting is both something we actively, agentively do and something that arises out of natural capacities of perceptual responsiveness to the world. A similar point applies to verbal representation. It too arises out of natural expressions of pain, alarm, and interest in the form of calls and cries, and it too is then something we do, as we come to articulate natural expressions into representational language.

This similarity points us to a set of deeper questions. How and why do we come to be makers and users of representations – visual and verbal alike – at all? How are the capacities and interests that are developed through the making and using of representations in general related to artistic representation? What makes a representation – a presentation of a subject matter – artistic? With some developed responses to these questions, the antithesis – representations are matters of game-playing versus representations are matters of natural responsiveness to nature – begins to emerge as a false one.

Like at least other chordates, human beings are perceptually aware of and responsive to features of their environments. Unlike other animals, human beings are aware to a very high degree of aspects of things and of multiple ways of classifying the same object. For us – as Michael Tomasello puts it, developing Wittgenstein's work on linguistic reference as a social phenomenon and on aspect-seeing –

> In different communicative situations one and the same object may be construed as a dog, an animal, a pet, or a pest; one and the same event may be construed as running, moving, fleeing, or surviving; one and the same place may be construed as the coast, the shore, the beach, or the sand, all depending on the communicative goals of the speaker.[40]

Tomasello hypothesizes that there is a natural human capacity to become acculturated and aware of multiple perspectives on the same object or event. But this natural capacity becomes actualized into an explicit ability only in and through social interaction.[41] It is through participating in

---

[40] Michael Tomasello, *The Cultural Origins of Human Cognition* (Cambridge, MA: Harvard University Press, 1999), pp. 8–9.

[41] The distinction between capacities or second-order, natural abilities to develop abilities and explicit first-order abilities traces to Aristotle. See Richard Eldridge, *On Moral Personhood: Philosophy, Literature, Criticism, and Self-Understanding* (Chicago, IL:

what Tomasello calls "extended joint attentional interactions,"[42] particularly in cases in which we become aware of others as agents who may have both multiple goals and multiple available means for achieving a goal, that we become aware that *how* objects are picked out can vary and that this matters. Other nonhuman primates can also shift goals and see the same object as either a weapon or a tool for digging. But we can see differing aspects and identities of things much more quickly and flexibly, we can do so simultaneously, not only sequentially, and, most importantly, we can internalize different ways of identifying things. This internalization "creates a clear break with [the] straightforward perceptual or sensory-motor representations [that we share with other nonhuman primates and sentient creatures]."[43]

As a result, as we come both phylogenetically and ontogenetically to develop this internalized awareness of different ways of seeing and identifying things, in and through the development of representational systems, visual and verbal alike, we are particularly aware of ourselves *as* representers, as *using* images or cries for one communicative purpose or another. Whatever the roots in biological evolution of this socially actualized, flexible representational capacity, it offers us a clear evolutionary advantage. It has survival value, in enabling more flexible and culturally accumulative responsiveness to our natural environment. We can plan and learn and cooperate much more flexibly and effectively than other animals.

But not only does our awareness of aspects and our ability to represent them promote survival, it also confers on us new interests. As we represent things *as* this or that (either as a developing linguistic community or as an individual coming to an already developed language), we can both make mistakes and develop new representations. In the course of doing this, we can become interested in further representation for its own sake, not

---

University of Chicago Press, 1987), p. 31 and p. 193, n. 15 for the relevant references. The idea that we have a natural language capacity that becomes an explicit ability to speak some particular language or other only and necessarily through social interaction is defended by many Wittgensteinians. See Eldridge, *Leading a Human Life*, pp. 203–04.

[42] Tomasello, *Cultural Origins of Human Cognition*, p. 36. Compare also Donald Davidson on what he calls "triangulation" in Donald Davidson, "The Second Person," in D. Davidson, *Subjective, Intersubjective, Objective* (Oxford: Clarendon Press, 2001), pp. 107–21 at pp. 117–21.

[43] *ibid.*, p. 126.

just for the sake of survival. We can become interested in truth, in how things are (or are this or that), whether or not acquiring awareness of further aspects of things has immediate survival value. Second, we can become interested in the aspects or appearances of our representational devices themselves. We can be interested in how *their* aspects enable us to become aware of and communicate aspects of things. For example, can a visual image communicate the relative spatial position of objects, and is it important for it to do so? If it is, then perspective drawing will answer to this purpose. Or is it important to use visual images more for narrative and less for spatial purposes? If so, then wealth of sequential detail may matter more than rendering of relative spatial position. Or we may simply enjoy the activity of experimenting with the media of visual representation: mud, blood, crushed berries, or acrylics, as may be. Likewise, we may become interested in the flow, rhythm, "feel," and memorability of verbal representational devices, so that song and chant and poetry may arise. Third, we can become interested in the development and presentation of a representational device (visual or verbal) to others as a form of performance that might command admiration and respect. We can want to become accomplished in representing aspects of things not only because we want to get them right, but also because we wish to be admired as representers.

Artistic representation as a human activity then arises when these latter interests – in truth, in what different kinds of representations can communicate, and in representation as commanding performance – come to the fore. In light of this, we can now make more sense of Aristotle's treatment of the value or point of artistic representation. According to Aristotle,

> Two causes seem to have generated the art of poetry as a whole, and these are natural ones.
> (i) Representation is natural to human beings from childhood. They differ from the other animals in this: man tends most toward representation and learns his first lessons through representation.
> Also (ii) everyone delights in representations...The cause of this is that learning is most pleasant, not only for philosophers but for others likewise...For this reason they delight in seeing images [mimemata], because it comes about that they learn as they observe and infer what each thing is.[44]

---

[44] Aristotle, *Poetics*, p. 4.

Representation, that is to say, arises out of our normal interactions with others and with our environment; it is natural to us. Our representations are more flexible and aspect-oriented than are those of other animals. We are aware of our thoughts and beliefs as *our* products. They are not simply and only the results of sensory-motor processes; they express points of view and manners of interest in things and their aspects. We delight in them in that by means of them we learn about things and their aspects – we learn which aspects of things may matter to us in different contexts – and we delight in the communicative achievement that is involved in a successful medium-specific representation in a medium itself. Hence we can delight directly in the representation as a medium-specific achievement as well as delighting in what we may learn from it.

Functions of artistic representation

The success of an artistic representation, as of much specifically human cultural representation more generally, involves the achievement of sense or meaning, the casting of a certain light on things and connections among things. A simpler animal sensory-motor representation may succeed in representing a present particular threat or possibility. The eye of the frog succeeds in communicating the presence of a fly and so prompts the darting of the tongue. But human cultural representations present more than this; they present instances of kinds and connections among kinds that matter to us by engaging our broader interest in truth, over and above survival. They aim at more than mere recording. Hence

> It is the function of a poet not to relate things that have happened, but
> things that may happen, i.e. that are possible in accordance with
> probability or necessity...For this reason poetry is a more philosophical
> and more serious thing than history; poetry tends to speak of universals,
> history of particulars. A universal is the sort of thing that a certain kind
> of person may well say or do in accordance with probability or
> necessity – this is what poetry aims at, although it assigns names [to the
> people].[45]

---

[45] *ibid.*, p. 12. Note that what Aristotle means by "history" is what we would more naturally call mere chronicle or a list of particular events. Serious narrative history is just as much a fully cultural representation that illuminates kinds of things and our interests in them as is poetry.

Likewise, it is the function of a photographer or a still-life painter not simply to *record* this vase of flowers, but instead to display or present a vase as an instance of a kind of thing that may engage human interest, attention, and feeling from a point of view. There must be a point – an achievement of illumination of significance for us – to artistic representation. Mere detailed reproduction of reality is not by itself enough (unless *that* may have a point in a certain context). A full body cast sculpture is not necessarily a successful work; a hologram is not automatically a successful artistic representation.

Aristotle goes on to make it clear that in the case of tragic drama in particular the point of artistic representation is the *catharsis* of emotions.[46] *Catharsis* is a term in Greek with multiple senses, ranging from that of a medical purgative to that of clarifying or making clear an object of attention. To say that a successful tragic drama brings about the catharsis of emotions is to say that it makes clear the natures of the objects toward which emotions are appropriately felt: it presents the genuinely pitiable and fearful as pitiable and fearful. In doing so, it further engages and trains the emotions, so that the right emotion is felt toward the right object on the right occasion.

These points about tragic drama naturally extend to other media of art. Epic presents the heroic as heroic; history painting presents terrible, pitiable, or heroic actions as such; landscape painting presents a scene as beneficent for human life or awe-inspiring; architecture affords and presents a sense of space and its uses for work or worship or family life. The special point of *artistic* representation, over and above cultural representations in general, involves the highlighted and emphasized engagement of feeling. Not only are meaning and truth presented, but the sort of meaning and truth that are in question in art have distinctively to do with how it is appropriate to feel about and respond to the presented subject matter.

Aristotle further develops a richly worked out account of the specific subject matter, plot, characters, thought, diction, spectacle or staging, and song that are proper to a successful tragic drama in particular.[47] In each case, the proper form of the element in question is derived from the account of how that element may best contribute to the aim or end of the tragedy.

---

[46] See *ibid.*, p. 48.   [47] See *ibid.*, pp. 7ff.

Here Aristotle's account displays an interesting tension. On the one hand, he does specify requirements that must be satisfied by the elements of a tragedy in order for it to work well. Not every element of any kind works on any occasion, however its maker might wish or think it should. For example, "nature itself teaches [poets] to choose [the verse form] that is appropriate to a given action."[48] There are objective constraints on the elements that may be used and on how they may be combined, if the aim of tragedy is to be achieved. On the other hand, there can be "an error [that is] correct, if it attains the end of the art itself"; for example, it is impossible that Achilles should have pursued Hector for as long and as intensely as he did, yet Homer's description of this pursuit nonetheless works in the context of the other incidents and characters of the *Iliad*.[49] Similarly, richness of metaphorical and other figurative language that lights up aspects of things and is itself required in successful tragedy "is an indication of genius"[50] that, it seems, cannot quite be taught. In both these respects, Aristotle leaves more room for successful artistic originality, against the grain of rules, than his specifications of required elements suggest.

Overall, it is arguable, however, that Aristotle's view of the subject matter that a successful tragic drama may present is too narrow, largely because his sense of value in human life is too circumscribed by the norms of the Greek city-state.[51] Notoriously, Aristotle claims that the worst plot presents a character who is "about to act in full knowledge, but [does] not do it"[52] – a pretty good one-phrase description of *Hamlet*. In general, human life and success and failure within it change their shapes as there are changes in technology and social organization. The materials and media available for presenting a subject matter and the techniques of presentation also change. As Dewey usefully remarks in noting these changes, any formulaic prescriptions for realism in presentation "leave us cold; by the time we arrive at them, the elements that stirred the blood and aroused admiration in the concrete have vanished."[53] While it is true that we are to be "carried on to a refreshed attitude [i.e. to an engagement and clarification of our emotions] toward the circumstances and exigencies of

---

[48] *ibid.*, p. 38.   [49] *ibid.*, p. 37.   [50] *ibid.*, p. 32.

[51] For a full discussion of the limitations of Aristotle's discussion of tragedy, connected with a discussion of the limitations of his moral philosophy, see Richard Eldridge, "How can Tragedy Matter for Us?," in Eldridge, *Persistence of Romanticism*, pp. 145–64.

[52] Aristotle, *Poetics*, p. 18.   [53] Dewey, *Art as Experience*, p. 151.

ordinary experience"[54] by an artistic representation, these circumstances and exigencies themselves change. Artists must often respect some rough precepts that are abstracted from what has worked in the past, and practice on the model of prior artistic successes helps. But artists must also be free to explore new materials, techniques, and subject matters in response to changes in life.

Representation – verbal, visual, or otherwise – is then the product of human activity in response to the object or subject matter of the representation. Mere matching between two things to the point of perfect resemblance is neither necessary nor sufficient for representation. Instead, as Walton notes, "for something to be an object of a representation [i.e. something that the representation presents], it must have a causal role in the production of the work; it must in one way or another figure in the process whereby the representation came about, either by entering into the intentions with which the work was produced or in some more 'mechanical' manner."[55] Even such perhaps *prima facie* mechanical a means of representation as photography involves the intention on the part of the maker to make a representation of a certain subject matter. The camera must be aimed and the shutter switch pushed. The subject matter may be immediately fictional, particularly in verbal representation, in that nonexistent persons and incidents are described (or painted). But what is described must nonetheless be the kind of thing that can be experienced and can be illuminated via its representation. (This may include such things as a marked surface or a sound pattern as things to be experienced.)

When the representation is specifically artistic, then it will present things or aspects of things from a point of view and with an emotional attitude of engagement, fascination, horror, pity, and so forth that the audience will be invited to share. Through this emotional engagement, the subject matter will be illuminated and clarified. In particular, its significance as an object of emotion within human life will be illuminated. In visual representation this will happen by means of visual exploration of the surface (for painting, photography, and other two-dimensional media) or of the object from multiple vantage points (for sculpture, architecture, and other three-dimensional media). For example, in exploring a lion-hunting painting by Delacroix we will imagine the excitement and terror of the occasion, the power of the lion, the apprehension of the hunters, and so forth, and so come to understand the incidents presented "from

---

[54] *ibid.*, p. 139.   [55] Walton, *Mimesis as Make-Believe*, p. 111.

the inside."[56] In verbal representation this will happen by our taking up the point of view, attitudes, and emotional engagements of the authorial intelligence. This may include identification with the attitudes and emotions of the characters presented, when the author is sympathetic with them, or it may include such things as horror at the successes of an unsympathetic character. In musical representation this will happen through our identification with the development of the melody, rhythm, and harmony, as we find ourselves "moving" in attention with the development of the work through its abstract patterns of statement, departure, resistance, return, and closure. Movies, dance, drama, song, and performance art combine elements of both visual and verbal representation.

In all these cases, when the work goes well there will be an achievement of engagement of attitude and its expression in the representation, in contrast with a more routinized statement. In Wollheim's useful term, the activity of mark-making or representation-making may itself be *thematized*,[57] in that our attention will be engaged with just how the materials and medium have been worked to present just this subject matter in a significantly new emotional and attitudinal light. We may be successfully invited to become attentive to just how these words or marks or sounds have been chosen to present just this subject matter in just this emotional light.

Dewey usefully distinguishes in this connection between artistic representation and ordinary representation, that is, between "expression and statement."

> [Statement] is generalized. An intellectual statement is valuable in the degree in which it conducts the mind to many things all of the same kind...The meaning of an expressive object, on the contrary, is individualized. The diagrammatic drawing that suggests grief does not convey the grief of an individual person; it exhibits the *kind* of facial "expression" persons in general manifest when suffering grief. The esthetic portrayal of grief manifests the grief of a particular individual in connection with a particular event. It is *that* state of sorrow which is depicted, not depression unattached. It has a *local* habitation...[Its significance] is a function of what is in the actual scene in its interaction with what the beholder brings with him.[58]

56 See Scruton, *Art and Imagination*, pp. 128–29.
57 See Wollheim, *Painting as an Art*, p. 20.
58 Dewey, *Art as Experience*, pp. 90–91, 87.

A work of art must present a subject matter in such a way that the emotional and attitudinal significance of it can be explored through inter-action with the work itself, as that work is achieved through the working of a medium. In this sense, a work of art must be a representation. But this also suggests the extent to which success in artistic representation, as opposed to ordinary representation, is indissolubly wedded to both the explorative, formal working of the medium and the achievement of expressiveness.

3   Beauty and form

Beauty, absorption, and pleasure

It has long been recognized that human beings find various visual and auditory appearances to be deeply absorbing. Certain sunsets, flowers, birdsongs, and beautiful bodies, among natural things, and certain pots, carvings, vocalizations, and marked surfaces, among humanly made things, seem to engage eye or ear together with attentive mind. In experiencing such things, we feel we want the experience to continue for "its own sake," at least for some further time. Greek uses the phrase *to kalon* – the fine, the good, or the beautiful – to describe many sorts of things that are attractive to mind and eye or ear, without sharply distinguishing natural beauty from artistic merit (or moral goodness). In the *Symposium*, Socrates reports that the priestess Diotima once instructed him in how "a lover who goes about this matter correctly must begin in his youth to devote himself to beautiful bodies,"[1] first loving one body, then many (as he comes to understand that they are alike in beauty), next beautiful minds, beautiful laws and customs, beautiful ideas and theories, until finally he will come to love "the Beautiful itself, absolute, pure, unmixed, not polluted by human flesh or colors or any other great nonsense of mortality."[2]

It is natural to think of the affording of such experiences as a central aim of art. Many artists seem to seek to engage and entrance eye or ear and mind. They monitor and revise their products – rearranging colors, shapes, notes, words, or postures – with a view to deepening the product's affordance of absorbing experience, where this affordance seems to be a function of the arrangement, form, or pattern of elements composing the work.

---

[1] Plato, *Symposium*, trans. Alexander Nehamas and Paul Woodruff (Indianapolis, IN: Hackett, 1989), 210A, p. 57.
[2] *ibid.*, 211E, p. 59.

In thinking about the special nature of art compared to other things, reference to this kind of experience naturally comes to the fore. According to the traditional formula of Horace (following Aristotle), the office of art was to "please and instruct." Yet many representations that are not particularly artistic *are* instructive, including computer manuals, scientific theories, assembly instructions, mathematical proofs, and recipes. Attention to how art is distinctly pleasurable seems naturally to claim pride of place in the theory of art.

Historically a shift away from representation theories of art to pleasure- and experience-oriented theories was specifically motivated by a growing sense of the claims of the modern mathematical-experimental sciences of nature to have a central title to accuracy of representation and instruction, apparently leaving no room for art in fulfilling these functions. Sir Francis Bacon, for example, writing in 1605, held that reason, exemplified in experimental inquiry, "doth buckle and bow the mind unto the nature of things";[3] that is, it gets things right. In contrast, poetry is "Feigned History." It submits "the shews of things to the desires of the mind";[4] that is, it produces appearances – not recordings of the real – that please by giving the mind what *it* wants.

Theorists concerned to describe how art satisfies the desires of the mind were led to talk of both a special faculty for a distinct kind of satisfying experience and special objects of that faculty. In England, Joseph Addison in his *Spectator* essays developed the idea of works of art as objects of *taste*, "a faculty of the soul, which discerns the beauties of an author with pleasure, and the imperfections with dislike."[5] In Germany, Alexander Baumgarten developed the concept of *aesthetics* in its modern sense. *Aisthesis* in Greek means simply "sensation." Beginning from the idea that

[3] Sir Francis Bacon, *Two Books of the Proficience and Advancement of Learning, Human and Divine* in Bacon, *Works*, ed. Spedding, Ellis, and Heath, 3 vols. (London: Longmans, 1879), vol. I, pp. 343–44, cited in Monroe Beardsley, *Aesthetics from Classical Greece to the Present: A Short History* (University, AL: University of Alabama Press, 1975), p. 170.

[4] *ibid.*

[5] Joseph Addison, *The Spectator*, ed. Alexander Chalmers (New York: D. Appleton, 1879), paper no. 409, vol. V, p. 20, cited in Peter Kivy, "Recent Scholarship and the British Tradition: A Logic of Taste – The First Fifty Years," in *Aesthetics: A Critical Anthology*, ed. George Dickie and Richard J. Sclafani (New York: St. Martin's Press, 1977), pp. 626–42 at p. 628. Kivy's essay is a fine survey of the logical shape and structure of seventeenth-century theories of taste.

aesthetics is "the science of sensory cognition"[6] in general (as opposed to "pure" mathematical or logical thinking), Baumgarten went on under this heading to discuss what he called *"perfect sensate discourse,"*[7] that is, discourse that merely by the arrangement of its parts pleases the mind in the mere apprehension of it, without regard for accuracy or correctness. Following this lead, the seventeenth and eighteenth centuries are then populated with sensibility-oriented discussions of pleasure in both art and nature. Taxonomies of various kinds of objects – both natural and artistic – that please (or horrify) in mere apprehension were developed. The beautiful, the sublime, the grotesque, and the pastoral, among others, were identified as occasions of distinct kinds of emotionally powerful apprehensions. For most theorists, including Burke, Kant, and Wordsworth, these experiences tend to fall into two very broad classes: the beautiful, understood as harmonious, absorbing, and calming; and the sublime, understood as unruly, awe-inspiring, and invigorating.[8]

Experiences, however, prove to be things that it is particularly difficult to describe and classify. As the metaphor of taste already suggests, one may try to describe experiences as having qualitatively different phenomenological "feels" or manners of felt presence to consciousness, just as, say, coffee and vanilla feel different to the tongue and mind. Yet it proves difficult to identify any phenomenologically distinct feel that is experienced by all suitably attentive apprehenders of works of art. The experience of reading Homer's *Iliad* seems not to *feel* very like the experience of looking at a Claude landscape or listening to a Mozart symphony, except in the sense that all these experiences are in some way pleasing and absorbing. Different sensory modalities are used for each of them, and different modes of attention are required.

Hence theorists of art as what pleases in experience have tended instead to focus either on distinct features of our *manner of attending* to beautiful objects in both art and nature or on distinct features of the *object* of art-relevant pleasure in apprehension. It has been argued by

---

[6] Alexander Baumgarten, *Aesthetica* (1750), §1, cited in Beardsley, *Aesthetics from Classical Greece to the Present*, p. 157.

[7] Baumgarten, *Aesthetica*, §§3, 4, cited *ibid.*, p. 158.

[8] For a discussion of these two types of experiences and their significance in Wordsworth's poetry, see Richard Eldridge, "Internal Transcendentalism: Wordsworth and 'A New Condition of Philosophy,'" in Eldridge, *Persistence of Romanticism*, pp. 102–23.

Addison, Shaftesbury, Burke, Kant, and Schopenhauer, among others, that we pay attention to beauty in nature or in art in a specially *disinterested* way, without regard for any use of the object apprehended in any practical project.[9] We do not undertake to build with beautiful paintings or poems or sunsets; we simply regard them.

Taken by itself, however, this approach to both beauty and art seems to leave the status of something as either naturally beautiful or artistically successful too much in the control of the apprehender. It suggests that any object – the remains of a cat's nightly kill, or a cheap plastic fork – can become naturally beautiful or artistically successful "for us," if we simply decide to attend to it in a disinterested way and then manage to do so. While this suggestion has its charms in allowing that anything could be art as far as its intrinsic features go, and in holding that its status as artistically successful or naturally beautiful "depends on us,"[10] it seems nonetheless not to answer to the powerful idea that initially motivates experience-oriented theories: that something *in* the object nonoptionally claims and holds our attention. This something seems to invite, hold, and reward the attentive eye and ear.

Efforts to characterize this something-in-the-object have, however, proved elusive. Specifications of its nature cannot reasonably be regarded as empirical generalizations about causes of experience in everyone, for not everyone in fact has the same pleasures in apprehension with regard to the same objects. Hence we seem to have to identify artistically success-ful and naturally beautiful objects first, in order to know whose pleasures in particular are on the mark.[11] The situation is quite different from the case of establishing the standard for normal vision, say, by reference to a physically healthy majority. Whose identifications of artworks and art-relevant properties shall count, and why?

Specifications of a property in the object that *counts* as relevant to aesthetic pleasure are best regarded, therefore, not simply as causal

---

[9] For a useful survey of the emergence of disinterestedness as a central mark of our mode of attention to artistic and natural beauty, see Jerome Stolnitz, "Of the Ori-gins of 'Aesthetic Disinterestedness,'" in *Aesthetics: A Critical Anthology*, ed. Dickie and Sclafani, pp. 606–25, as well as Kivy, "Recent Scholarship and the British Tradition."

[10] Theories that *do* focus centrally on the authority of critics and other apprehenders in *deciding* what is art will be considered further in chapter 7 below.

[11] Unless, of course, Hume is right that we can agree on independent criteria for expertise in apprehension. Again, I postpone this topic until chapter 7.

generalizations about normal response, but rather as efforts on the part of those captivated by beauty to articulate something about the nature of their experience. These articulations typically are given less in phenomenological terms than they are in either metaphysical or functional terms. Francis Hutcheson, for example, identifies "uniformity amidst variety" as the feature in objects that "excite[s] in us the ideas of beauty," whether natural or artistic,[12] adding that objects might also be "agreeable on other accounts, such as *grandeur, novelty, sanctity,* and some others."[13] Hutcheson regards these as empirical claims about what causes a distinct art-relevant sensation or aesthetic experience in him and, presumably, like-minded others. But, again, this claim will not do, in the face of wide disagreements about which objects occasion which experiences. What makes Hutcheson's claim seem specially metaphysical is its combination of empirical inadequacy and vagueness. Almost any object seen or heard might be thought by someone to possess uniformity amidst variety. Any single object that has parts – from a dog to a teacup to a safety pin – might be thought automatically to possess it. A similar objection applies to Clive Bell's account of art as that which possesses *significant form.*[14] Almost anything might seem to have it, and no empirical generalization about normal experience of pleasure in significant form is available to resolve disagreements.

Kant on natural and artistic beauty

Instead, then, of following Hutcheson and Bell in their efforts to make empirical claims about causes of aesthetic experience, we might instead embrace the vagueness and metaphysical character of their descriptions of art-relevant features in an object. The point of an account of uniformity amidst variety or significant form or some other defining feature that causes aesthetic pleasure would then not be empirical adequacy in the first instance so much as the further articulation of the *significance* of a certain kind of pleasurable experience. In the *Critique of the Power of Judgment,* Kant moves explicitly in this direction, in proposing "the form of the

---

[12] Francis Hutcheson, *An Inquiry Concerning Beauty, Harmony, and Design,* ed. Peter Kivy (The Hague: Martinus Nijhoff, 1973), p. 40.

[13] *ibid.*

[14] See Clive Bell, *Art* (1914), chapter 1, "The Aesthetic Hypothesis," reprinted in *Philosophy of Art,* ed. Neill and Ridley, pp. 99–110, at pp. 100ff.

purposiveness of an object"[15] that causes "the harmonious free play of the cognitive faculties"[16] in us as the defining feature in any beautiful object, natural or artistic. The point of Kant's terminology is not to enable the clear resolution of disagreements by specifying an art-relevant property in objects about whose instances everyone will immediately agree. He is quite aware that the phrase "form of purposiveness" is so vague that its application will be reasonably disputed (even if underlying such disputes there is in principle a genuine question of correctness).[17] Rather, the point of Kant's phrases is to begin to suggest why the experience of beauty, natural and artistic alike, matters to us. It is more than a mere affirmative buzz or tingle. It is a pleasurable feeling with a distinct causal history and, in virtue of that history, a distinct significance for us.

In pleasing us, natural and artistic beauty, according to Kant, serve no exterior purpose. The experience of beauty does not yield knowledge, and it does not of itself enable the satisfaction of desires for material goods. Yet it is not nonetheless merely agreeable or pleasant;[18] instead, the experience of beauty matters. Beauty in nature makes us *feel as though* the natural world were congenial to our purposes and projects. In feeling the beautiful natural object to be "as it were" intelligible or made for us to apprehend it, we further feel that nature as a whole – which seems to "shine forth" in beauty – is favorable to our cognitive and practical interests as subjects. To experience a beautiful sunset, according to Kant,

---

[15] Purposiveness without a purpose or finality without an end (*Zweckmässigkeit ohne Zweck*) is the subject of the "Third Moment" of the "Analytic of the Beautiful," §§10–17 of the *Critique of the Power of Judgment*. See in particular Kant's "Definition of the beautiful inferred from this third moment" in *Critique of the Power of Judgment*, trans. Paul Guyer and Eric Matthews (Cambridge: Cambridge University Press, 2000), p. 120.

[16] Kant initially develops the idea of the harmonious free play of imagination (focusing on a single object or work) and understanding in the *Critique of the Power of Judgment*, introduction, section 7. To say that imagination and understanding "play freely" is to say that we intuit or focus on an object without seeking or arriving at any definite knowledge of the object intuited; to say that they do this harmoniously is to say that in our focusing on the object it is nonetheless "as though" understanding takes place.

[17] See *Critique*, trans. Guyer and Matthews, p. 163. Kant's defense of the intersubjective validity of judgments of taste and his explanation of how there can nonetheless be disagreement in overt verdicts issued by apprehenders will be considered in chapter 7.

[18] Kant distinguishes the (morally) good from the merely agreeable from the beautiful in *ibid.*, §5, pp. 94–96.

is to feel (though not to know theoretically) that nature makes sense. Pleasure in the beautiful

> is also in no way practical, neither like that from the pathological ground of agreeableness nor like that from the intellectual ground of the represented good. But yet it has a causality in itself, namely that of *maintaining* the state of the representation of the mind and the occupation of the cognitive powers without a further aim. We *linger* over the consideration of the beautiful because this consideration strengthens and reproduces itself...[19]

Though Kant's terminology may be difficult, the experience he is describing is a familiar one. Beautiful objects of nature or art engage our attention. We *enjoy* them in paying active, cognitive attention to them, even if we acquire from them neither definite theoretical knowledge of nature nor material goods nor mere (passively received) pleasant sensations.

The experience of successful art then combines the experience of natural beauty with the invigorating experience of the natural sublime.[20] In stemming from genius, "the talent (natural gift) that gives the rule to art,"[21] the successful work of art is necessarily original. It proceeds not from copying or aping (*Nachmachung*), but from taking up and freely imitating (*Nachahmung*), following after, or being inspired by prior artistic work.[22] Genius

> cannot describe or indicate scientifically how it brings its product into being... [T]he author of a product that he owes to his genius does not know himself how the ideas for it come to him, and also does not have it in his power to think up such things at will or according to plan, and to communicate to others precepts that would put them in a position to produce similar works.[23]

---

[19] *ibid.*, §12, p. 107.

[20] Kirk Pillow has argued persuasively that the work of art is seen by Kant as having a sublime content – an indeterminately large and not quite wholly unified fund of ideas, emotions, and attitudes that challenges the imagination in attempting to trace and present it – somehow coherently housed within a beautiful form. See Kirk Pillow, *Sublime Understanding* (Cambridge, MA: MIT Press, 2001), especially chapter 3, "Sublime Understanding."

[21] Kant, *Critique*, trans. Guyer and Matthews, §46, p. 186.

[22] See *ibid.*, §47, p. 188; see also §49, p. 196, on aping and copying versus inspiration and serving as a model.

[23] *ibid.*, §46, p. 187.

In thus springing forth chthonically in and through the genius in its maker, rather than according to any definite plan, the successful work of art resembles such sublime, terrifying yet invigorating natural phenomena as overhanging rocks, storms at sea, and raging torrents. Arguably Kant overstates the point, in that makers of art must have some rough conception of what they are trying to do (compose a sonata or paint a still life or write a novel, say). Moreover, the ability to produce art successfully *can* be cultivated through training and practice. But (like Aristotle in remarking that sometimes rules can be broken successfully) Kant captures our sense that in artistic production some free experimentation with the materials and formal possibilities of a medium normally takes place. This free experimentation or improvisation, beyond mere aping, is a source of our interest in the artistic product. The work of art and the power of free production that it evidences inspire us, its audience. Our own cognitive powers are "animated,"[24] as we are brought to feel that we have like powers that might likewise be brought to expression in fully achieved, exemplary action and its products.

Yet despite being chthonically original in stemming from natural genius, the genuine work of art must also be *exemplary*. "Since there can also be original nonsense"[25] that is not art, the genuine work of art must be intelligible or make sense. While being original, the products of genius "must at the same time be models."[26] As in the experience of beauty in nature, the audience must feel *as though* the product is favorable to our cognitive and practical interests as subjects, something we can or could take as a model and follow after. It must seem to us to model and anticipate a world of subjects who act all at once fully, freely, expressively, and according to deeply purposive reason, without coercion or constraint.

Kant's accounts of both natural and artistic beauty have considerable appeal. Natural and artistic beauty seem to engage and absorb the eye or ear together with the attentive mind, and they seem valuable "for their own sake," rather than for the sake of any exterior cognitive or practical interest. Dewey notes that attention to the formed work of art *resembles* an experience of thinking *about* something else via the use of signs and symbols, yet the focus remains on the work itself and on its qualities,

---

[24] See *ibid.*, §12, p. 107 and §48, p. 194, for references to animation.
[25] *ibid.*, §46, p. 186.   [26] *ibid.*

which are evident in attentive perception.[27] Attending to formal qualities and interrelations in the work may well produce the kind of pleasurable absorption and have the kind of value that Kant says it has. The satisfying arrangement of qualities or formal elements is *a* criterion of art.

Yet we may also doubt whether Kant's account is wholly adequate to the varieties of art. Kant's central terms "form of purposiveness" and "harmonious free play of the cognitive faculties" *are* vague and metaphysical. They do not point to any neutral, uncontestable procedures for identifying successful works. Though he holds that works of art do express indefinite "aesthetic ideas" – ideas such as justice and freedom that can only be figuratively symbolized, not directly embodied in things present to sense experience[28] – his focus on formal elements and the pleasure of apprehending them may underrate the representational and cognitive dimensions of some art. Many works of twentieth-century art, including much of Dada, conceptual art, and performance art, seem more provocative and "assertational" than intended to provide pleasure in the apprehension of formal elements.

Nonetheless, where provocative and assertational intentions wholly override the imperative to achieve satisfying form in a medium, then the status of the product as art becomes subject to some doubt. The result of wholly provocative or assertational intentions swerves toward tract, screed, or propaganda, and away from art. As Dewey puts it, "doing or making is artistic," as opposed to exclusively theoretical, symbolic, communicative, political, and so forth, "when the perceived result is of such a nature that *its* qualities *as perceived* have controlled the question of production."[29] Practitioners in the studio and workshop *do* pay special attention to formal elements and their interrelationships. They typically monitor and correct their production in order to achieve an absorptive coherence of elements. Likewise, critics typically attend to the formal details of the presence or absence of such an achievement in a work. While it is true that all objects have form, attention to singular arrangements of elements that invite and sustain absorptive engagement is central to the artistic enterprise. In Dewey's phrasing,

---

[27] See Dewey, *Art as Experience*, p. 38.

[28] On aesthetic ideas see Kant, *Critique*, trans. Guyer and Matthews, §49, pp. 191–96, and on symbolization see §59, pp. 225–27.

[29] Dewey, *Art as Experience*, p. 48.

Objects of industrial art have form – that adapted to special uses. These objects take on aesthetic form, whether they are rugs, urns, or baskets, when the material is so arranged and adapted that it seems immediately the enrichment of the immediate experience of the one whose aesthetic perception is directed to it...Where the form is liberated from limitation to a specialized end and serves also the purposes of an immediate and vital experience, the form is aesthetic and not merely useful.[30]

General versus individual form

Form, pattern, and arrangement can be thought of at two distinct levels. *General form* is an arrangement or manner of composition that might be shared by a number of separate works. Examples include: sonata form; the Petrarchan sonnet form; organization according to the classic three unities of time, place, and action in drama; and the triangular arrangement of multiple figures in a history or story painting. In each case, the maker will be aware of working within the parameters of an established formal genre in a medium. It is often useful for students to practice within such formal genres, and experimentation within such general forms, carried out in relation to subject matters and manipulations of elements, may offer possibilities for new absorptive and expressive achievement.

Individual form or what some have called the organic unity of the elements of a work is closer to being a distinctive mark of exemplary artistic achievement. As Dewey puts it, "In a work of art, different acts, episodes, occurrences melt and fuse into a unity, and yet do not disappear and lose their own character as they do so."[31] In the distinctly successful work, that is to say, the different elements – for example, musical motifs, apples presented in impasto, beams and girders, occurrent thoughts in a protagonist of lyric – seem somehow to "fit" one another and the overall subject matter and expressive tenor of the work. The formal elements seem to require one another in just their particular places in the work. Any substitution or alteration of them would diminish the work's solicitation of and support for absorbed perception.

---

[30] *ibid.*, p. 116.   [31] *ibid.*, p. 38.

Beardsley's theory of individual form

Monroe Beardsley has developed the most detailed theory of the achievement of individual form in the various media of art. He takes being intended, through formal arrangement, to solicit and sustain an aesthetic
experience or an absorption in formal arrangement as the definition of
art.

> My answer [to the question, "What is art?"] is that an artwork is an
> arrangement of conditions intended to be capable of affording an
> experience with a marked aesthetic character – that is, an object (loosely
> speaking) in the fashioning of which the intention to enable it to satisfy
> the aesthetic interest played a significant causal part... Experience has a
> marked aesthetic character when it has some of the following features,
> including the first one: attention firmly fixed on a perceptual or
> intentional object; a feeling of freedom from concerns about matters
> outside that object; notable affect that is detached from practical ends;
> the sense of powers of discovery; and integration of the self and of its
> experiences.[32]

This definition clearly echoes both Kant's account of the art object's appealing to our cognitive powers in perception, without having any further
purpose, and Dewey's account of how, in attending to art, we focus on the
organization of perceptual qualities for its own sake. Beardsley adds that a
successful work of art invites and sustains "absorption in form and quality,
a giving-in to their force."[33]

It is not, however, required that all things that are rightly called art
actually afford such an experience, nor is it ruled out that other things
that are not works of art *do*. Beardsley remarks that "To define artworks
in this way does not entail either (1) that their aesthetic intentions are in
fact fulfilled, or (2) that other things besides artworks (natural and technological objects) cannot also afford experiences with marked aesthetic
character."[34] The point of Beardsley's definition is not to cast works of art
as all and only in fact successful aesthetic objects. Beautiful natural objects surely have marked aesthetic features. Beardsley's point is rather to
highlight the fact that the practice of making works of art is significantly
informed, perhaps even controlled, by an intention to afford aesthetic experience (though other intentions – to win renown, make money, or use

[32] Beardsley, *Aesthetics*, pp. xix, lxii.   [33] *ibid.*, p. lxxii.   [34] *ibid.*, p. xix.

up some leftover canvas) may also be present. Audiences attend to works *as art* when they explore in attentive perception whether this intention is in fact realized. It does seem true both that the work of artists is frequently significantly informed by such an intention and that audiences in engaging with art frequently explore in perception its manner and degree of realization. Distinctive, successful, absorbing formal arrangement (or the intention to achieve it) is one criterion of art.

Against the background of this general characterization of art, Beardsley goes on to develop detailed accounts of the features of formal arrangements in visual art, music, and literature that artists can manipulate in order to produce aesthetic experience. An initial distinction that is central to these detailed accounts is between the *parts* of a work (for example, a red brush stroke, a particular pitch, or a single word) and *emergent regional properties* of a work.[35] Emergent regional properties belong to a complex or to the whole work, but not to any of its parts. For example, a set of dots or brush strokes might produce an emergent squarish figure, or a series of pitches might produce a falling motive in a key. Emergent regional properties are constituted out of proper parts of the work, but they serve as independent foci of perceptual attention. Typically we see the squarish figure or hear the falling motive, rather than attending to each brush stroke or pitch one by one. Likewise, we read words in the context of whole thoughts, attending to the function of a word in expressing the thought, not centrally to single word after single word.

As aspects of visual design, itself emergent out of both parts and emergent regional properties, Beardsley lists color, which may vary in hue, brightness, or saturation; line, which may vary in length, orientation, or curvature; visual density; depth; rhythm (that controls the movement of the eye); and relative dominance (of figures and of figure vs. ground).[36] Aspects of sound design include duration, volume, timbre, pitch, auditory movement, rhythm, tonality, cadential drive, melody, mode, and harmony.[37] Literary form involves "the concrescence of patterns"[38] of significance and "semantical thickness"[39] achieved in a variety of ways, including metaphor, imagery, irony, multiple relatedness of themes, point of view, and emotive meaning. Crucially such concrescence and thickness

[35] *ibid.*, pp. 82–88.   [36] *ibid.*, pp. 87–107.   [37] *ibid.*, pp. 87–107.
[38] *ibid.*, p. 128.   [39] *ibid.*, p. 129.

occur in and through relations of *semantic* elements (words with their meanings), not in virtue of the mere shape or look of words alone. These semantic relations themselves become a focus of attention in part for their own sake, over and above any message they might convey. What matters for aesthetic experience of a literary work is that webs of words-with-meanings form such a focus for attention. (Beardsley cites with approval Cleanth Brooks' dictum that "The language of poetry is the language of paradox";[40] that is, beyond any message, the verbal pattern that is its vehicle is also a focus of attention in its own right.) Though Beardsley does offer a theory of aesthetically significant form in literature, as in other media of art, the form that is relevant is semantic, not merely syntactical.

Beardsley's remarks about the importance of visual design, sound design, and verbal design are well confirmed in the practice of many important working critics. For example, Michael Baxandall echoes Beardsley in regarding paintings as objects of "intentional visual interest,"[41] where we may take "legitimate satisfactions"[42] in the "superior organization – perceptual, emotional, constructive"[43] that a painting can display. Michael Fried has developed at length the language of *absorption* to describe the character of the satisfaction of our interest in visual pleasure (including how the design or arrangement presents its subject) by major paintings in the western tradition from Chardin through abstract expressionism.[44] Formal criticism focusing on patterns of development and significance (motivic, harmonic, rhythmic, etc.) has been the norm in the criticism of music. In literary criticism, not only Brooks and the New Critics, but also any critics who explicate the significance of semantic patterns (thematic, imagistic, emotive, point-of-view related, etc.) by focusing on their details, work within Beardsley's general idiom.

---

[40] *ibid.*, p. 152, note 9D, citing Cleanth Brooks, "The Language of Paradox," in *The Language of Poetry*, ed. Allen Tate (Princeton, NJ: Princeton University Press, 1942), pp. 358–66, later reprinted as chapter 1 of Brooks, *The Well Wrought Urn* (New York: Reynal & Hitchcock, 1947).

[41] Michael Baxandall, *Patterns of Intention: On the Historical Explanation of Pictures* (New Haven, CT: Yale University Press, 1985), p. 43.

[42] *ibid.*, p. viii.   [43] *ibid.*, p. 135.

[44] See Michael Fried, *Absorption and Theatricality: Painting and Beholder in the Age of Diderot* (Berkeley, CA: University of California Press, 1980), and Michael Fried, *Art and Objecthood: Essays and Reviews* (Chicago, IL: University of Chicago Press, 1998).

In sum, for Beardsley "the form of an aesthetic object is the total web of relations among its parts,"[45] including both its proper parts and its emergent regional properties. The web of relations may be instanced as both *texture* or relations among small-scale elements and *structure* or relations among large-scale elements.[46] When aesthetic experience (perceptual attention to the total web of relations) is *unified*, *intense*, and *complex* then there is successful art.[47] The unity of an experience is a matter of its "hanging together"; there is closure, or a beginning, middle, and end, or the experience is "unusually complete in itself." When there is intensity there is "a concentration of experience" and an emotion "characteristically bound to its object" (the work and what it presents). When there is complexity the elements of the work function as "heterogeneous but interrelated components of a phenomenally objective field," that is, as interrelated foci of absorbed, perceptual (including semantic) attention to the work.[48] Successful art invites and sustains unified, intense, and complex perceptual experience – absorption – and all genuinely artistic making properly aims at doing so (even where the result may be a failure, a partial success, or a mere exercise piece).

Criticisms of formalist-aesthetic theories of art

Despite (or because of) their intuitive plausibility and appeal, aesthetic theories of art have been subjected to considerable criticism. To many of their critics, such theories have seemed to domesticate art to an idle plaything of empty pleasure and in doing so to scant its cognitive, political, and spiritual significance. This line of criticism begins as early as Wordsworth's complaint in his 1800 "Preface" to the second edition of *Lyrical Ballads* that talk of *taste* is

> the language of men who speak of what they do not understand; who talk of Poetry as of a matter of amusement and idle pleasure; who will converse with us as gravely about a *taste* for Poetry, as they express it, as if it were a thing as indifferent as a taste for rope-dancing, or Frontiniac or Sherry.[49]

---

[45] Beardsley, *Aesthetics*, p. 168.   [46] *ibid.*, p. 169.   [47] *ibid.*, p. 462.
[48] *ibid.*, pp. 527–28.
[49] William Wordsworth, "Preface to *Lyrical Ballads*," in Wordsworth, *Selected Poems and Prefaces*, ed. Jack Stillinger (Boston, MA: Houghton Mifflin Company, 1965), pp. 445–64 at p. 454.

It continues in Duchamp's stance – definitive for a great deal of Dada and avant-garde art – that he is "interested in ideas – not merely in visual products."[50] The production of visual or aural or semantic beauty came to seem to many artists to be less interesting and important than the production of striking meaning or provocation or ironic wit. The philosophical claim that art is a thing of pleasure seemed to many practitioners itself to be a way of all at once misunderstanding, devaluing, and repressing the real cognitive, political, and spiritual insights (or wit) that art may have to offer. As Arthur C. Danto trenchantly puts this thought,

> Distinguishing the fine from the applied arts, and identifying the former as *les beaux arts*, constitutes a form of repression masked as exaltation paralleled only by the perception of women as the Fair Sex. To put works of art or to set women at what came to be known as an "aesthetic distance" – as objects whose essence and fulfillment consists in pleasing the senses – was a brilliant political response to what were felt as dark dangers in both...[In the arts] aesthetic distance then does what frames and pedestals do to icons and effigies, isolating them conceptually from the practical world and humiliating them as objects fit only to caress the disinterested and refined eye.[51]

In the face of their ambition to achieve "something closer to transformation rather than visual satisfaction"[52] – to achieve and embody striking meaning and insight – why should artists be required by theory to focus on form, arrangement, and the production of pleasure? Central traditions of conceptual art, of performance art, of various forms of constructivism in music (Boulez) and theatre (Brecht, Beckett), and of self-conscious modernism in narrative literature (Calvino, Barth) seek prominently to undo and criticize stale, perhaps bourgeois, obsessions with what they see as escapist pleasure. They work for the sake of ideas and insight, not absorption in form. Robert Rauschenberg notoriously once carefully erased a de Kooning drawing and then framed and exhibited it as "Erased De Kooning

---

[50] Marcel Duchamp, "Interview with James Johnson Sweeney," reprinted in *Theories of Modern Art*, ed. Chipp, p. 394.

[51] Arthur C. Danto, "The Space of Beauty: Review of *The Power of the Center: A Study of Composition in the Visual Arts* by Rudolf Arnheim," *New Republic* (November 15, 1982), pp. 32B–35B at p. 32B.

[52] Danto, *Embodied Meanings: Critical Essays and Aesthetic Meditations* (New York: Farrar, Straus, & Giroux, 1994), p. x.

Drawing" in order to make a point, presumably a piece of wit about artistic creativity and visual pleasure. As Timothy Binkley sums up these developments,

> Art in the twentieth century has emerged as a strongly self-critical discipline. It has freed itself of aesthetic parameters and sometimes creates directly with ideas unmediated by aesthetic qualities. An artwork is a piece: and a piece need not be an aesthetic object, or even an object at all.[53]

Perhaps worse yet, as both Kendall Walton and Arthur Danto have argued, *which* aesthetic response – absorption or disgust; awe, or indifference, or amusement – a given work properly produces is a function *not* of its arrangement or form alone, but of its independently established artistic identity and meaning. Walton, for example, invites us to notice that if Picasso's *Guernica* is regarded by us as one member of the class of *guernicas* – works that all possess the surface design of Picasso's, but some of which are molded into variously jagged or rolling bas-reliefs – then we would in all likelihood find it "cold, stark, and lifeless...or perhaps bland, dull, [and] boring" in comparison with other *guernicas*; it is only when we regard it (correctly) as a painting that we feel it to be "violent, dynamic, vital, [and] disturbing."[54] Which aesthetic properties a work has and displays is a function of which independently historically established class of works it inhabits. Aesthetic properties are not immediately evident in perception to the nonhistorical eye or ear alone. Danto has similarly argued that there can be "perceptually indistinguishable counterparts" – works that look exactly like each other: for example, a monochrome red square painted by a follower of Josef Albers, a canvas primed in red lead by Giorgione (but never painted any further), and a painting once imagined by Kierkegaard "The Israelites Crossing the Red Sea" (the Israelites have all crossed over, and the Egyptians have drowned), among other possible "red square" paintings.[55] These works all look exactly alike, yet they have quite

---

[53] Timothy Binkley, "Piece: Contra Aesthetics," *Journal of Aesthetics and Art Criticism* 35 (1977), pp. 265–77, reprinted in *Philosophy Looks at the Arts*, revised edn. ed. Joseph Margolis (Philadelphia, PN: Temple University Press, 1978), pp. 25–44 at p. 26.

[54] Kendall Walton, "Categories of Art," *Philosophical Review* 79 (1970), pp. 334–67; reprinted in *Philosophy Looks at the Arts*, ed. Margolis, pp. 88–114 at p. 99.

[55] Danto, *The Transfiguration of the Commonplace* (Cambridge, MA: Harvard University Press, 1981), p. 1.

distinct meanings and aesthetic properties. Giorgione's primed canvas is a mere thing with no artistic meaning; "The Israelites Crossing the Red Sea" might be deeply moving. Beardsley had claimed that "two objects that do not differ in any observable properties cannot differ in aesthetic value";[56] given Walton's and Danto's examples, this seems wrong.

Building on such cases, Danto argues further that artworks cannot be defined or identified as all and only those things that produce a certain kind of favorable, absorbing aesthetic experience. We have to know first – on independent historical grounds – whether the thing before us is an artwork, and if so which one, in order to know how to feel in attending to it.

> If knowledge that something is an artwork makes a difference in the mode of aesthetic response to an object – if there are differential aesthetic responses to indiscernible objects when one is an artwork and the other a natural thing – then ... we should have to be able to distinguish works of art from natural things or mere artifacts in order to define the appropriate kind of response. Hence we could not use that kind of response to define the concept of the artwork.[57]

That is, artworks cannot be picked out as all and only those things that afford absorptive pleasure, independently of historical knowledge, and art cannot be defined as that which produces such pleasure independently of historically determined representational and expressive meaning. Moreover, as Danto adds, not all works of art produce pleasure at all: "we are repelled, disgusted, even sickened by certain works of art."[58]

Defenses of the aesthetic interest of art

These criticisms of aesthetic theories of art are based on accurate observations. Works do have aesthetic properties in relation to their historically determined category memberships. There can be perceptually indistinguishable counterparts with different aesthetic properties. Some art, and some successful art, is horrifying. Yet it is not clear that these points hit their mark and succeed in undermining aesthetic theories of art.

Recall that for Beardsley the formal elements whose arrangement pleases in a successful work of literary art are words-plus-their-meanings.

---

[56] Beardsley, *Aesthetics*, p. 503.   [57] Danto, *Transfiguration of the Commonplace*, p. 91.
[58] *ibid.*, p. 92.

Semantic features of words and sentences – including not only reference and sense, but also imagery, metaphor, irony, point of view, etc. – are among the elements that are to be arranged so as to absorb the attentive mind. One need not dwell on the mere look or shape of marks alone. (Kant similarly notes that aesthetic ideas – semantic complexes bound up with the arrangement and symbolized by it – are a focus of our interest in art.) Likewise for visual and aural art. Any broadly representational features of works are included as elements of the arrangement to which audiences are to attend. There is no requirement that aesthetic pleasure be afforded in the act of immediate perception of the work, independently of any awareness of what it is about or what it expresses. Likewise there is no requirement in aesthetic theories that the audience prescind from prior historical knowledge of the genre of a work at hand or of its place in a line of historical development either within a genre or across genres. Instead, according to aesthetic theories the audience is standardly to attend to *how* representational and expressive features are embodied in the formal arrangement. Is the arrangement – including the arrangement of representational and expressive features (motives, images, descriptions of actions and perceptions, etc.) unified, intense, and complex? Does it display purposiveness without a purpose in satisfying the attentive mind that contemplates not the meaning for its own sake, but the meaning as it is singularly embodied in the arrangement? If so, then the work succeeds in the aims of art.

It is true that there can be successful work that is immediately horrifying or disgusting. But it does not follow that it is not also pleasing and absorbing. Our disgust or horror may be directed to the subject matter, but we may also be pleased by and absorbed in how that subject matter is wholly rendered by the form. Quite arguably such a mix of horror or disgust *and* absorption is just what is going on in our relations to cases such as Picasso's *Guernica* or Philip Roth's description in *Letting Go* of a child dying from a fractured skull. Horrified, disgusted, repelled, sickened, or enraged as we are by what is presented, we nonetheless go on looking or reading, as the work embodies in its arrangement a kind of *saturated* authorial point of view on its subject: nothing is shirked; attention is wholly fixed on the subject matter and *its* significance within human life; all the elements of the formal arrangement serve to fix authorial attention; in dwelling on the arrangement we, the audience, participate in that authorial attention, finding horror in the subject matter but also aesthetic satisfaction in both the fullness of attention and the fullness of its embodiment in the arrangement.

The further one moves in attending to a given work away from dwelling on the arrangement (in relation to what is represented or expressed) and to dwelling *only* on what is represented or expressed, the more the work will seem to drift away from successful art and toward propaganda or therapeutic (but ill-formed) venting or treatise or advertising. When our attention is, in contrast, to some extent solicited and sustained by how just this formal arrangement presents its subject matter, then and only then is it the kind of attention that is appropriate to and characteristic of successful art.[59] Pleasure in formal arrangement is one criterion of art. This is the point that Dewey is making when he contrasts "complete surrender in perception"[60] to the work of art with the tendency to withdraw from perception, message in pocket, in order to act. Similarly, Roger Scruton notes that we take an aesthetic interest in an object *x* or an interest in *x* "for its own sake" if and only if the answer to the question "Why are you interested in *x*?" consists in a further description of *x*.[61] Our attention must be held by just *this* formal arrangement (of material-representational-expressive elements). Dewey notes that "one does not want the object for the sake of something else."[62]

It is easy, however, to overstate this point and so to suggest that *only* formal arrangement, independent of representational and expressive dimensions, matters for the experience of art. Kant, Bell, and Beardsley, among others, are often accused of this sort of overstatement, with some initial plausibility even if without final justice.[63] Dewey is correcting both Kant and his own overstatement when he immediately adds that the

---

[59] See Richard Eldridge, "Form and Content: An Aesthetic Theory of Art," *British Journal of Aesthetics* 25 (1985) reprinted in *Philosophy of Art*, ed. Neill and Ridley, pp. 239–53.

[60] Dewey, *Art as Experience*, p. 269.   [61] Scruton, *Art and Imagination*, p. 143.

[62] Dewey, *Art as Experience*, p. 254.

[63] For useful accounts of how even Bell, despite his remarks about significant form as the sole focus of attention to art, in the end takes significant form itself to have a further representational function in presenting the reality of "things in themselves," see Thomas M. McLaughlin, "Clive Bell's Aesthetic: Tradition and Significant Form," *Journal of Aesthetics and Art Criticism* 35, 4 (summer 1977), pp. 433–43.

aesthetic experience is characterized by "not absence of desire and thought but their thorough incorporation into perceptual experience."[64]

It is also important to remember that the absorptive pleasure that is afforded by successful arrangement is not a mere sensory buzz or tingle. Instead it involves the active use of cognitive powers of imagination and conceptualization in order to explore the representational and expressive significance of formal elements and their interrelation. Moreover, this absorptive pleasure is itself significant within human life, not gratuitous. We seem to see clearly and to feel the significance of (perhaps very abstractly) presented actions and objects in relation to human life in time. As Dewey puts it, both echoing Hegel and anticipating Heidegger,

> A work of art elicits and accentuates the quality of being a whole and of belonging to the larger, all-inclusive whole which is the universe in which we live. This fact, I think, is the explanation of that feeling of exquisite intelligibility and clarity we have in the presence of an object that is experienced with esthetic intensity. It explains also the religious feeling that accompanies aesthetic perception. We are, as it were, introduced into a world beyond this world which is nonetheless the deeper reality of the world in which we live in our ordinary experience.[65]

Beauty in nature can induce this feeling of being in the presence of a world beyond this world, a world which is nonetheless the deeper reality of our world. A successful work of art can seem to embody and exemplify full action and full meaningfulness as such – a meaning wholly fused to material elements in arrangement – and so to anticipate and promise a human world suffused with meaningful action, rather than emptiness and coercion. In both cases, the object of absorptive pleasure is something considerably more significant than an occasion for idle sensory delectation. We are pleased in and through actively exploring the beautiful natural scene or object and the formal arrangement of the successful work. This active exploration discloses in continuous attention dimensions of meaning and presence.

But this difference between genuine aesthetic pleasure and mere delectation also makes it clear that success in formal arrangement is not at all separable from success in either artistic representation or artistic

---

[64] Dewey, *Art as Experience*, p. 254.   [65] *ibid.*, p. 195.

expression. The achievement of formal success involves both the presentation of some subject matter as a focus for thought fused to perception and the presentation of an emotional attitude toward both the subject matter and its material vehicle. Kant remarks that the successful work of art will "make sensible [*versinnlichen*]"[66] via its arrangement a deep sense of the meaning of things in relation to human life. To understand this more fully, we must consider not only artistic representation and formal arrangement, but also artistic expression.

---

[66] Kant, *Critique*, trans. Guyer and Matthews, §49, p. 192.

4 Expression

Feelings about subject matters in life: Wordsworth, Tolstoy, and Collingwood

Against the idea that works of art present a subject matter and the idea that works of art embody pleasing formal arrangements, it can seem important to emphasize that works of art are products of human action – *made* things, not just either imitations or forms. Without this emphasis artworks can seem either too much like gratuitous reproductions of reality (like mirrors or reflections in ponds) or too much like objects of idle pleasure and amusement (like pretty decorations). When we instead focus on works of art as things that human beings make, then these misemphases can be corrected. Though they do present a subject matter and please through arrangement, works of art are also made in order somehow to communicate something – an attitude, a point of view, or a feeling about a subject matter – that lies in some sense "in" the maker. Audiences typically approach a work with an interest in what it *says*, that is, with an interest in which attitudes and emotions toward its subject matter on the part of its maker it makes manifest. It is natural therefore to think that artworks are *expressive* objects and that it is distinctive of *artistic* representations and formal arrangements – in contrast with scientific treatises and decorations – that they have as a central function the *expression* of attitudes and emotions toward their subject matter. Only by attending to art as expression can we properly engage with its distinctive kind of significance: the communication of emotion and attitude.

In the 1800 preface to the second edition of *Lyrical Ballads*, Wordsworth eloquently sketches an expression theory of poetry as a way of establishing its importance in human life, in contrast with decadent and idle entertainment. His principal purpose in his poems, he tells us,

> was to choose incidents and situations from common life, and to relate or describe them, throughout, as far as was possible in a selection of

language really used by men, and, at the same time, to throw over them a certain colouring of imagination, whereby ordinary things should be presented to the mind in an unusual aspect...Humble and rustic life was generally chosen, because, in that condition, the essential passions of the heart find a better soil in which they can attain their maturity, are less under restraint, and speak a plainer and more emphatic language; because in that condition of life our elementary feelings co-exist in a state of greater simplicity, and, consequently, may be more accurately contemplated and more forcibly communicated.[1]

Crucially, "the feeling therein developed gives importance to the action and situation, and not the action and situation to the feeling."[2] That is, the ordinary affairs of life are chosen as subject matters, *not* in order simply to communicate information about them (such as median age of marriage, or average income tax paid, say) but rather because these subject matters are objects of forceful feeling, when feeling is healthy, and because here feelings can best be *understood* (contemplated) and *shared* (communicated). Here the poet serves as a kind of bootstrapping device through which people in general may come themselves both to have more appropriate feelings toward the stuff of ordinary life and to be more aware of those feelings: to be clearer about their character and their appropriateness to their objects. The poet feels more readily than do the rest of us, but nonetheless typically and on our behalf.

The Poet is chiefly distinguished from other men by a greater promptness to think and feel without immediate external excitement, and a greater power in expressing such thoughts and feelings as are produced in him in that manner. But these passions and thoughts and feelings are the general passions and thoughts and feelings of men.[3]

As a result of the poet's expression of *our* feeling, "the understanding of the Reader must necessarily be in some degree enlightened, and his affections strengthened and purified."[4]

Wordsworth's sense of the expressive task of the poet seems readily to extend to other media of art. When Cervantes juxtaposes Don Quixote's idealism against Sancho Panza's common sense, when Van Gogh paints walking shoes strewn on the floor, when Anthony Caro presents an array

---

[1] Wordsworth, "Preface to *Lyrical Ballads*," pp. 445–64 at pp. 446–47.
[2] *ibid.*, p. 448.   [3] *ibid.*, p. 457.   [4] *ibid.*, p. 448.

of beams and girders, or when Balanchine choreographs for the music of Stravinsky, we are in each case invited to partake in and so to come to understand a feeling about what is presented or arranged for us. We are to see and to feel the comparative virtues (and the complementarity and tension between them) of Don Quixote and Sancho Panza; we are to see and to feel what these shoes (and the countryside in which he walks and paints) mean to Van Gogh and may mean to us; we are to feel the experience of space and point of view, both as they are invited by Caro's arrangement and as Caro's arrangement makes us aware of point of view in life; and we are to see how Stravinsky's musical form can be responded to in felt motion that we, in turn, follow with feeling. Even Sol LeWitt, in his abstract, geometric constructions is inviting us to follow and partake in the work of construction, and in doing so to feel the values of order and constructive proceduralism that are embodied in the work, in the face of but hence in relation to the rest of life. Artists seem typically to attend to and seek to embody their own feelings about a subject matter or experience in their forms and representations, therein inviting us to share in both those feelings and their expressive clarification in the work. Expressiveness is a criterion of art.

Significantly, the expression in question in a work of art is *not* achieved through an immediate gush of feeling into the work. It is different from the immediacy of horror one might feel in witnessing a terrible traffic accident or from the immediacy of empathy one might feel for those stuck in grinding poverty. Instead, when artistic expression is aimed at, then the emotion is, as Wordsworth puts it, "recollected in tranquility."[5] There is a sense of *working through* the subject matter and how it is appropriate to feel about it, a working through undertaken by the artist and subsequently followed and recapitulated by the audience. Feeling is here mediated by thought and by artistic activity. The poet must, Wordsworth observes, think "long and deeply" about the subject, "for our continued influxes of feeling are modified and directed by our thoughts."[6] One must "look steadily at [one's] subject,"[7] attending to both the specificity of this situation, object, experience, or action and its place in human life in general: how this situation, object, experience, or feeling is affiliated with further possible subject matters and routes of feeling.

Here the enterprise of art seems very different from undertaking simply to please and absorb an audience. Wordsworth claims that only

---

[5] *ibid.*, p. 460.   [6] *ibid.*, p. 448.   [7] *ibid.*, p. 450.

through the achievement of artistic expressiveness might his contemporaries hope to overcome the "savage torpor" of his times (a general indifference and callousness toward life and feeling) and a consequent "degrading thirst after outrageous stimulation"[8] (an addictive need for vulgar spectacle in order to feel anything at all). For Wordsworth, talk of works of art as pleasurable objects of taste encourages both passivity in the audience and addictive attachment to passively received spectacle. When all one can say about a work is "I like it" or "it was fun," then the task of expressiveness – of working through how it is appropriate to feel about a difficult, real subject in ordinary life – is being shirked. As Aristotle held in characterizing *catharsis* as the purpose of tragedy, a working through and clarification of feeling must take place, in order for there to be genuine artistic expressiveness. But in contrast to Aristotle's focus on fixed forms of plot or arrangement through which *catharsis* might be achieved, Wordsworth and other theorists of expression are struck by the changing material of ordinary life, about which feeling is to be clarified, by the need for new forms of art in order to achieve this clarification (the genuine poet must "create the taste by which he is to be enjoyed"[9]), by the resistances to the work of clarification that are set up by the common pursuit of spectacle and amusement, and by the crucial role of the creative artist in overcoming repressiveness and opening up authentic routes of feeling on behalf of us all.

Wordsworth's emphasis on the centrality to art of the task of the expression of feeling is taken up in a good deal of subsequent theorizing about art. Tolstoy claims that

> To evoke in oneself a feeling one has once experienced, and having evoked it in oneself, then, by means of movements, lines, colors, sounds, or forms expressed in words, so to transmit that feeling that others may experience the same feeling – this is the activity of art.
>
> Art is a human activity consisting in this, that one man consciously by means of certain signs, hands onto others feelings he has lived through, and that others are infected by those feelings and also experience them.[10]

---

[8] *ibid.*, p. 449.

[9] Wordsworth, "Essay Supplementary to the Preface (1815)," in Wordsworth, *Selected Poems and Prefaces*, ed. Stillinger, p. 477.

[10] Leo Tolstoy, *What is Art?*, trans. Aylmer Maude (Indianapolis, IN: Bobbs-Merrill, 1960), p. 51.

Like Wordsworth, Tolstoy emphasizes that an artwork is a made thing –
a product of human activity, not a mere pleasing natural object – and a
thing made with a purpose: the communication of feeling that has been
"lived through" within the framework of ordinary life. The feeling must
be "evoked in oneself" ("recollected in tranquility"), not simply suffered,
and it must be embodied in the arrangement of movements, lines, colors, sounds, or forms expressed in words that is the work. Art is "not a
service of Beauty,"[11] for that service too easily, even typically, degenerates
into class-bound, decadent worship of spectacle, exemplified for Tolstoy by
opera, a "counterfeit"[12] art that furthers a "stunting of human life" and
makes those devoted to it "dull to all the serious phenomena of life and
skillful only at rapidly twisting their legs, their tongues, or their fingers."[13]
The office of art is rather to call our attention to ordinary life, real life,
and how it is appropriate to feel about it, not to fob us off with either
decadent titillation or narcotic, vapid prettiness.

The English philosopher R. G. Collingwood, in developing his own
expression theory of art, likewise stresses the difference between passive
and narcotic response to a putative "aesthetic quality" in things and active
engagement on the part of an audience with art as expression.

> Aesthetic theory [i.e. the philosophy of art] is the theory not of beauty
> but of art. The theory of [artistic] beauty ... is merely an attempt to
> construct an aesthetic on a "realistic" basis, that is, to explain away the
> aesthetic activity by appeal to a supposed quality of the things with
> which, in that experience, we are in contact; this supposed quality,
> invented to explain the activity, being in fact nothing but the activity
> itself, falsely located not in the agent but in his external world.[14]

Instead of looking for an art-relevant formal *quality* in things, we should
in theorizing turn our attention to what we actually and actively do with
art, when we engage with it properly as expression. The proper experience of art "arises from within; it is not a specific reaction to a stimulus proceeding from a specific type of external object";[15] it is, rather,
an active grasping of what is expressed, a recapitulation of and participation in the artist's working through of feeling in relation to subject

---

[11] *ibid.*, p. 131.   [12] *ibid.*, pp. 131, 133.   [13] *ibid.*, p. 10.
[14] R. G. Collingwood, *The Principles of Art* (Oxford: Clarendon Press, 1938), p. 41.
[15] *ibid.*, p. 40.

matter. To suppose otherwise is to confuse art with amusement and spectacle – a confusion that is all too common in the modern industrial world.

A way of life can die when people become unable to confront it, to feel toward it, and to believe in it, but instead fall into boredom and the pursuit of distractions from life. Collingwood argues that this kind of loss of emotional commitment to a way of life is what brought about the downfall of the Roman Empire. He then claims that we are ourselves not much better off.

> We live in a world in which most of what goes by [the] name [of art] is amusement...[A long-growing and deep-seated conviction that its own way of life was not worth preserving – the disease that felled Rome] is notoriously endemic among ourselves. Among its symptoms are the unprecedented growth in the amusement trade, to meet what has become an insatiable craving; an almost universal agreement that the kinds of work on which the existence of a civilization like ours most depends (notably the work of industrial operatives and the clerical staff in business of every kind, and even that of the agricultural laborers and other food-winners who are the prime agents in the maintenance of every civilization hitherto existing) is an intolerable drudgery; the discovery that what makes this intolerable is not the pinch of poverty or bad housing but the nature of the work itself in the conditions our civilization has created; the demand, arising out of this discovery, and universally accepted as reasonable, for an increased provision of leisure, which means opportunity for amusement, and of amusements to fill it; the use of alcohol, tobacco, and many other drugs, not for ritual purposes, but to deaden the nerves and distract the mind from the tedious and irritating concerns of ordinary life; the almost universal confession that boredom, or lack of interest in life, is felt as a constant or constantly recurring state of mind; the feverish attempts to dispel this boredom either by more amusement or by dangerous or criminal occupations; and finally (to cut the catalogue short) the discovery, familiar *mutatis mutandis* to every bankrupt in last stages of his progress, that customary remedies have lost their bite and that the dose must be increased.[16]

---

[16] *ibid.*, pp. 104, 96–97.

In contrast, serious art is not a matter of amusement, spectacle, and increasing doses of narcotic. It engages with ordinary life. The genuine artist will attend to ordinary life, with all its "tedious and irritating concerns," and to the conditions of modern labor and of the reproduction of social life. Genuine art will present the stuff of ordinary life as a subject matter of feeling, as it arises in the responsive artist and is communicated creatively through the expressive work. Honest work will be presented *as* worthy of respect; tedium arising from meaninglessness will be presented *as* dispiriting; self-importance will be lampooned *as* dangerous and comical. The faithful presentation of modern life, and especially of conditions of work and of social reproduction, as subjects for feeling, is a central office of genuine, expressive art. One might think of Philip Roth's reverent presentation of the process of glove manufacturing in 1950s Newark, New Jersey, in *American Pastoral*, or Cindy Sherman's investigations of Hollywood "processing" or "counterfeiting" of women's identities, or Sam Mendes' attentions to various repressions, distractions, and discoveries of American suburban life in his film *American Beauty*, among many other examples. In Wordsworth's phrasing, the aim here is "truth which is testimony"[17] about how the phenomena of life are to be felt about. The genuine work of art expresses and communicates participation in apt feeling.

Any expression theory of art must further provide answers to three closely interrelated questions:

(i) What is expressed in art? In particular, is it the individual artist's feeling or attitude, or is it a collective-cultural feeling in which the artist participates?

(ii) How is artistic expression achieved? In particular, is there a distinctive psychodynamic process of expression, or is expression rather a matter more either of surface, "physiognomic" similarities between works and human facial, vocal, and postural configurations or of the successful formal working of materials in a medium?

(iii) Why does artistic expression matter? How, and how well, does an account of our interest in expression elucidate our interest in art?

What is expressed in art? Hegel versus Danto

G. W. F. Hegel argues that a central task of art is the expression of the spirit and the sense of what is highest that is held in common by a nation

---

17 Wordsworth, "Preface to *Lyrical Ballads*," p. 454.

or people. There can be merely decorative art, individualist art that is frivolously expressive, and in general art determined by extrinsic purposes. "Art can be used as a fleeting play, affording recreation and entertainment, decorating our surroundings, [and] giving pleasantness to the externals of our life."[18] But

> Fine art…only fulfils its supreme task when it has placed itself in the same sphere as religion and philosophy, and when it is simply one way of bringing to our minds and expressing the *Divine*, the deepest interests of mankind, and the most comprehensive truths of the spirit. In works of art the nations have deposited their richest inner intuitions and ideas, and art is often the key, and in many nations the sole key, to understanding their philosophy and religion.[19]

Hegel's account of art as *cultural* expression of a shared sense of what is highest has clear advantages. It enables us to see collectively produced, culturally central works such as Rouen Cathedral (*c.* 1160–*c.* 1600) or Angkor Watt, the Khmer Buddhist temple at Angkor, Cambodia (early twelfth century) as expressive objects, without having to specify any individual whose particular emotions or attitudes such works express.

Hegel's account further enables us to see how and why expression might matter as other than an item of an individual maker's biography. Collectively produced, culturally central works of art make manifest emotions and attitudes that themselves inform whole cultures. Hegel argues that the emotions and attitudes toward what is highest that inform any one culture are internally related to – that is, are variations of – the emotions and attitudes that inform any culture. "Works of fine art," he claims, are "the first reconciling middle term between pure thought and what is merely external, sensuous, and transient, between nature and finite reality and the infinite freedom of conceptual thinking."[20] That is to say, human beings in general can think and reason, in the sense that they can articulate and respond to arguments and to what count as good reasons for doing something. They seek to exercise this power so as to make within nature, itself partly hostile and partly beneficent, a cultural world in which they can in general act according to shared reasons, not only

---

[18] G. W. F. Hegel, *Aesthetics: Lectures on Fine Art*, trans. T. M. Knox (Oxford: Clarendon Press, 1975), vol. I, p. 7.
[19] *ibid.*   [20] *ibid.*, vol. I, p. 8.

according to the brute demands of survival or in response to coercion, and so come to feel themselves to be at home.

Collectively produced, culturally central works of art are ways of articulating and furthering this ambition in sensuous form. Any such work will embody a strategy for anticipating and promoting freedom within cultural life. It will express a sense of what is worth caring about and worshiping, will express a sense of the point or purpose of human life and practice. Therefore any such work will be comparable with other such works, as embodying such a strategy. Strategies of cultural freedom are hence of inherent interest to human beings in any cultural situation, as they struggle to live more freely. "The universal need for art...is man's rational need to lift the inner and outer world into his spiritual consciousness as an object [*Gegenstand*: object of experience] in which he recognizes again his own self."[21]

> Art's vocation is to unveil the *truth* in the form of sensuous artistic configuration, to set forth the reconciled opposition just mentioned [*viz.* that between abstract law, duty, and responsiveness to reasons, on the one hand, and the abundance of phenomena, natural necessity, and sensuous inclinations and impulses, on the other], and so to have its end and aim in itself, in this very setting forth and unveiling.[22]

In art, that is to say, and especially in collectively produced, culturally central works of free or fine art, a sense of what human rational activity is *for* is articulated and embodied, thence to be further worked through, as our understandings of ourselves and our possibilities of cultural life advance. For example, Sophocles' *Antigone* – written by Sophocles, but developing a conflict central to Greek culture – presents an opposition between the value of positive, human political authority, embodied in Creon, and the values of family piety and respect for the gods, embodied in Antigone. Both sets of values legitimately have authority over us, and here they come into tragic conflict. Yet although *Antigone* is a tragedy, it also further presents "the vision of an affirmative reconciliation and the equal validity of both the powers that were in conflict."[23] It shows

---

[21] *ibid.*, vol. I, p. 31.

[22] *ibid.*, vol. I, p. 55; see pp. 53–54 for Hegel's specification of the terms of the opposition.

[23] *ibid.*, vol. II, p. 1216.

that each power or set of values requires the other in order itself to be furthered in ongoing social life. Without families and piety there are no cultivated individuals formed by family and religious training to enter into the life of the political community; without positive political authority, there is no stable framework within which family life and religious training might be carried on.

The oppositions between abstract law, duty, and responsiveness to reason (itself capable of attaching to either civic life or family life, among other things), on the one hand, and the abundance of phenomena, natural necessity, and sensuous inclinations and impulses, on the other, are real ones that human beings face and seek to overcome in experience.

> These are oppositions which have not been invented at all by the
> subtlety of reflection or the pedantry of philosophy; in numerous forms
> they have always preoccupied and troubled the human consciousness,
> even if it is modern culture that has first worked them out most sharply
> and driven them up to the peak of harshest contradiction.[24]

In modernity, people care about this and that as natural inclinations move them, within the bustle of divided labor and the framework of class antagonisms, typically without noticing or understanding what many others do. But though these oppositions are sharp, they can nonetheless be worked through. Their "mediation," Hegel claims, "is no mere demand, but what is absolutely accomplished and is ever self-accomplishing."[25] Art – and especially art that is collectively produced and culturally central – matters because it expresses sensuously an initial sense of the possibility of this mediation and a direction for its development.

Hegel then argues that fine art's initial, sensuous expression of the possibility of a life of cultural freedom declines in importance with the advent of new, more adequate forms of expression of this possibility: Christian religion and Hegelian philosophy. "Art, considered in its highest vocation is, and remains for us" – we moderns – "a thing of the past."[26] The Symbolic form of art, for example the pyramids of Egypt, gave mute and inchoate expression to this possibility, abstracted from any effective development of cultural life.[27] Classical art – preeminently Greek sculpture of the gods in human shape – effectively presented human life as a locus of freedom,

---

[24] *ibid.*, vol. I, p. 54.   [25] *ibid.*, vol. I, p. 55.   [26] *ibid.*, p. 11.
[27] On symbolic art, see *ibid.*, pp. 76–77.

meaning, and value, but only in visual images and in connection with freedom made available only for a few. In its images, it presents *"implicitly the unity of the divine nature with the human."*[28] Modern art, or what Hegel calls Romantic art, represents a cultural world of achieved freedom as a nonactual object of inner longing and feeling, hence as something to be achieved through real cultural practice, guided by religion and philosophy. Hence Romantic art matters less than does Classical art. Romantic art – first in Christian paintings of the Crucifixion, and then in modern literature and music – "has won a content which goes beyond and above the classical form of art and its mode of expression...Inwardness celebrates its triumph over the external world and manifests its victory in and on the external itself, whereby what is apparent to the senses alone sinks into worthlessness."[29] Romantic art expresses feeling in relation to the thought that present culture can and should be recast so as to achieve freedom, even if the actual shape of free life must be sketched in detail more by religion and philosophy than by art.

While Hegel's theory offers a clear account of the expressive meaning and function of a number of collectively produced, culturally central works of art – including especially temples, cathedrals, altarpieces, and other forms of religious liturgical and monumental art – it is easy to doubt that it is satisfactory as a theory of art in general. It is not clear that all human beings and all cultures in fact have exactly the same problem of the achievement of freedom, nor is it clear that that problem is solvable. Perhaps oppositions between ways of life cannot wholly be worked through, culturally and politically. The idea that they might be strikes many nowadays as an implausible theodicy: Hegel's last-ditch and failed effort to posit comprehensive, God-centered meaning at work in the world. Even if one reads Hegel's remarks about God and freedom as requiring no external agency beyond the doings of human beings themselves (as Hegel surely intends), the claim that oppositions between ways of life and consequent value commitments can be wholly mediated seems implausible. Not only are there oppositions between different cultures with different conceptions of what is highest, cultures are themselves mongrelized, in being composed of individuals with divergent backgrounds and changing commitments. Even if it is true that works of art – the highest and best works of art that fulfill art's "supreme function" – express in sensuous form a

---

[28] *ibid.*, p. 79.   [29] *ibid.*, pp. 79, 81.

conception of what is highest and embody an anticipation of human freedom in its service, it is not clear that all such expressions will be quite
commensurable with and transparent to one another. They may remain
significantly shaped by the local and particular, in the form of existent
practices of art and other contingent practical commitments. Exactly *how*
freedom is anticipated and how a sense of what is highest is embodied
in sensuous form may differ significantly among a university scientist, a
migrant farm worker, a middle-class suburban teacher, and an urban club
owner, to say nothing of the differences associated with ethnicity, race, or
gender. As Stanley Cavell once observed, "the Spirit of the Age is not easy
to place, ontologically or empirically."[30] While there can be commanding
works that bring together many audiences – Louis Armstrong's *West End
Blues*, say, or Victor Fleming's *The Wizard of Oz* – oppositions nonetheless
remain. Perhaps we need a somewhat more individualist and pluralized
theory of expression.

In *The Transfiguration of the Commonplace*, Arthur C. Danto develops just
such a theory. He begins his account by arguing that works of art, like bits
of language, have *aboutness*; they present a subject matter. Only in virtue
of this is a given artwork distinct from a mere thing that is perceptually
indiscernible from it. Duchamp's readymade sculpture *Bottle Dryer* (1914)
is visually indistinguishable from any of a number of pieces of manufactured ironwork used in restaurants and wineries, since it began life as one
of these pieces. Unlike the others, however, Duchamp's sculpture is *about*
something: say, the presence of striking form *in* ordinary objects, the overcoming of boundaries between art and life, the paramount importance of
conception and wit in art making, and so forth. As Danto puts the general
point:

> Artworks as a class contrast with real things in just the way in which
> words do, even if they are "in every other sense" real…Art differs from
> reality in much the same way that language does when language is
> employed descriptively [i.e. when *it* is about something]…This is not at
> all to say that art is a language, but only that its ontology is of a piece
> with that of language, and that the contrast exists between reality and it
> which exists between reality and discourse.[31]

[30] Stanley Cavell, "Aesthetic Problems of Modern Philosophy," in S. Cavell, *Must We
Mean What We Say?* (New York: Charles Scribner's Sons, 1969), p. 73.
[31] Danto, *Transfiguration of the Commonplace*, pp. 82, 83.

That artworks unlike mere real things are representations, have about-ness, or have a semantic dimension does not yet suffice to distinguish them from *other*, nonartistic representations. There are representations such as "the picture of a cat in the child's alphabet book...whose status as art is pretty moot."[32] Such representations, together with many words and sentences used descriptively, are what they are in virtue of their semantic dimension, in virtue of their being interpreted as they are.

> But then the question of when is a thing an artwork becomes one with the question of when is an interpretation of a thing an *artistic* interpretation. For it is a characterizing feature of the entire class of objects [viz. representations] of which artworks compose a subpopulation that they are what they are because interpreted as they are. But since not all members of this class are artworks, not all these interpretations are artistic interpretations.[33]

What, then, makes an interpretation an interpretation *of art*? How does art manage to mean or represent *artistically*?

To answer these questions, Danto turns to the theory of expression. "Works of art," he proposes, "in categorical contrast with mere representations, use the means of representation in a way that is not exhaustively specified when one has exhaustively specified what is being represented... An artwork expresses something about its content, in contrast with an ordinary representation."[34] This observation, however, is just a first step. The crucial notion of a representation expressing something about its content is still underarticulated. Any representation – even the humblest sentence in an elementary logic textbook or a casual doodle in the margin of a student's notebook – will express some attitude or other on the part of its maker toward its content. All representations (of whatever quality, artistic interest, or banality) exist because their makers had the attitude that this subject matter was at least marginally worth representing in this way. What, then, makes an expression of an attitude toward a content *artistic*?

Here Danto proposes that "the point of intersection between style, expression, and rhetoric must be close to what we are in pursuit of."[35] Ordinary sentences in textbooks or illustrations in some alphabet books have no particular style. They are not rhetorically effective (nor are they intended to be) in bringing their audiences to feel something in relation

---

[32] *ibid.*, p. 127.   [33] *ibid.*, p. 135.   [34] *ibid.*, pp. 147–48, 148.   [35] *ibid.*, p. 165.

to their contents. Unlike metaphors, they do not invite their audiences actively to see their subject in a new light. (Metaphor, for Danto, is a central device of rhetoric.) Works of art, in contrast, *do* have distinctive style and *do* invite us to "see" their subject actively in a new way. "It is as if a work of art were like an externalization of the artist's consciousness, as if we could see his way of seeing and not merely what he saw."[36] Rembrandt, for example, paints Hendrijke Stoeffels – his mistress and mother of their daughter – *as* Bathsheba. In doing so, he includes all her folds and wrinkles

> because they are part of the woman he loves. And *that woman*, with just those marks of life upon her, *is* Bathsheba, a woman of beauty enough to tempt a king to murder for possession of her. And that is the metaphor of the work: to show that plain dumpy Amsterdam woman as the apple of a king's eye *has to be an expression of love*.[37]

In a fully artistic representation, then, we actively *participate in* a way of seeing the world with feeling that the work expresses, enables, and solicits from us. We encounter not just the thing seen, but another seeing and feeling mind in whose modes of attention we can participate.

> What, then, is interesting and essential in art is the spontaneous ability the artist has of enabling us to see his way of seeing the world – not just the world as if the painting were like a window, but the world as given by him. In the end we do not simply see that naked woman sitting on a rock, as voyeurs stealing a glimpse through an aperture. We see her as she is seen with love by virtue of a representation magically embedded in the work.[38]

Danto further provides a subtle account of what a *way of seeing* is, in which he attempts to balance the social and individual dimensions of this achievement. Meanings, attitudes, and emotions do not spring *ex nihilo* from an isolated experiencing consciousness. Rather, "meanings more or less come from the world in which the artist lives;...they must belong to the world the artists find themselves in, and are part of that historical moment."[39] That is, there are, one might say, historically afforded patterns of grief, love, awe, and honor in relation to appropriate objects, and no one comes to have such emotions and attitudes except by way of engaging

---

[36] *ibid.*, p. 164.   [37] *ibid.*, p. 195.   [38] *ibid.*, p. 207.
[39] Danto, *Embodied Meanings*, p. xiii.

with (and then perhaps altering) such patterns. In this respect, meaning is social in nature. The achievement of the artist is not to invent meanings out of whole cloth, but to embody them. "The originality of the artist comes from inventing modes of embodying meanings she or he may share with communities of very large circumference."[40]

But it is also true that it is the individual artist's distinctive, personal way of seeing (itself achieved against a historical background of emotion and attitude) that is embodied in the successful work. "The greatness of the work is the greatness of the representation the work makes material. If style is the man, greatness of style is greatness of person."[41] Hence Danto's theory of expression is considerably weaker than Hegel's. Though meanings, emotions, and attitudes arise in any individual out of historically afforded patterns, such patterns can be refigured within any individual. There is no logic of or plan for appropriate emotions toward appropriate objects in which all persons, or even all persons of a given time and place, must participate. In that sense, there is, for Danto, no necessary Spirit of an Age. There are only embodied meanings that the artist may share with communities of very large circumference – or may not. The emotional-attitudinal "inside" of a person that is embodied in an expressive work is a kind of mere factual-historical inside: something a given person in interaction with a collectivity of some extent will happen to have in one way or another. There is no necessarily shared common human project of freedom, and there are in consequence no necessarily shared emotions and attitudes toward embodiments of strategies of freedom.

This is in many ways a great virtue, and Danto is himself happy with this result. There is no governing logic of culture and cultural expression in which art, criticism, and the philosophy of art must all participate. Many critics, Danto remarks, have

> an agenda. I have none...For me the essence of art [viz. expressing and embodying some meaning or other] must be shared by everything that is an artwork, so there is nothing that exhibits this essence more than anything else, nor is it important that it should do so. In a way, what makes artworks interesting is the *accidents*, what changes from artist to artist and period to period...I can like it all.[42]

---

[40] *ibid.*   [41] Danto, *Transfiguration of the Commonplace*, p. 207.
[42] Danto, *Embodied Meanings*, pp. 11, 13, and Arthur Danto, "Learning to Live with Pluralism," in A. Danto, *The Wake of Art: Criticism, Philosophy, and the Ends of Taste*, ed.

"Learning to live with pluralism"[43] is, in criticism, the path of virtue. Danto's own critical reviews of exhibitions of painting and sculpture are distinguished for their cosmopolitanism and generosity.

Despite the virtues of his criticism, it is possible nonetheless to wonder whether or not Danto has quite captured the conditions for success in art. As Cynthia Freeland observes, "Danto's open-door theory of art says 'Come in' to all works and messages, but it does not seem to explain very well *how* an artwork communicates its message."[44] Artists do seem to seek to hold the attentions of their audiences by arranging their materials so as wholly to absorb those attentions in presentation of a subject matter as a focus for thought, fused to both emotional attitude and material vehicle. Danto's cosmopolitan expressivism underrates the efforts of artists to achieve *singularity* in their work as a focus for expression, over and above either representation or the expression of feeling. It also underrates the effort to embody in a singular work centrally human emotions of pride and humility in relation to work, themselves aspects of an aspiration to live freely in Hegelian terms. Gregg Horowitz and Tom Huhn capture this point by remarking that "art is also, regardless of whatever meanings it occasions, a symbol of our inadequacy."[45] That is, the work of art is not just a representational and expressive something; it is also the always-failed material precipitate of an effort to achieve full and absolute meaningfulness in action and its products: as Horowitz and Huhn put it, "to become self-determining."[46] Beethoven laboring in his sketchbooks, Pollock improvising in his studio, and Mallarmé crafting his lyrics were not simply and only trying to express an emotion or attitude. They were trying to achieve – as an exemplar for us all – meaningfulness as such in thoroughly worked form. Danto's theory of artistic expression undervalues this ambition as a central element in artistic making.

Guy Sircello has argued cogently that "any serious and reasoned determination of what is art and what is not [and so, *eo ipso*, Danto's] [will] project some attitude or personal characteristic" and that "if philosophy

---

Gregg Horowitz and Tom Huhn (Amsterdam: Overseas Publishers Association, 1998), pp. 81–95 at p. 95.

[43] *ibid.*, the title of the essay.

[44] Cynthia Freeland, *But is it Art?* (Oxford: Oxford University Press, 2001), p. 58.

[45] Gregg Horowitz and Tom Huhn, "The Wake of Art: Criticism, Philosophy, and the Ends of Taste," in Danto, *Wake of Art*, p. 51.

[46] *ibid.*, p. 49.

is to have any role in this activity, it will be to determine which attitude or which character it is *best* to have."[47] As a skeptical cosmopolitan, Danto adopts a pose of avoiding all such projection, but projection there nonetheless is. "Disavowal" – especially disavowal of all salvationist aspirations – is the obverse side of Danto's cosmopolitanism; it is central "to his aesthetic taste and judgment,"[48] and it is projected throughout his writing. It is an enormously generous and admirable stance, but it is not clear either that it can recognize itself as a stance or that it properly engages with some of the defining aspirations of some of the most serious art.

Are works of art, then, centrally expressive objects where what is expressed is to some extent both personal and affiliated with contingencies of different culture, as Danto's cosmopolitan theory of expression urges? Or are works of art centrally expressive objects where what is expressed is a shared and essentially human aspiration (inflected within a cultural framework, which itself necessarily articulates such an aspiration) for full meaningfulness and freedom, exemplified in commanding artistic beauty, as Hegel urges? One might well hope to avoid, overcome, or at least mitigate this dichotomy, and to see works of art as expressive somehow of both personal-cultural contingencies *and* of a defining human aspiration, hence as *really* mattering. In order to move in this direction, however, it will help to consider both *how* expression is achieved and *why* expression matters.

How is artistic expression achieved?

Expression theories of art take as their point of departure the insight that works of art, whatever else they are, are products of human action. Just as there are different theories of the nature of human action, however, there are also various ways of conceiving of how expressiveness enters into a work of art. Theories of artistic expression can be usefully divided into three main groups: psychodynamic theories, physiognomic-similarity theories, and "working-through" theories.

Collingwood's psychodynamic theory
In *The Principles of Art*, Collingwood develops a rich psychodynamic theory of mental processes that may occur or be undertaken in relation to

---

[47] Guy Sircello, "Arguing About Art," in *Aesthetics Today*, ed. Philipson and Gudel, pp. 477–496 at p. 494.
[48] *ibid.*, p. 51.

emotion. For Collingwood, every state of awareness possesses an emotional charge. At the level of brute sensate awareness, without conceptualization, this emotional charge comes immediately welded to a sensum or quality of one's experiential field. *Feeling* is Collingwood's term for this immediate unity of sensum and emotion.[49] This immediate emotional charge is invariably discharged in bodily reaction. For example, one might unthinkingly brush one's hand against a hot oven and immediately feel a sensed quality (heat and resistance) coupled with pain and then all but instantaneously jerk away. Sensate creatures in general have these kinds of responses to their environment.

Above the level of immediate, nonconceptual consciousness, however, Collingwood distinguishes two further levels: conceptual consciousness and thinking. In conceptual consciousness we focus our awareness on an object or event that we have learned to identify as a kind of thing, through having assimilated patterns of attention from others. For example, in conceptual consciousness one will see that object as a *book* or a *cup*, or one will hear the rain outdoors *as rain* or the passing car *as a car*, over and above immediate sensory awareness. In thinking, one considers relations among claims, including deductive following from, inductive evidence for, contradiction, consistency, and overall coherence.

At each of these more than simply animal levels of consciousness, emotions are likewise welded to mental activity and its product. In seeing a tree or hearing a birdsong recognitively, we feel something or other, and so too for thinking about problems in physics or the factors that affect the growth of an economy. These *emotions of consciousness* and *emotions of thought* are not, however, immediately discharged in bodily activity. Though they occur, they can be suppressed, with attention held on the object of recognition or thought. It can often be important to do this, when one wishes to solve problems of either recognition or theory. Typically it does not help to foreground in one's awareness one's own emotions when one is factoring polynomials or trying to distinguish a broken head gasket from a leaking radiator.

When, however, the emotions of consciousness and the emotions of thought are not immediately discharged in bodily activity and also suppressed, not acknowledged, then we can lose our emotional sense of why we are doing what we are doing. Conceptually structured activity and the labor associated with it can become dead to us. We are bored, or horrified,

---

[49] See Collingwood, *Principles of Art*, pp. 160ff.

or even entrancingly absorbed in what we are doing, yet we fail to be aware
of this fact about ourselves.

There are, then, a number of things that can happen. Emotions of
consciousness and thought might be *betrayed*, *described*, *aroused*, or *expressed*.
Betraying an emotion is a matter of "exhibiting symptoms" of it – for
example, "turning pale and stammering" when afraid.[50] Though the fear
is expressed in one natural sense of the word *expression*, it is more natural
to say that it is exhibited, displayed, or evidenced involuntarily in bodily
activity. One may not oneself become conscious of the particular object
and quality of one's fear, but may remain wholly caught up in it, in such
a way that others can "read it off" one's behavior causally.

Describing an emotion is a matter for psychologists or oneself in taking an external attitude to what one feels as a kind of thing. "To describe
a thing is to call it a thing of such and such a kind: to bring it under
a conception, to classify it"[51] – for example, to say, "I am angry." While
description may have its uses, both in psychological science and in self-
observation and self-control, it is not the same thing as turning one's
attention to a particular emotion and its quality, wedded to a cognitive
experience on an occasion. To say "I am bored," for example, is quite different from saying

> I grow old...I grow old...
> I shall wear the bottoms of my trousers rolled.
>
> Shall I part my hair behind? Do I dare to eat a peach?
> I shall wear white flannel trousers, and walk upon the beach.
> I have heard the mermaids singing, each to each.
>
> I do not think that they will sing to me.[52]

This latter expression "individualizes,"[53] as Collingwood puts it. It is specific to a certain quality of life as brought under conceptual attention, and
it is distinctively expression proper or artistic expression. (It bears adding
that the emotion expressed in art is, for Collingwood, invariably its author's. The expression of this emotion can happen, however, by way of expressing an author's attitude toward a character's quite distinct emotion.

---

[50] *ibid.*, pp. 121, 122.   [51] *ibid.*, p. 122.

[52] T. S. Eliot, "The Love Song of J. Alfred Prufrock," in *The Norton Anthology of English
Literature*, 3rd edn, ed. M. H. Abrams *et al.* (New York: W. W. Norton, 1974), vol. II, pp.
2164–67 at p. 2167, lines 120–25.

[53] Collingood, *Principles of Art*, p. 112.

For example, *Hamlet* expresses Shakespeare's emotions – including interest – at increasing uncertainties in modern life, the breakdown of moralities of honor, the growth of individualism, the dangers and importance of conscience, and so forth, and it does so by way of Shakespeare's interest in Hamlet's melancholy and other moods. But Hamlet's melancholy is not necessarily Shakespeare's. Likewise, T. S. Eliot both identifies with Prufrock's emotion and its expression, but also achieves a certain situating distance on it, with its own expressive tenor.)

Arousal of emotion is a matter of effecting or setting up causally an emotion in an audience, quite standardly the province of propaganda, advertising, or some other form of craft. It is a matter of providing a stimulus that will work, according to disinterested knowledge of more or less prevailing causal patterns of response.[54]

Expression proper or artistic expression is quite different from betrayal, description, and arousal. In genuine expression, one begins

> conscious of having an emotion, but not conscious of what this emotion is. All [the incipient expresser] is conscious of is a perturbation or excitement, which he feels going on within him, but of whose nature he is ignorant. While in this state, all he can say about his emotion is: "I feel...I don't know what I feel." From this helpless and oppressed condition he extricates himself by doing something we call expressing himself. This is an activity which has something to do with the thing we call language: he expresses himself by speaking. It has also something to do with consciousness: the emotion expressed is an emotion of whose nature the person who feels it is no longer unconscious. It has also something to do with the way in which he feels the emotion. As unexpressed, he feels it in what we have called a helpless and oppressed way; as expressed, he feels it in a way from which this sense of oppression has vanished. His mind is somehow lightened and eased.[55]

The character and importance of the expressive lightening and easing of emotion become somewhat clearer in Collingwood's account of a bad work of art.

> A bad work of art is an activity in which the agent tries to express a given emotion, but fails...A bad work of art is the unsuccessful attempt to become conscious of a given emotion: it is what Spinoza calls an inadequate idea of an affection.[56]

---

[54] see *ibid.*, pp. 110–11.   [55] *ibid.*, pp. 109–10.   [56] *ibid.*, p. 282.

For Spinoza, an action arises out of an adequate idea that embodies a clear and distinct understanding of its object. A passion – a felt determination to do something – arises out of an inadequate idea, one that does not embody clear and distinct understanding. To have an inadequate idea of an affection is then to misunderstand what it is worthwhile to care about and feel about in which ways. An inadequate idea of an affection gives rise to passions wherein we become passive victims of our own feelings, buffeted into action this way and that by failing to care about and respond in feeling to the right things in the right ways. Hence it is no surprise that Collingwood adds that "Bad art...is the same thing as... corrupt consciousness...Bad art, the corrupt consciousness, is the true *radix malorum*."[57] If we try, but fail, to express our emotions, and so deceive ourselves about what we have done, we remain in the grip of inadequate and mistaken ideas of what is worth caring about in what ways. All too readily we become victims of hucksters, whether political or commercial or therapeutic, who will fill the gap in conviction by telling us what we should care about or what others care about, distracting us from achieving our own full agency, informed by genuinely felt, appropriate concern. Artistic expression of emotion, leading to adequate ideas of affection, is the only remedy.

Collingwood's distinctions and his account of the value of artistic expression have considerable plausibility. Dewey similarly distinguishes the artistic expression of emotion from "mere discharge"[58] of it, and he distinguishes artistic expression, which involves the working of materials employed as a medium of art in order to achieve clarity in feeling toward objects, from artificial expression, which is insincere and employs preconceived means to ends (as in advertising and propaganda), and from artful expression, which is a matter of craft and social grace. The idea that through artistic expression we unburden ourselves of confusion in feeling and achieve a genuine, individualized understanding of how one "really feels" about some difficult matter is plausible and attractive. It has affinities with Aristotle's conception of catharsis, and it seems to describe well one thing that many artists try to do. James Joyce in *Ulysses* is surely working out for himself and inviting us to discover with him how stretches of life in Dublin on June 16, 1904, may be felt about – with just *this* mixture of excitement, disgust, frustration, and acceptance. Paul Cézanne in the

---

[57] *ibid.*, p. 285.   [58] Dewey, *Art as Experience*, p. 62.

Mont Sainte-Victoire series is articulating and embodying his own feelings for that inhabited and natural landscape and enabling us to see and feel with him.

Despite its attractions, a number of questions can be raised about this view. Is all centrally successful art successful through expressing and inviting feeling in this way? Conceptual art and Dada seem colder, more austere, even where they are ironic and witty. More crucially, does the notion of *individualized understanding* of emotion make sense? Joyce, for example, is describing scenes and incidents about which it is appropriate to feel in certain ways. What makes his feeling – and ours in following him – distinctly individual? Would not another set of scenes and incidents that are largely similar, but not identical, rightly inspire the same feelings? Furthermore, does the notion of the *lightening, alleviation,* or *easement*[59] of oppressed consciousness that Collingwood takes to occur through expression make sense, without reference to the kind of *aesthetic pleasure* that is achieved in successfully working the materials of a medium? Perhaps Collingwood is confusing an aesthetic satisfaction in artistic working with the discharge of emotional oppression. Most crucially, Collingwood's emphasis on the psychodynamics of the expression of emotion seems to make expression too *biographical* a phenomenon. Was Beethoven in the grip of a singular melancholy passion in writing the Appassionata sonata? His care, displayed in his notebooks, in working through motives and developments suggests more craft and concentration on materials than overwhelming feeling. Even if Beethoven was in the grip of some singular passion, do we need to recreate that very passion ourselves in order to understand the work? Do we not instead understand the sonata by following the development? And if all these questions arise with Beethoven, do they not arise even more forcefully with such more cerebral artists as Pierre Boulez or Anthony Caro or Jorge-Luis Borges?

Physiognomic similarity theories

Troubled by these kinds of worries, a number of theorists of expression in the latter half of the twentieth century have developed radically nonpsychodynamic or nonpsychological theories of expression. These latter theories are often inspired by Wittgenstein's remark in *Philosophical Investigations,* that one "might speak of a 'primary' and 'secondary' sense of

---

[59] See Collingwood, *Principles of Art*, pp. 110, 117 for these terms.

a word."[60] For example, knowing the primary senses of *fat* and *lean*, we might feel strongly inclined to say that Wednesday is fat and Tuesday is lean rather than vice versa.[61] Here the words *fat* and *lean* are used against the background of their primary sense in a secondary, *descriptive* sense that is not metaphorical.[62] Just so, when we describe the face of a basset hound as sad or the babbling of a brook as joyful we are using *sad* and *joyful* descriptively, in secondary senses, in order to pick out a surface or *physiognomic* similarity between this dog's face (compared to other dogs' faces) or this brook (compared to more languid ones), without any emotion or feeling occurring in either the dog or the brook. A *physiognomic similarity* theory of expression seems to account especially well for the use of emotion terms to describe the comparative contours of themes and developments in works of music, and Peter Kivy[63] and Stephen Davies[64] have worked out this view in detail with special reference to music. Alan Tormey, one of the earliest developers of this view, summarizes it aptly in claiming that

> statements attributing expressive (or physiognomic) properties to works of art should be construed as statements about the works themselves; the presence of expressive properties does not entail the occurrence of a prior *act* of expression ... The expressive qualities of a work of art are logically independent of the psychological states of the artist, and humor (or sadness) in a madrigal is neither necessary nor sufficient for amusement (or despair) in a Monteverdi.[65]

Such a physiognomic similarity theory of expression seems aptly to spare us the oddity of seemingly having to investigate Beethoven's mind in order to understand his work rather than the other way round.

The most complete version of a physiognomic similarity theory of expression for the arts in general has been developed by Nelson Goodman in *The Languages of Art*.[66] According to Goodman there are three conditions

---

[60] Wittgenstein, *Philosophical Investigations*, part 2, p. 216e.   [61] *ibid.*   [62] *ibid.*

[63] Peter Kivy, *The Chorded Shell: Reflections of Musical Expression* (Princeton, NJ: Princeton University Press, 1980).

[64] Stephen Davies, *Musical Meaning and Expression* (Ithaca, NY: Cornell University Press, 1994).

[65] Alan Tormey, "Art and Expression: A Critique," in *Philosophy Looks at the Arts*, ed. Margolis, pp. 346–61 at pp. 351, 358.

[66] Goodman, *Languages of Art*, pp. 85–95.

that are individually necessary and jointly sufficient for a work of art to express something. The first two conditions are that the work must *possess* the property that is expressed and it must also *refer* to it, in the way that a paint chip both possesses and refers to the color that it has. Goodman's term for possession plus reference is *exemplification*. The third condition is that the possession, and hence the exemplification, must be *metaphorical*. That is, the term ascribing the property exemplified (i.e. both possessed and referred to) must be used in a secondary sense. As Goodman puts it, it must be used comparatively, in carrying along with it an intended range of contrasts with other related terms (compare "fat" contrasted with "lean"), and the comparisons must be invoked or brought to mind outside the habitual use or normal "realm" of application of these contrastive terms. In short, what happens in metaphor is that "A whole set of alternative labels, a whole apparatus of organization, takes over new territory. What occurs is a transfer of a schema, a migration of concepts, an alienation of categories."[67] For example, Wednesday is called fat, or the *Moonlight Sonata* is called melancholic. Expression is metaphorical (alien, unusual) exemplification. The interest or point of applying expression terms to works of art is to describe or capture – in novel ways – certain features of works and comparisons among works that are of interest to us. This interest is primarily cognitive; in applying expression terms, we capture how works of art (and the subject matters they present) are or may be seen. Reference to feeling to be recreated and worked through in the audience drops out. Emotion terms are about the work and its subject matter, and comparisons and contrasts among works can aptly be noted by deploying an emotion vocabulary metaphorically.

In a similar spirit, Monroe Beardsley argues that expression in the arts is a function of "human regional qualities" that are "emergent in" a work.[68] Given that these qualities are *in* the work, we do not need to talk about a composer's or painter's or writer's emotion; "expresses dignity," for example, can be adequately replaced by "has dignity."[69] Expressive works of music are instances of processes of development that are of interest in themselves, not as symbols for something else,[70] certainly not primarily as evidence about composers' states of mind.

Tormey, Goodman, Beardsley, and others are surely right to emphasize that works of art are produced through detailed and attentive working

---

[67] *ibid.*, p. 73.   [68] Beardsley, *Aesthetics*, p. 328.   [69] *ibid.*, p. 332.   [70] *ibid.*, p. 338.

and reworking of materials in an expressive medium, not simply via an upsurge of powerful emotion. Collingwood too, after all, distinguishes the expression of emotion from its betrayal, and Dewey distinguishes it from brute discharge. A coherent expression of melancholy, say, in relation to a subject matter will not exist in a work unless its maker has made apt use of the expressive possibilities that are available in the medium and through its history of use. These expressive possibilities are not determined by either decisions or feelings in individual minds alone. The processes that give rise to successfully expressive works are more than internal psychodynamic processes; they involve using historically afforded expressive possibilities in media.

It is doubtful, however, whether expressive qualities in works of art can be regarded as wholly "secondary" and independent of human mental states. As Guy Sircello observes, "what all anthropomorphic predicates [such as "sad," "joyful," etc.] ultimately relate to are human emotions, feelings, attitudes, moods, and personal trait;...[they] finally relate to various forms of the 'inner lives' of human beings."[71] That is to say, there would be no point or possibility of describing works of art in anthropomorphic, expressive terms were there not also the practice of describing both the looks and feeling states of human beings in these terms. It is true that the possession of a contour or "look" that is expressive of sadness does not *entail* that either a work or a person that has that look is in fact feeling sadness.[72] Persons can feign looks, and works of art do not themselves have feelings. Moreover, it is true that expressive predicates do in the first instance describe looks, contours, or physiognomies.[73] But "any attempt to save [pure physiognomic similarity theories] by 'eliminating' descriptions of artistic acts [of artists *doing* something in making the work] in favor of 'logically equivalent' descriptions of formal elements and/or represented subject matter is doomed to fail."[74] Like grimaces and cries, works of art have expressive properties because they are the products of what human beings in general *do*.

---

[71] Guy Sircello, *Mind and Art: An Essay on the Varieties of Expression* (Princeton, NJ: Princeton University Press, 1972), p. 39. See also Scruton, *Art and Expression*, p. 38: in comparison to the use of emotion terms to describe emergent perceptual properties, "the use to refer to an emotional state is primary," and the former use would not be intelligible without the latter.

[72] See Sircello, *Mind and Art*, p. 46.   [73] *ibid.*   [74] *ibid.*

Sircello's emphasis on the importance of artistic *acts* of making the work allows him to capture the importance of *point of view* in presentation of a subject matter as a focus for thought and perception. To cite just two of his many examples:

> *Wedding Dance in the Open Air* is an ironic painting because Brueghel *treats* the gaiety of the wedding scene ironically.

> Prokoviev's Grandfather theme is witty because the composer wittily *comments* on the character.[75]

These works would not have the expressive physiognomic qualities that they have, nor would these qualities be available to us and be of interest, were it not the case that the painter or composer from a point of view *put* them there and made a point of view on what is presented available to us. In each case, "the respective anthropomorphic predicate is applied to the work of art in virtue of what the artist *does* in that work."[76]

A pure physiognomic similarity theory of expression that makes no reference to artistic acts and points of view also has difficulty in explaining why we want to read or listen to or look at a work of art *again*. In emphasizing as Goodman does *only* the invitation by the work of a new set of comparisons among looks, surfaces, contours, and so forth of things, such theories construe the presence of expressive qualities as primarily a matter of cognitive interest. As Roger Scruton observes against Goodman, "No cognitive theory of aesthetic experience can explain why one should desire to listen to a symphony again, any more than one should wish to reread a scientific treatise or repeat a successful experiment."[77] When, however, we take into account the importance of artistic acts and points of view, this desire becomes transparent. In reading and rereading (hearing and rehearing, etc.) a work, we take up an authorial point of view, and we participate – as Collingwood rightly emphasized – in how a subject matter is experienced in feeling by an authorial subject. Through this participation, we can ourselves progressively explore contours of feeling and their aptness to their objects.

In favor of physiognomic similarity views, however, it must be conceded that the achievement of a point of view in relation to a subject matter and its expression in a work cannot be a matter only of "psychic" action independent of media of art and their histories of use. Having a

---

[75] ibid., p. 25.   [76] ibid., p. 26.   [77] Scruton, *Art and Imagination*, p. 226.

point of view – a way of looking at things – and associated emotions pre-supposes participation in a socially shared space or pattern of reasons for taking an interest in things under a description. Having a point of view is not simply a matter of being in a physicotemporal location. It is rather a matter of *from* a location identifying and attending to things under a description. When queried, one must be able to some extent to say *what* one is attending to – a cup, a birdsong, a slip, a face – and *why* one construes the object of attention as one does. That is, one must be able to some extent to paraphrase the content of one's attention. Attention to objects is not purely a matter of physiological response; it is a socially learned achievement. Collingwood himself makes this point in developing his own theory of expression beyond its initial presentation as an individual psychodynamic theory into a theory of expression as an achievement of the extension and rearticulation of communal patterns of attention and response.[78]

Hence psychodynamic and physiognomic similarity theories of expression can be usefully integrated with one another, when we come to realize both that conceptual recognitive consciousness is not itself purely an individual psychic phenomenon *and* that attending to a subject and responding with feeling (and then further embodying attention and response in a work) are things that situated individual agents *do*.

"Working-through" theories

Yet it is not clear that even a sophisticated theory of historically enabled expressive action will quite wholly capture either the nature of artistic expression or our interest in attending to it. In *The Brown Book*, Wittgenstein distinguishes between what he calls the "transitive" and "intransitive" uses of the terms *peculiar* and *particular*.[79] In the first, transitive use, there is something more that one is prepared to say about what it is that is peculiar or particular. For example, in elaboration of the remark "this soap has a peculiar smell," one might add: "it is the kind we used as children."[80] Here the term *peculiar* serves transitively to introduce a

---

[78] See Collingwood's discussion of attention in *Principles of Art*, especially pp. 203–06, 225–28, and 234–41, and his final argument that conceptual or recognitive consciousness cannot be a purely individual achievement, pp. 250–51.

[79] Ludwig Wittgenstein, *The Brown Book*, in Wittgenstein, *The Blue and Brown Books* (New York: Harper & Row, 1958), p. 158.

[80] *ibid.*

further comparison or specification. In contrast, we might also use the term *peculiar* intransitively, simply to highlight the fact that there is something – one cannot quite say what – that is "out of the ordinary" "uncommon," or "striking"[81] about what is experienced.

Drawing on Wittgenstein's distinction, Richard Wollheim[82] and Garry Hagberg[83] have each argued that *expressive* can also be used in an intransitive sense. In this usage, to say that a work is expressive is not to relate it to any independent or distinctly identifiable emotion or feeling. It is rather to say that the work is striking, out of the ordinary, uncommon, and uncommonly successful in its arrangement of its materials. Our interest in expressiveness is then an interest in following out such a striking, uncommon, and successful arrangement of materials, as itself a piece of virtuosity. Hence this construal of expressiveness can be termed the *working of materials* view.

Drawing on work by Benedetto Croce, Colin Lyas has argued that what is expressed in a work need not be an emotion at all. "One can," Lyas writes, "as well seek to express one's ideas of how, say, a requiem should sound, or how a hard-boiled San Francisco detective might behave. When one solves one's problem by making the work as one wanted it, then that is achieved expression in Croce's sense."[84] Here too the expression thus achieved is intransitive, in the sense that it is a quite particular expression, achieved in just this successful arrangement of materials, not the expression *of* something that might be displayed or embodied otherwise. Our interest in achieved expressiveness is again an interest in this singular, virtuoso success.

While it rightly emphasizes the importance of virtuoso work to the achievement of artistic expressiveness, the working of materials view is unable to account easily for the fact that emotions are centrally among the things that works of art are said to express. To revert to Sircello's examples, we do say that Brueghel's painting is ironic, or Prokoviev's theme is witty. What is expressed is centrally a subject's emotions and attitudes. The working of materials view here overlooks the importance of a subject's point of view – achieved by the artist in the work and proffered to the

---

[81] *ibid.*   [82] See Wollheim, *Art and its Objects*, pp. 93–96.

[83] See G. L. Hagberg, *Art as Language: Wittgenstein, Meaning, and Aesthetic Theory* (Ithaca, NY: Cornell University Press, 1995), pp. 103–09.

[84] Colin Lyas, *Aesthetics* (Montreal: McGill-Queen's University Press, 1997), p. 102.

audience for participation – in the experience of expression in art. But then – as the working of materials view rightly emphasizes – not just any instancing of a point of view or any unburdening will suffice either, in order for there to be artistic expression. The coherent working through of materials does matter.

The moral we should draw from these three accounts is that artistic expressiveness is not fully explicable in psychodynamic terms alone, in physiognomic terms alone, or in formal terms alone. Felt response, patterns of emotion and attitude, and formal success all matter to artistic expressiveness. Felt response or attitude toward a subject matter must be blended with cognitive attention to it, over and above raw feeling and its mere discharge. Felt response or attitude and cognitive attention together must be sustained and developed through the articulate working of materials. With this result in hand, we are now able to address more clearly the question of why artistic expression matters to us.

Why does artistic expression matter?

In an individualistic and therapeutic age, we are likely to think at first blush that expression matters as a form of relief: the discharge of some burdensome feeling that would otherwise fester and corrupt the psyche. Whatever the merits of such a view of expression as therapy, however, it does not account for the interest or importance of distinctively artistic expression. Though they form a continuum, what distinguishes artistic expression from ordinary expression – as theorists from Aristotle to Collingwood to Dewey have emphasized – is the achievement through the working of materials that present a subject matter of increased focus on and clarity about what one feels. Therapeutic discharge may sometimes bring increased focus and clarity as well, but it rarely does so in and through the virtuosic working of materials. When it does so, it begins to verge on artistic dramatic monologue or standup comedy. How and why, then, might artistic expression matter over and above immediate therapy?

In *What is Art?*, Tolstoy suggests that it is the communicative or transmissive dimension of artistic expression that in the first instance distinguishes it from mere individual unburdening. "Art," he tells us, "is one of the means of intercourse between man and man...The peculiarity of [this] means of intercourse, distinguishing it from intercourse by means of words, consists in this, that whereas by means of words a man transmits his thoughts to another, by means of art he transmits his feelings."[85]

Though successful communication and communion of feeling may mark a difference from therapeutic expression, it cannot yet be a sufficient condition for artistic expression. Art is more than a matter of simply a man causing "another man to yawn when he himself cannot help yawning, or to laugh or cry when he himself is obliged to laugh or cry, or to suffer when he himself is suffering – that does not amount to art."[86] Hence Tolstoy claims that "by art, in the limited sense of the word, we do not mean all human activity transmitting feelings, but only that part which we for some reason select from it and to which we attach special importance," and he then specifies that "feelings flowing from . . . religious perception"[87] are the particular province of art. It is unclear, however, why it is just these feelings whose expression should matter in art, other than for the sake of bringing people together, under the assumption – surely dubitable – that such feelings are shared. This suggestion also competes, however, with a further specification of Tolstoy's that for artistic expression communication of feeling must take place "by means of movements, lines, colors, sounds, or forms expressed in words."[88] Though Tolstoy is on the right track in emphasizing the importance for artistic expression of both communicative success and arrangement of artistic materials, we still need to know more about exactly how this is done and why it matters. As Colin Lyas comments, "Tolstoy has not made clear when a vision is embodied in a work. Moreover, we are given no clear idea why we feel so moved by sharing the expressed visions of artists."[89]

According to Ralph Waldo Emerson in "Self-Reliance," "In every work of genius we recognize our own rejected thoughts: they come back to us with a certain alienated majesty."[90] This thought points toward both a way between Hegel and Danto on what is expressed and to a more plausible account of why artistic expression matters for us. Human life is lived in relation to modifiable routines of practice that are afforded by culture. Any culture, that is to say, presents a tangled ensemble of ways of working, eating, playing, reproducing, dwelling, and so on. There is no distinctively

---

[85] Tolstoy, *What is Art?*, p. 49.   [86] *ibid.*, p. 50.   [87] *ibid.*, p. 53.   [88] *ibid.*, p. 51.
[89] Lyas, *Aesthetics*, p. 66.
[90] Ralph Waldo Emerson, "Self-Reliance," in *Selections from Ralph Waldo Emerson*, ed. Stephen E. Whicher (Boston, MA: Houghton Mifflin, 1957), pp. 147–68 at p. 147.

human action without engaging in the routines that compose such an ensemble. No one comes *ab novo* simply to work, eat, play, reproduce, and dwell as a distinctively human agent altogether on one's own.

In coming to engage with such an ensemble of routines, anyone will have attitudes and emotions about whether what one does oneself is done fluently, expressively, and aptly, both for oneself and in the eyes of others. One will feel that one has made a suitable home or not, found suitable work or not, enjoyed this meal or not, and so on. Attitudes and emotions toward the affairs of life can run from pride, enjoyment, delight, and self-respect, on the one hand, to shame, guilt, self-abasement, and resentment, on the other, with infinite shades of variation.

It is easy and frequently reasonable just to get on with the business at hand rather than to dwell in any such attitudes and emotions. Perhaps one simply must work in order to earn a wage; perhaps possibilities of pride, delight, and enjoyment are vanishingly slim, so that it would be better not to dwell on their absence; perhaps it is simply best not to make too great a show of one's feelings.

Yet the attitudes and emotions that we continue to have persist, and they bespeak certain possibilities of change and development. With shame in being stuck in this way of work or family life or consumption comes at least the bare aspiration or sense that it might be otherwise. With pride, enjoyment, delight, and self-respect comes a wish to continue or further one's routes of engagement in practice. When, then, Emerson writes that in works of genius we recognize our own thoughts returning with a certain alienated majesty, he can be construed as suggesting that the office of art is to bring our emotions and attitudes toward the affairs of life more actively into the forefront of consciousness. The majesty of these returning thoughts consists in their having a certain command over us and our aspirations and resentments. They are *our* emotions and attitudes, as complex as the affairs of life in which we are engaged, and they variously nurture, inhibit, and otherwise inhabit both what we do and how we do it: with patience and love, or with resentment and bitterness, among many other shades of possibility. The fact that these returning thoughts are alienated from us consists in our having failed to acknowledge them, having failed quite wholly to feel them and to accept them as our own. To the extent that we have failed to do this, our emotions and attitudes are not integrated with our practices, and we live less than fully coherently and fluently.

Hence Collingwood's neo-Spinozist view of the function of expression, developed as Collingwood himself develops it in quasi-Hegelian, communalist terms, correctly specifies the central function of artistic expression. It brings into consciousness and clarifies, on behalf of a people caught up in a shared and contested way of life, what in that way of life is worth caring about in which specific ways: with pride or love or bitterness or disgust. "What the artist has to utter," as Collingwood puts it,

> is not, as the individualist theory of art would have us think, his own secrets. As spokesman of his community, the secrets he must utter are theirs. The reason why they need him is that no community altogether knows its own heart; and by failing in this knowledge a community deceives itself on the one subject concerning which ignorance means death. For the evils which come from that ignorance the poet as prophet suggests no remedy, because he has already given one. The remedy is the poem itself. Art is the community's medicine for the worst disease of mind, the corruption of consciousness.[91]

Dewey makes a similar point when he observes that artistic expression involves the "progressive organization of 'inner' and 'outer' material in organic connection with each other."[92] The outer material includes not only the materials of art – paint, words, bodily motions, stone, and so on – but also the material of life: the tangled ensemble of contested and changing cultural routines through which human life is reproduced. The outer materials of art include as well nature as a scene of human habitation (or its frustration) and natural objects as fit for the human eye (or repellent to it). The inner material of art includes the emotions and attitudes – the rejected thoughts – that anyone will have in relation to the outer material. Any culture will enable some degree of satisfaction and fluency in cultural routines, with associated pride, enjoyment, and self-respect, for some of its members some of the time. To this extent, Hegel is right that an aspiration toward full satisfaction, fluency, and self-respect is part of the inner life of any culture. But no culture has yet enabled full satisfaction, fluency, and self-respect in cultural routines for all of its members all of the time, and different cultures offer to some extent complementary, but to some extent deeply opposed, routines for its pursuit. There is always, in any culture, both room for and need for departure and revision, for

---

[91] Collingwood, *Principles of Art*, p. 336.   [92] Dewey, *Art as Experience*, p. 75.

individual vision striking out on its own against the grain of culture, and there is also both room for and need for the understanding and appreciation of the fluencies and possibilities of pride, enjoyment, and self-respect that are afforded in different cultures. To this extent, Danto is right that a certain cosmopolitanism and appreciation of both cultural and individual varieties of expression is in order. It is even arguable that the deepest and fullest artistic expressions of emotions and attitudes toward cultural routines must include a sense of their own partiality and finitude, rather than bluster, assertion, and self-important attitudinizing. Artists will typically not be fully aware of the success or failure of their efforts at artistic expression until they find that others actually do actively come to clarify *their* own emotions and attitudes toward life through engagement with the work. Artistic expression in its uncertainties is the opposite of propaganda, and fragmentariness, abstraction, the inclusion of multiple voices and points of view, and awareness of culturally particular traditions of framing, presentation, treatment, and subject matter are fixtures of modern art – as Hegel saw in describing what he called Romantic art.

Dewey captures well the continuing interplay between the particular dimensions of artistic expression, cultural and personal, on the one hand, and its more objective dimensions, in involving common emotions and attitudes toward a common cultural repertoire, on the other.

> A poem and picture present material passed through the alembic of personal experience. They have no precedents in existence or in universal being. But, nonetheless, their material came from the public world and so has qualities in common with the material of other experiences, while the product awakens in other persons new perceptions of the meanings of the common world. The oppositions of individual and universal, of subjective and objective, of freedom and order, in which philosophers have reveled, have no place in the work of art. Expression as personal art and as objective result are organically connected with each other.[93]

Why do writers write, painters paint, choreographers choreograph, and so on? To express and in expressing to clarify inner emotions and attitudes – their own and others' – in relation to specific elements of the common materials of outer life. Readers read, the eye follows attentively the painting or the dance, as the ear follows the piece of music, in order to

---

[93] *ibid.*, p. 82.

participate in this expression and clarification. Its achievement is not an "internal" psychic process alone and not a matter of surface organization alone, but is inseparable from the presentation and treatment of a subject matter, drawn from the outer material of life, toward which emotions and attitudes are held, and from the effective, coherent, and fully attentive formal arrangement of color, line, shape, motion, tone, and word.

5 · Originality and imagination

Genius and the pursuit of the new: Kant

In presenting a subject matter as a focus for thought and emotional attitude, distinctively fused to the imaginative exploration of material, works
of art are evidently *special*. Where does this special character of art come
from? Are successful artists a special class of people, with capacities the
rest of us altogether lack? Or do they rather exercise in a special way an
imaginative capacity in which we all have a share? What are the roles of
training, artistic tradition, and common culture in the development of
artistic ability? Can art be taught?

It is commonly thought, and especially widely so in modernity, that
artworks are in some way distinctively new and original. Ezra Pound,
translating a dictum of Confucius, titled his 1934 collection of critical
essays on literature *Make it New*.[1] John Dewey remarks on "the qualita-
tive novelty that characterizes every genuine work of art."[2] In Plato's *Ion*,
Socrates and Ion agree that though Homer and other poets "all treat of
the same subjects," one of them – Homer – "speaks well and the rest
of them speak worse," and this because Homer, like all the good poets,
is "inspired, possessed."[3] Exactly what is going on *in Homer* that makes
his poetry different and special? How does the sort of creative capacity
that Homer displays have to do with making things that are distinctively
new?

In a useful survey essay, Timothy Gould proposes that our own "modern and more unified concept of genius"[4] arises out of a constellation of
five conceptual elements evident in Greek thought, particularly in Plato,

---

[1] Ezra Pound, *Make it New* (London: Faber & Faber, 1934).

[2] Dewey, *Art as Experience*, p. 288.   [3] Plato, *Ion*, 532a, p. 218; 533e, p. 220.

[4] Timothy Gould, "Genius: Conceptual and Historical Overview," in *Encyclopedia of
Aesthetics*, ed. Kelly, vol. II, pp. 287–92 at p. 288A.

that were then modified through the establishment of Christianity in the West and the development of the modern world. These five elements are *mantike* or possession by something divine and immortal; *enthousiasmos* or the mental and emotional state of being thus possessed; *techne* or craft, skill; *daimon* or a more personal tutelary spirit or muse, distributed distinctively to some individuals; and *demiourgous* or a divine principle that brings about the creation of the world.[5] Possession by one's personal *daimon* or muse, putting one in a state of enthusiasm that results in an upsurge of productive power, itself then mediated by craft, results in distinctively artistic making, which is analogous to the divine creation of the world out of nothing. With the advent of Christianity, the image in the Gospel of John of divine creation as self-realizing *logos* displaces the image of the demiurge, but the conception of artistic creativity as involving these five elements is largely continued. Petrarch's possession by Laura, Dante's inspiration by Beatrice, Shakespeare's captivation by the Dark Lady, Milton's prayer to the Muses, and Wordsworth's invocation of Milton as precursor all show something of this constellation of ideas.

With the slow development of modernity, these ideas are significantly naturalized and internalized, subjected to what Gould calls "the somewhat paradoxical secularization of the divine, without which the idea of genius is impossible."[6] Genius is seen as an internal gift of nature, a special and specially distributed talent or election that occurs naturally in some but that cannot be explained. Interwoven with the development of the modern conception of genius and creativity is the development of the modern system of the fine arts. As Gould notes, the fine arts such as painting, poetry, and music are now distinguished *as* fine or high arts from craft, domestic, or industrial arts; *expression* of inner productive power displaces imitation as a principal aim of art; the creator of art who manifests expressive power is seen as more important than any traditional rules, forms, or genres; and creative artists are seen as or as like *sublime* forces

---

[5] *ibid.*, p. 288A–B.

[6] *ibid.*, p. 288B. Gould notes that this secularization and internalization are already to some extent present in Socrates. On the theme of internalization of creative possession by the divine, see also Northrop Frye, "The Drunken Boat," in *Romanticism Reconsidered*, ed. N. Frye (New York: Columbia University Press, 1963), pp. 1–25.

of nature: raging torrents of creative energy.[7] When this creative energy as a gift of nature surges forth, then the result is a moment of inspiration, an epiphany, or, as Francoise Meltzer notes, something very like the reception of grace.[8] Craft and reworking of material may be necessary in order to give this moment of inspiration satisfactory outward shape, and its genuineness may have to be confirmed in the responses of others, but it remains crucial as the fount of artistic making.

Though a conception of the importance of inspiration is increasingly shared from the early seventeenth century onwards, the most well worked out and influential conception of artistic genius is put forward by Kant in sections 46–50 of *The Critique of the Power of Judgment*. According to Kant, "*genius* is the talent (natural gift) that gives the rule to art...a *talent* for producing that for which no determinate rule can be given."[9] Since no determinate rule for artistic making can be formulated, then, as already noted, genius "cannot itself describe or indicate scientifically how it brings its product into being."[10] Kant immediately notes that lack of any determinate rule for production in works of genius explains how the German word "genius [*Genie*] is derived from [the Latin] *genius*, in the sense of the particular spirit given to a person at birth, which protects and guides him, and from whose inspiration those original ideas stem."[11] Inspiration comes or is given divinely-naturally; genius "is apportioned [to one who receives it] immediately from the hand of nature, and thus dies with him, until nature one day similarly endows another, who needs nothing more than an example in order to let the talent of which he is aware operate in a similar way."[12]

---

[7] *ibid.*, p. 289A. On the emergence of the modern system of the fine or high arts in the seventeenth century, see also Paul Oskar Kristeller's classic essay, "The Modern System of the Arts," in the *Journal of the History of Ideas* 12 (1951, 1952), reprinted in *Art and Philosophy*, ed. Kennick, pp. 7–33. Kristeller's account of the rise of the modern system of the arts is usefully qualified in Meyer Schapiro, "On the Aesthetic Attitude in Romanesque Art," in M. Schapiro, *Romanesque Art: Selected Papers* (New York: G. Braziller, 1977), pp. 1–28. On the shift toward expression as a central aim of art, see M. H. Abrams, *The Mirror and the Lamp* (Oxford: Oxford University Press, 1953).

[8] Francoise Meltzer, "Originality in Literature," in *Encyclopedia of Aesthetics*, ed. Kelly, vol. III, pp. 413–16 at p. 414A.

[9] Kant, *Critique*, trans. Guyer and Matthews, §46, p. 186.   [10] *ibid.*, §46, p. 187.

[11] *ibid.*   [12] *ibid.*, §47, p. 188.

It is not the case, however, that every unpredictable and spontaneous production will be successful art. Craft is also required. "Genius can only provide rich *material* for products of art; its elaboration and *form* require a talent that has been academically trained, in order to make a use of it that can stand up to the power of judgment."[13] Without craft, training, and form, inspiration "in its lawless form" is all too likely to produce "nothing but nonsense."[14] In order to avoid this, the artist must hold

> up his work [to the demands of taste], and, after many, often laborious
> attempts to satisfy it...[find] the form that contents him;...this is not as
> it were a matter of inspiration or a free swing of the mental powers, but
> a slow and indeed painstaking improvement, in order to let [the form of
> the work] become adequate to the thought and yet not detrimental to
> the freedom in the play of the mental powers.[15]

Nonetheless, "it is in regard to [genius and imagination] that [a work] deserves to be called *inspired*, [even though it is] only in regard to [taste and judgment] that it deserves to be called...*beautiful*."[16]

The work of genius serves crucially as the vehicle of *free* meaning making of and in culture, over and above the necessities of survival and commerce. The product of genius serves others "as a model...against which [they] may test their own talent."[17] When others respond to the work of genius, then its power and status as a work of genius are confirmed, and those who take it up become successors to its maker-as-precursor.

> In this way the product of a genius...is an example, not for imitation,
> but for emulation by another genius, who is thereby awakened to the
> feeling of his own originality, to exercise freedom from coercion in his
> art in such a way that [that successor art] thereby itself acquires a new
> rule, [through] which the [precursor] talent shows itself as exemplary.[18]

The making of a meaningful work that is in this way free from coercion is our means of creating human culture as second nature, as a fit home for humanity.

> The imagination (as a productive cognitive faculty) is, namely, very
> powerful in creating, as it were, another nature out of the material

---

[13] *ibid.*, §47, p. 189.   [14] *ibid.*, §50, p. 197.   [15] *ibid.*, §50, p. 191.

[16] *ibid.*, §50, p. 197.   [17] *ibid.*, §47, p. 188.

[18] *ibid.*, §49, pp. 195–96; translation corrected.

which the real one gives it. We entertain ourselves with it when experience seems too mundane to us; we [also] transform [merely given] nature...in accordance with principles that lie higher in reason...in this we feel our freedom from the law of association (which applies to the empirical use of [imagination]), [so that]...material...lent to us by nature...can be transformed by us into something entirely different, namely into that which steps beyond nature.[19]

In artistic making, that is to say, a new cultural world is imagined and anticipated. The making of art serves as an exemplary gesture that demonstrates the possibility of free, coherent, and satisfying meaning-making as such.

Partly by way of Kant's influence, and partly by way of developing independently the streams of thought that Kant crystallized, these ideas about genius as exemplary, free, and original imaginative making have been widely taken up. Coleridge's conception of imagination as an esemplastic power (molding, shaping, and unifying power of making) as opposed to merely associative fancy derives from Kant and Schelling.[20] Michael Baxandall describes influence – the *active* and liberative taking up by a successor of motifs, subject matter, materials, and so forth from the work of a predecessor: for example, Picasso's active taking up of Cézanne's way of "registering...two separate planes...as one superplane" – in similar terms.[21] Harold Bloom's well-known theory of the anxiety of influence describes a similar play of active response and Oedipal contestation in the relation between successor and precursor, as successors are first threatened by the sublime energy of a predecessor genius and then in active response to this threat are liberated to the exercise of their own creativity.[22] A

---

[19] *ibid.*, §49, p. 192; my interpolations. For more on Kant's thought concerning culture as second nature, see Eldridge, *Persistence of Romanticism*, pp. 38–39, 62–63.

[20] Samuel Taylor Coleridge, *Biographia Literaria*, ed. George Watson (London: J. M. Dent, 1965), especially chapter 12, "On the Imagination, or Esemplastic Power," pp. 161–67.

[21] Baxandall, "Excursus Against Influence," in *Patterns of Intention*, pp. 58–62. The quoted phrases come from p. 61. Baxandall's point in writing *against* influence is to emphasize that influence is active, agentive, taking up of strategies from a predecessor, *not* a passive, merely conditioned response – exactly along the lines of Kant's account of a successor actively using the work of a predecessor as a model.

[22] Harold Bloom, *The Anxiety of Influence: A Theory of Poetry* (Oxford: Oxford University Press, 1973).

generally Kantian theory of imagination, creativity, and influence captures the importance of "direct experience" of original works, as opposed to copies, descriptions, or paraphrases.[23] It enables us to understand the possibility of training in artistic making that can never be reduced to recipe or rote. Instead, models must be put before the novice, practice works in response to them must be criticized and revised, and then one must wait – for active, imaginative creativity in the novice either to come to the fore or not. For generations, teachers of poetry, painting, music, acting, and dance have worked in this way, hoping for that magical moment when precursor work is all at once fully internalized, taken up, and actively transformed by the student as nascent successor.

Hegel's criticisms of subjectivism

While he broadly accepts Kant's conception of art as in the service of freedom, Hegel also criticizes Kant's picture of creativity as too individualist and subjectivist. "This apparently perfect reconciliation [of freedom and sensuous embodiment in the gesture of genius] is still supposed by Kant at the last to be only subjective in respect of the...production [of art], and not itself to be absolutely true and actual."[24] According to Hegel, Kant "makes [the] dissolution [of the opposition between freedom and sensuousness] and [their] reconciliation into a purely *subjective* one...not one absolutely true and actual."[25] In order to *be* the genuinely true and actual sensuous embodiment of freedom, the work of art must, according to Hegel, proceed not from individual genius alone and its subjective psychological needs and powers, but further from the engagement of creative genius with a widely shared and lived conception of freedom. Shared and lived conceptions of freedom themselves have a definite, progressive logic of development, Hegel claims. Instead of emphasizing the capacities and action of the individual maker, we should, Hegel argues, note how "the sequence of definite conceptions of the world, as the definite but comprehensive consciousness of nature, man, and God, *gives itself artistic shape.*"[26] Notoriously, Hegel supposes that this explains why certain

---

[23] See Kant, *Critique*, trans. Guyer and Matthews, §47, p. 188, where Kant observes that only "models" and not "mere descriptions" can serve to transmit freely formed, genuinely artistic ideas "to posterity."

[24] Hegel, *Aesthetics*, vol. I, p. 60.   [25] *ibid.*, vol. I, p. 57.

[26] *ibid.*, vol. I, p. 72; emphasis added.

nonwestern cultures did not manage to create great art, for they lacked a proper *conception* of the freedom that art is to embody.

> So, for example, the Chinese, Indians, and Egyptians, in their artistic shapes, images of gods, and idols, never get beyond formlessness or a bad and untrue definiteness of form. They could not master true beauty because their mythological ideas, the content and thought of their works of art, were still indeterminate, or determined badly, and so did not consist of the content which is absolute in itself. Works of art are all the more excellent in expressing true beauty, the deeper is the inner truth of their content and thought.[27]

Here Hegel is right, against Kant, that centrally successful works of art – those that fulfill art's highest function – may not be about anything whatsoever, just as their maker subjectively chooses. Instead, they must have "content and thought" that are the "inner truth" of a culture. They must be about or must represent and express attitudes toward what a significant number of people who share a significant stretch of culture most deeply care about in common: romantic love, honor, family, the cultivation and expression of individuality, duty, eschatological vision (and conflicts among all these), as may be. Artists, and especially distinctively successful ones, typically do pay close attention to what one might call the inner agenda of their culture, rather than creating only out of their own whims independently of any such attention. As Collingwood notes in criticizing pure artistic individualism, "everything that [an artist] does he does in relation to others like himself...[People] become poets or painters or musicians not by some process of development from within, as they grow beards; but by living in a society where these languages are current."[28]

Against Hegel, however, we are likely to be suspicious of the idea that conceptions of freedom have a fixed logic of progressive development with which nonwestern cultures fail to engage. There *are* significant differences between cultures, and western (post-Hellenic, post-Christian) conceptions of freedom, right, and justice are important. But to some extent these conceptions are shared outside the West more widely than Hegel was aware, and to some extent where they are not then the countervailing conceptions – for example, of the importance of stillness and reverence, or of the importance of familial piety – can be readily understood by

---

[27] *ibid.*, vol. I, p. 74.   [28] Collingwood, *Principles of Art*, pp. 318–19.

us as reasonably contesting and correcting certain elements of the western heritage. No culture, moreover, is an altogether coherently organized whole of valuable repertoires and practices. Within any culture, conflicts among values remain, and the worth of practices and repertoires remains contested. While it is true that the creative making of centrally successful art must take up and express what people in a culture most deeply care about, the task of doing this is not made straightforward by a governing logic of the development of cares in cultures. Individual makers of art will have more to do in order to identify, assess, and develop certain threads of care and commitment than Hegel supposes. Instead of thinking as Hegel does of centrally successful art as essentially illustrative of cares and commitments that might better be understood otherwise (for example, philosophically or philosophico-historically), we might better think of the work of genius as, in Stanley Cavell's phrase, the enactment of "the promise that the private [what I or a few care about] and the social [what we care about] will be achieved together"[29] – in the face of continuing obscurities and difficulties that trouble such enactments. "The problem . . . of the artist is not to discount his subjectivity, but to master it in exemplary ways. Then his work outlasts the fashions and arguments of a particular age. That is the beauty of it."[30]

Why originality matters: Adorno on free meaning-making

How and why might anyone come to wish to produce work that outlasts the fashions and arguments of a particular age? How and why might originality in the making of forms that represent subject matters about which communities care deeply and that express attitudes toward those subjects come to matter "for its own sake"?

The practice of making art does not begin historically from any individual intention alone. It arises out of practices of the making of both immediately useful objects and objects for ritual-liturgical purposes. (Recall Nietzsche's account of the birth of tragedy, considered in chapter 1.) In Adorno's formulation, "in the most authentic works the authority that

---

[29] Stanley Cavell, "Being Odd, Getting Even," in S. Cavell, *In Quest of the Ordinary: Lines of Skepticism and Romanticism* (Chicago, IL: University of Chicago Press, 1988), pp. 105–49 at p. 114.

[30] Cavell, "Aesthetic Problems of Modern Philosophy," pp. 73–96 at p. 94.

cultic objects were once meant to exercise over the *gentes* became the immanent law of form."[31] Initially, that is to say, the making of certain objects and images and sounds – perhaps the cave paintings at Lascaux; perhaps the decorated and costumed bodies of those preparing for war or the hunt; perhaps ritualized drumming; perhaps chanting and remembering the deeds of ancestors – is centrally part of the sustaining of life in tribal communities. These objects and images and sounds and words are used magically to invoke higher powers, reinforce commitment, and maintain common focus and discipline. As the making of these objects, and also of utilitarian objects such as pots and cloth, goes on, however, it surely becomes evident that some of the objects thus made are especially striking and that certain individuals are specially apt at this making. Practices of training in the making of cultic objects develop, as can still be seen in the training of New Guinea totem carvers. Somewhere in the course of these developments, pride in and attention to the making of distinctive form as itself a valuable achievement – apart from the use of any object, image, or sound to fulfill a cultic function – comes to the fore. In monitoring their own products and the products of others, people begin to admire this achieved image or look or sound as itself an achievement of art. People begin to take pride in achieving this striking form or image, or to admire that configuration of rhythm. A sense of the development and significance of form-making power dawns. The exercise of form-making power for its own sake comes to be seen as a valuable instancing of a human capability for free meaning-making. The modern system of the fine and high arts that develops in the early seventeenth century is an outgrowth and refinement of an earlier sense of artistic making and its significance, as certain media – music, poetry, drama, painting, sculpture, dance, and architecture – are seen to offer specially powerful possibilities for the making of forms in which human powers of making can be displayed for their own sake and pride can be taken directly in their exercise. But surely some sense of these powers is present in any human culture, woven through its productions of cultic and utilitarian objects.

Distinctively artistic practice, then, emerges out of cultic and utilitarian production when pride in powers of the making of new meaningful forms becomes relatively foregrounded, in a progressive and never quite complete development. Adorno is describing the results of this

---

[31] Adorno, *Aesthetic Theory*, p. 17.

foregrounding when he remarks that "only artworks that are to be sensed as a form of comportment [Verhaltensweise] have a raison d'être."[32] The making of art, that is to say, exemplifies free meaning-making. Adorno overstates the point somewhat, in that meaning-making never becomes entirely free and for its own sake, independently of other psychological, social, economic, utilitarian, and so forth motives. Works of art that have decorative, liturgical, and utilitarian functions surely do have a raison d'être. The worthwhile point that is embodied in Adorno's remark, however, is that attention to meaning-making for its own sake, in the forming of wood, paint, clay, stone, sound, or words, is a defining aim of practice that can be recognized as artistic, over and above or in addition to being a practice of either utilitarian or cultic making. (Compare Hegel on art's supreme function with the fact that genuine works of art can also be decorative, useful, status-asserting, etc.) Through free meaning-making, distinctively human powers of envisioning and shaping for the sake of eye and ear in conjunction with the mind are exercised and appreciated. As Adorno puts it, "The autonomy [art] achieved, after having freed itself from cultic function and its images, was nourished by the idea of humanity."[33]

In order, then, for distinctively human powers of free meaning-making to continue to be exercised and appreciated, newness must be pursued. If a work is instead made as a repetition, according to plan, and with the satisfaction of either some utilitarian need or cultic function comparatively foregrounded, then the exercise and appreciation of powers of free meaning-making are foregone. Particularly in opposition to the manufactured commodity, where each unit – each pin or plate or automobile – is immediately fungible with any other of like manufacture, the work of art must be new. Even the copying or immediate repetition of prior art (as opposed to being inspired to new production by the power of form-making that prior art manifests) will result in something other than art. As Adorno puts it, "art must turn against itself, in opposition to its own concept, and thus become uncertain of itself, right into its innermost fibre."[34] Again the point is overstated, as Adorno argues for a hypermodernism; contra Adorno, there can be practices of making works

---

[32] ibid., p. 12.   [33] ibid., p. 1.

[34] ibid., p. 2. Adorno makes a similar point about the importance of the free making of meaning in philosophy, which must, like art, pursue "non-identity thinking" or "open thinking." On "open thinking" that "points beyond itself" see Theodor Adorno, "Resignation," Telos 35 (spring 1968), p. 168; on nonidentity thinking see Theodor

of art that form a tradition, and works of art can and typically are made within genres, not as outbursts of pure iconoclasm. But Adorno is right that being made within a tradition or genre is not sufficient for distinctively successful art. Mere formula must be worked through and overcome: in Pound's phrase, the artist must "make it new," must find new possibilities of subject matter, formal handling, and emotional expression within a tradition or genre, if distinctively human powers of free meaning-making are to be exercised and appreciated. This imperative pushes artistic production increasingly toward abstraction and conceptual innovation, against what craft alone enables. Modern art becomes "abstract by virtue of its relation to what is past; irreconcilable with magic, it is unable to speak what has yet to be, and yet must seek it, protesting against the ignominy of the ever-same."[35]

The point of protesting in artistic work against the ignominy of the ever-same is concretely and specifically to remind ourselves that our lives can be more than mere repetitions, that they can themselves be media of free and satisfying meaning-making, at least in principle and prospect. Instead of doing just this or that, again, as it has always been done, we can make objects and shape our lives freely and with full emotional investment. We need not succumb to lives of silent melancholy and quiet desperation. The making of original art is an anticipation and promise of original making in life more generally. As Adorno puts it, "the new is the aesthetic soul of expanded reproduction [of social life], with its promise of undiminished plenitude…Artworks detach themselves from the empirical world and bring forth another world… Thus, however tragic they appear, artworks tend *a priori* toward affirmation."[36]

Adorno, to repeat, overstates his points in tending to present craft, genre membership, and location within an artistic tradition as incompatible with originality, rather than in principle compatible with it but insufficient for it, and hence in tending to defend an esoteric, iconoclastic modernism. He remarks, for example, on "the decline of aesthetic genres as such."[37] Yet – especially in his later views about historical developments

---

Adorno, *Negative Dialectics*, trans. E. B. Ashton (New York: Continuum, 1973), especially part 2, "Negative Dialectics. Concept and Categories," pp. 135–207.

[35] Adorno, *Aesthetic Theory*, p. 22. See also on the development of increasing abstraction in music Dahlhaus, *Idea of Absolute Music*.

[36] Adorno, *Aesthetic Theory*, pp. 21, 1.   [37] *ibid.*, p. 199.

in music – he does elsewhere concede that original works of art must take inherited materials and strategies as points of departure.[38]

In any case – no matter how things stand with his sometime emphasis on esoteric, iconoclastic modernist works as exemplars of the original – Adorno's account of the importance of originality in art as the bearer of a *promesse de bonheur*[39] in social life more generally has been widely shared. Not only are there the briefs in favor of originality already alluded to[40] that have been put forward by Emerson and Thoreau, as well as the accounts of Kant and Harold Bloom, there is also Wordsworth's sense of the redemptive power of original artistic making in the face of the conformist traffic in commodities. Ordinarily, for Wordsworth, "The world is too much with us; late and soon / Getting and spending, we lay waste our powers."[41] There is a "tendency, too potent in itself, / Of use and custom to bow down the soul / Under a growing weight of vulgar sense / And substitute a universe of death / For that which moves with light and life informed / Actual divine and true."[42] But through participating as an audience in original artistic making – itself carried out in response to nature, for Wordsworth – we may hope to become "Powers ... minds truly from the Deity."[43] The experience of expressed originality, that is to say, is elevating and empowering for those who receive it – a fundamental working assumption of the so-called New Criticism in the United States and Practical Criticism in England, as practiced by Brooks, Leavis, and their circles. Similar accounts of the value of artistic originality appear in the structure-oriented and drama-oriented criticism of music, dance, painting, and sculpture. Even apart from these practices of criticism, original artistic making can seem immediately to serve as both the paradigm and promise of full human meaning-making as such, blending

---

[38] See Adorno, "Reaktion und Fortschritt," *Anbruch* 6, 12 (June 1930), cited in Max Paddison, *Adorno's Aesthetics of Music* (Cambridge: Cambridge University Press, 1993), p. 88.

[39] Adorno, *Aesthetic Theory*, p. 12.

[40] "Quiet desperation" is from the section entitled "Economy" in Thoreau's *Walden*; "silent melancholy" is from Emerson's essay, "New England Reformers."

[41] Wordsworth, "The World is too Much with Us," in Wordsworth, *Selected Poems and Prefaces*, p. 182, lines 1–2.

[42] Wordsworth, *The Prelude* (1850), in *Selected Poems and Prefaces*, Book XIV, lines 157–62, pp. 359–60.

[43] *ibid.*, Book XIV, lines 111, 112, p. 359.

spontaneity and sensuousness with reason and intelligibility. W. B. Gallie notes that achieving a "perfect union of spontaneity and discipline"[44] is a central problem of human life, and he points to both artistic making in general and Wordsworth's poetry in particular as the best exemplars of its solution. A wish for a perfect union of spontaneity and discipline, of sensuousness and thought, and of impulse and craft seems to inhabit many of our deepest relationships (or our aspirations within them), and the partial fulfillment of this wish seems to be something of what we admire in dance and in sports. Original art seems to express and nurture this wish, in offering further exemplary, partial fulfillments of it. Adorno remarks that "modern art constantly works the Münchhausean trick of carrying out the identification of the nonidentical,"[45] that is, of achieving spontaneous, new, and yet intelligible and intelligibly crafted artistic work. (According to the tale, Baron Munchausen is supposed to have pulled both himself and his horse out of a quagmire by his own hair.) Original artistic making serves as a central means of humanity pulling itself upward into more fully human, more meaningful life.

Criticisms of the pursuit of originality: postmodernism and feminism

Despite the attractiveness of this picture of the nature and importance of artistic originality, the idea that art can or should be original has had a relatively bad press in the past forty or so years in advanced criticism in the arts and humanities. Already in 1975 Tom Wolfe was complaining that the pursuit of individual artistic heroism in abstract expressionist painting had degenerated into a stale game of scandalizing the bourgeoisie, in which the artist undertook – all too predictably – "to look at the world in a way they [the bourgeoisie] couldn't see, to be high, live low, stay young forever – in short, to be the bohemian."[46] The cultivation of originality, at least by those means, had become a cliché. Writing in 1983 principally about the visual arts, but generalizing to literature as well, Hal Foster notes that nowadays "a poem or picture is not necessarily privileged, and

---

[44] W. G. Gallie, "Is *The Prelude* a Philosophical Poem?," *Philosophy* 22 (1947), pp. 124–38, reprinted in Wordsworth, *The Prelude 1799, 1805, 1850*, ed. Jonathan Wordsworth, M. H. Abrams, and Stephen Gill (New York: W. W. Norton, 1979), pp. 663–78 at p. 665.

[45] Adorno, *Aesthetic Theory*, p. 23.

[46] Tom Wolfe, *The Painted Word* (New York: Farrar, Straus, & Giroux, 1975), p. 15.

the artifact is likely to be treated less as a *work* in modernist terms – unique, symbolic, visionary – than as a *text* in a postmodernist sense – 'already written,' allegorical, contingent."[47] Under the pressure of structuralist awareness of the pervasiveness of both linguistic and social codes that seemed to dominate artistic production, and in opposition to the veneer of refinement and to refinement as a value that seemed to dominate so-called high art, an interest in the originality of individual vision and work gave way in some circles to an interest in the authentically common experience, it was assumed, of the dispossessed: workers, women, gays, the racially outcast, and others. John Barrell, for example, complained that balanced art, supposedly fully blending spontaneity and craft, both proceeded from and addressed "a [bogus] middle point between and above all merely partial and particular situations" and in doing so bore "a close resemblance to a certain ideal construction of the situation of the middle class – neither aristocratic nor vulgar, neither reactionary nor progressive."[48] In reaction he undertook against the grain to read in the voice and interest of the dispossessed, to show that "much of the poetry in the canon of English literature can also be read as writing produced by and about a particular class and gender, and that it will produce 'universal meaning' only for those who define the universal in the image of that class and gender."[49] Why should we be centrally interested in so-called originality in vision and in work that in fact reveals itself as both stale and bound by class and gender? Why not instead follow Lillian S. Robinson and take an interest in the two-page autobiography of an "anonymous Seamer on Men's Underwear" who participated in one of the "Summer Schools for Women Workers held at Bryn Mawr in the first decades of the [twentieth] century"? True, the piece is, as Robinson notes, "a circumstantial narrative in which events from the melancholy to the melodramatic are accumulated in a somewhat hackneyed style," but it is at least "honest writing" and, Robinson argues, "clichés or sentimentality need not be signals of meretricious prose."[50]

---

[47] Hal Foster, "Postmodernism: A Preface," in *The Anti-Aesthetic: Essays on Post-Modern Culture*, ed. H. Foster (Port Townsend, WA: Bay Press, 1983), pp. ix–xvi at pp. x–xi.

[48] John Barrell, "Introduction," in J. Barrell, *Poetry, Language and Politics* (Manchester: Manchester University Press, 1988), pp. 5–6.

[49] Barrell, "Preface," in *ibid.*, p. ix.

[50] Lillian S. Robinson, "Treason our Text: Feminist Challenges to the Literary Canon," *Tulsa Studies in Women's Literature* (1983), reprinted in *Critical Theory Since 1965*, ed.

Or one might, in a deconstructive spirit, follow Jacques Derrida's efforts to unmask the imperialist but always failed efforts of philosophers, critics, and theorists to "neutralize or reduce" the play of language and of social codes by giving them "a center or... referring [them] to a point of presence, a fixed origin" so as "to orient, balance, and organize the structure."[51] Perhaps such orienting efforts cannot be quite wholly foregone. But they cannot, Derrida argues, be completed either, and the canny critic can decipher their fractures and self-contradictions: no text is a completely unified and univocal whole. Such canny reading might help us to cease to dream quite *so* heavy-handedly and tactlessly "of full presence, the reassuring foundation, the origin and end of the game"[52] and thus help us at least to be more open-minded. After all, as Walter Benjamin worried, might not the pursuit of a fully formed, final, original vision of humanity and social life, involving "genius and creativity, eternal value and mystery" lead us to "the processing of data in the Fascist sense"?[53] If one is magically in possession of the correct vision of humanity and social life, then anyone who disagrees with it must simply be in error and hence properly subject to some form of discipline, correction, or removal.

Not only, however, has it been argued that the putatively original productions of artists are both structured by sectarian linguistic and social codes and interests and less than fully formed and coherent, it has also been argued that the very idea of a creative artist is a modern invention. Prior to the Renaissance, it has been claimed, the artist was regarded largely as a craftsman, principally serving the interests of the aristocracy or the Church according to rules. It is only when, first, in the Renaissance, individuality began to be valued and cultivated, and, second, in the eighteenth century, painters, writers, and musicians lost court patronage and had to earn livings through sales, that the modern idea of the creative

---

Hazard Adams and Leroy Searle (Tallahassee, FL: Florida State University Press, 1986), pp. 572–82 at p. 581A.

[51] Jacques Derrida, "Structure, Sign and Play in the Discourse of the Human Sciences," in *The Structuralist Controversy: The Languages of Criticism and the Sciences of Man*, ed. Richard Macksey and Eugenio Donato (Baltimore, MD: Johns Hopkins University Press, 1972), pp. 247–65 at p. 247.

[52] *ibid.*, p. 265.

[53] Walter Benjamin, "The Work of Art in the Age of Mechanical Reproduction," in W. Benjamin, *Illuminations*, trans. Harry Zohn, ed. Hannah Arendt (New York: Harcourt, Brace, & World, 1968), cited in Gould, "Genius," p. 291A.

artist emerged. To suit this new social situation, the idea arose – urged by writers such as Wordsworth and theorists such as Kant – that artists and authors have been specially touched by inspiration or genius. This claim served conveniently to explain and justify why artists and authors – unlike ordinary craftsmen in the industrial and domestic arts – deserve a uniquely high price for their products. As Martha Woodmansee sums up this line of argument, "The 'author' in the modern sense is a relatively recent invention, a product of...the emergence in the eighteenth century of writers who sought to earn their livelihood from the sale of their writings to the new and rapidly expanding public."[54]

Similarly, Michel Foucault argues that in Velasquez's *Las Meninas* (1656)

> representation undertakes to represent itself here in all its elements, with its images, the eyes to which it is offered, the faces it makes visible, the gestures that call it into being...Perhaps there exists, in this painting by Velasquez, the representation, as it were, of Classical [i.e. seventeenth- and eighteenth-century] representation, and the definition of the space it opens up to us.[55]

What Foucault means by this is that during this period a new social formation of modern subjects – who understand themselves as masters of their own gaze, as potential owners of property, as bearers of rights under the law, as able to make enforceable contracts, and so forth – comes into being. This new social formation is quite different from the medieval world of fixed social roles that were taken to reflect a larger cosmological order. Instead, in the modern world individuals emerge as sovereign over their experience and commitments, a political sovereign in the form of a monarch is installed (and then later held accountable to the individuals governed: political individualism and absolute monarchy develop together), and artists and authors perforce come to make their ways in the world through sales. Velasquez's painting both illustrates and participates in these developments. It is not so much that Velasquez is himself an inspired, original painter as that in his work the emerging order of individualist representation "undertakes to represent itself." Foucault himself

[54] Martha Woodmansee, *The Author, Art, and the Market: Rereading the History of Aesthetics* (New York: Columbia University Press, 1994), p. 36.
[55] Michel Foucault, *The Order of Things*, trans. not named (New York: Random House, 1970), p. 16.

looks forward, together with Roland Barthes, to a new social formation mysteriously emerging, to the cessation of the cultivation and cult of individuality, and to the death of man. "It is comforting…and a source of profound relief," Foucault writes,

> to think that man is only a recent invention…a new wrinkle in our knowledge, and that he will disappear again as soon as that knowledge has discovered a new form…In attempting to uncover the deepest strata of western culture, I am restoring to our silent and apparently immobile soil its rifts, its instability, its flaws; and it is the same ground that is once more stirring under our feet.[56]

Individuals, artists, authors – these are all incomplete and unstable historical formations, arising in and through likewise incomplete and unstable historical social configurations. None of them is fully original, fully coherently expressive, or self-authorizing. As Barthes claims in announcing the death of the author,

> We know now that a text is not a line of words releasing a single "theological" meaning (the "message" of the Author-God) but a multi-dimensional space in which a variety of writings, none of them original, blend and clash. The text is a tissue of quotations drawn from the innumerable centers of culture…[T]he writer can only imitate a gesture that is always anterior, never original. His only power is to mix writings, to counter the ones with the others, in such a way as never to rest on any one of them.[57]

Or, in Foucault's formulation, "the subject…must be stripped of its creative role and analyzed as a complex and variable function of discourse."[58] In short, there is no there there: no creative subject to serve as a fount of original work, but only a historically constituted point of assignation of overlapping, mongrelized streams of discourse and image within complex currents of planless, self-evolving social life.

Perhaps worse yet, as the ideas of the modern individual and the creative artist were historically constructed, women were excluded from any

---

[56] ibid., pp. xiii, xiv.

[57] Roland Barthes, "The Death of the Author" (1968), reprinted in Philosophy of Art, ed. Neill and Ridley, pp. 386–90 at p. 388.

[58] Foucault, "What is an Author?," in Critical Theory Since 1965, ed. Adams and Searle, pp. 138–48 at p. 148A.

share in genius. On the basis of a detailed survey of conceptions of genius from the Greek world through the Renaissance, Romanticism, and the nineteenth and twentieth centuries, Christine Battersby has established that the standard image of genius was that of a "feminine" male. The prevailing rhetoric

> praised "feminine" qualities in male creators...but claimed females
> could not – or should not – create...The genius's instinct, emotion,
> sensibility, intuition, imagination – even his madnesses [all coded
> "feminine"] – were different from those of ordinary mortals...The
> genius was a male – full of "virile" energy – who *transcended* his
> biology...Creativity was displaced *male* procreativity: male sexuality
> made sublime...Indeed, the more psychically feminine genius appeared,
> the louder the shout that went up, "It's a boy."[59]

Inextricably interwoven socially with this prevailing conception of genius is "a continual blotting out of the contributions of women artists"[60] as their artistic labors, if allowed to take place at all, were by and large relegated to the "stereotypically female"[61] domestic arts of embroidery, pottery, lacemaking, flower arranging, and so forth.

Originality and imagination within common life

The central points made in these various deconstructions of the nature of genius and devaluings of the cultivation of individuality are surely correct. The heroism of abstract expressionist painting had by the early 1960s grown stale. Just as people grow up speaking one native language or another as a result of their linguistic circumstances, so too the production of art takes place against a background of multiple strategies, aims, examples, and conceptions of interest that are historically afforded. Artworks – whether paintings or poems, movies or pots or sonatas – typically *can* be read accurately and insightfully both as intended for certain preconceived sectarian audiences and as less than absolutely coherent, with rough edges, uncontrolled ambiguities, and conflicting attitudes and thoughts in play. It is true that the modern, post-Renaissance cultural

---

[59] Christine Battersby, *Gender and Genius: Towards a Feminist Aesthetics* (London: Women's Press, 1989; reprinted Bloomington, IN: Indiana University Press, 1990), pp. 3, 6.
[60] *ibid.*, p. 6.   [61] *ibid.*, p. 169.

world is significantly different from earlier and other worlds and true also that its special character shapes how the making and understanding of art are carried out. Some of the value of some art, as Mikhail Bakhtin has emphasized in discussing the novel,[62] comes from a polyphonic interplay of opposed points of view, not simply from magisterial individual vision preconceived by an isolated creator alone. Women have had less than a full share of opportunities to train in and to practice high art, and many valuable works by women have been dismissed as matters of mere domestic craft or decoration. Perhaps it is true that in the contemporary world we are so aware of varieties of social formation – both across different cultures and within any single culture – and hence aware of conflicting artistic traditions and directions of interest, that we find it hard to believe that an original artistic vision might command the absorption of everyone. Insistence that a given work of art requires and rewards the attention of everyone may well seem a piece of cultural tyranny.

It does not, however, follow from these points that originality either fails to exist or fails to be of central value in art. Works of art – including conceptual art and found art – are either made or put forward for attention as a result of human action. This action can be either original or stale, derivative, and imitative. Or it can be fraudulent. Even a perfect forgery – indiscernible to the eye or ear from an original or from other members of an œuvre – lacks the meaning and value of an original work, and this is because it does not result from the same original exploration of materials and possibilities of arrangement. Nelson Goodman has suggested that once we know, perhaps by means of chemical tests, that a given painting is a forgery, then we can learn to recognize it visually as such, even where previously we had failed to do so.[63] We can learn to see the action – fraudulent or original – that produced a painting *in* the painting. How the material is worked – fraudulently or originally – may become evident to the eye. Fraudulence may reveal itself as derivativeness.

Just as we speak our native languages by contingent inheritance, but can also speak or write them with a distinctive style, cadence, and impress of personality, attitude, and line of interest, so too then can the making of art take up and work through materials from a tradition in a distinctive,

---

[62] See Mikhail M. Bahktin, *The Dialogic Imagination*, ed. Michael Holquist, trans. Caryl Emerson and Michael Holquist (Austin, TX: University of Texas Press, 1981).
[63] Goodman, *Languages of Art*, pp. 99–112.

original way. Pot makers and painters, poets and architects, composers and quilters all know, if they are talented and things go well, the satisfaction of trying out a new motif, theme, shape, or mode of arrangement and having it work. Even if the result is not immediately intelligible and valuable to everyone, the satisfaction of presenting a subject matter as a focus for thought and emotional attitude, distinctively fused to the imaginative exploration of material, is available and valuable within a variety of artistic practices and traditions. Part of the value of this achievement comes from its being original, from its evidencing of powers of free meaning-making in the working through of subject matter and attitude within the materials of a medium of art. Artists of all kinds are the first audiences of their own works in process, and they monitor their ongoing work to establish whether, to what extent, and how they are managing to achieve original sense, with thought and attitude *distinctively* fused to the exploration of material. This is as true of appropriation art, found art, conceptual art, performance art, and other avant-gardisms as it is of work in more traditional media.

In modern art, artists in shaping and monitoring their work are often quite aware of the contingences of artistic achievement that are afforded by their particular artistic tradition and practice. Frequently they call attention to the work itself as a more or less coherent, but still incomplete, construction or assemblage, in order to highlight the open-ended, explorative, satisfaction-*seeking* quality of their work (and of the participation in that work that they invite from their audiences). Cézanne, for example, in his Mont Sainte-Victoire series increasingly leaves patches of canvas unpainted. In "Tintern Abbey" Wordsworth repeatedly qualifies his own thought with phrases such as "If this / Be but a vain belief"[64] and "I would believe,"[65] and in *The Prelude* he describes his courses of "lapse and hesitating choice, / And backwards wanderings along thorny ways,"[66] thus highlighting the explorative character of artistic making and its continuing uncertainties. Asides to readers or viewers are staples of modern literature and drama. Movies occur within movies. Composers introduce increasingly innovative dissonances in the history of composition. Either

---

[64] Wordsworth, "Lines Composed a Few Miles Above Tintern Abbey," in Wordsworth, *Selected Poems and Prefaces*, ed. Stillinger, pp. 108–11 at p. 109, lines 49–50.

[65] *ibid.*, p. 110, line 87.

[66] Wordsworth, *The Prelude*, in Wordsworth, *Selected Poems and Prefaces*, ed. Stillinger, p. 359, Book XIV, lines 136–37.

density, difficulty, and ambiguity of language (Mallarmé, Rimbaud, Pound, Hölderlin, Rilke) *or* unexpected directness and clarity (Carver, Kafka) may be highlighted. Process and exploration are foregrounded over any pre-formed message or effort to tyrannize a culture.

Creativity: Scruton and Coleridge on artistic imagination

In exploring the materials of a medium in relation to subject matter and attitude, makers of art will typically have a conception of the kind of thing they are making: a sonata, a sonnet, a novel, a *pas de deux*, a performance piece, a movie, a still life, and so forth. To some extent this conception will be drawn from a common background practice, and to some extent it will guide the shaping of the material. Yet exploring the material – the forms, motives, shapes, movements, words, and so on that are in the process of arrangement – freely and imaginatively remains crucial to artistic making. The word *imagination* can be used to describe both a faculty of mind and a process. The words *expression* and *creation* can be used to describe either a process or a product. It is difficult to say exactly what sort of explorative process involving imagination, expression, and creation is involved in artistic making. If the creative process could be broken down into parts or stages themselves governed by a law of succession in production or a rule for correctness, then the process would be mechanical or algorithmic, not free. As a result, it seems plausible to regard the product senses of "expression" and "creation" as primary. An expressive or creative process is deemed to have taken place when the product strikes us as freely formed and original; we do *not* determine free formation and originality by independently inspecting the process.

Although the process of free making cannot be characterized mechanically or algorithmically in such a way that imagination, creation, and expression are explained, it is possible nonetheless to say something about which aspects of the materials of art creative imagination and free making focus on. In discussing the aesthetics of music, Roger Scruton has offered a useful characterization of the focus of imaginative attention both in artistic making and in the apprehending of art. Works of music, he argues, are composed of *tones*, that is, sounds heard as leading away from and toward one another, not simply of pitches (of measurable wave length) experienced as discrete. Tones are part of an arrangement or order that we hear as a developing motive (or as one that fails to develop). They exist in and for hearing not one by one, but rather *as* elements of a developing musical order of which they are essentially a part. In being essentially elements *of* a developing arrangement or order, tones are what Scruton calls *tertiary qualities*. Primary qualities are observer-independent, in principle objectively measurable, qualities of objects, such as mass and chemical composition. Secondary qualities are qualities possessed by objects in relation to human or other sensory faculties: being red or blue, sour or sweet, loud or soft. They are real enough, but they are defined in relation to normal sensory responses of some class of sensate discriminators. Tertiary qualities are interrelations or arrangements of primary and secondary qualities. For example, tones are heard as elements of an interrelation, arrangement, or order of pitches. Tones – one leading to or away from another – and the arrangement or order of which they are essentially a part are, like secondary qualities, real enough. But unlike secondary qualities, they are defined not in relation to normal sensory responses alone but rather in relation also to the responses of beings with capacities of understanding or following a developing order or arrangement. As Scruton sums up his view,

> We might say that a work of music is a *tertiary* object, as are the tones
> that compose it. Only a being with certain intellectual and imaginative
> capacities can hear music, and these are precisely the capacities required
> for the perception of tertiary qualities.[67]

Here Scruton is essentially elaborating Kant's claim that the experience of beauty (in both nature and art) requires the involvement in a special way of both imagination and understanding. We must focus on an object, but do so freely and exploratively. Though we bring conceptual capacities (and not only sensory responses) to bear in exploring a work, we do so in an unusual way. We are especially alert to the developing *arrangement* or *order* of the work: to how its parts lead to or "fit" one another to compose a whole, embracing complexities, that sustains attention. That is, in Scruton's terminology, we attend to the work of art as a tertiary object: something that essentially exists in relation to this kind of exploration.

When things go well in this exploration, then the work is distinctively successful. Developing a Schopenhauerian stance, Scruton suggests that in successful music, at least, we can concretely experience through this

---

[67] Roger Scruton, *The Aesthetics of Music* (Oxford: Oxford University Press, 1997), p. 161.

exploration something that is otherwise mysterious and unavailable to us: autonomy or freedom according to law, over and above natural, causal processes. As Scruton puts it, in following the development of a successful musical work,

> the causality of nature has been set aside, discounted, hidden behind the acousmatic [pitches *as tones*] veil. In music we are given an unparalleled glimpse of the reality of freedom; and because, as Kant reminds us, reason deals only in necessities, we hear the free order of music as a necessary order: it is when each note *requires* its successor that we hear freedom in music.[68]

In being alert in exploring a work to an order of elements, regarded as developing both freely and with (rational) necessity so as to achieve a whole that can be followed, the imagination and understanding in responding to a work are on the lookout for concrete freedom. This seems true of the experience of art in general. (The only mistake in Scruton's passage is the word *unparalleled*: paintings, poems, movies, performance pieces, dances, and so on when successful are all tertiary objects. They too have freely achieved orders that can be followed by a being with imagination and understanding.) The role of imagination and creativity in exploring the materials of a medium in artistic making is to achieve this concrete freedom. What imagination focuses on in exploring materials in the process of arrangement is whether this free intelligibility or free order is being achieved.

This is what Coleridge meant in talking of imagination as an *esemplastic* or shaping power. He distinguishes imagination from *fancy*, which is a matter of associating materials from experience at whim, without any attention to making a freely intelligible order that can be followed. For example, we might fancy that there are centaurs or golden mountains. In simply thus fancying, there is no freely intelligible work to be explored; these are only an immediate combination of past elements of experience in a momentary act.

Imagination, according to Coleridge, is different.

> The imagination then I consider either as primary, or secondary. The primary imagination I hold to be the living power and prime agent of

---

[68] *ibid.*, p. 76.

all human perception, and as a representation in the finite mind of the eternal act of creation in the infinite I AM. The secondary I consider as an echo of the former, co-existing with the conscious will, yet still as identical with the primary in the kind of its agency, and different only in degree, and in the mode of its operation. It dissolves, diffuses, dissipates, in order to recreate; or where this process is rendered impossible, yet still, at all events, it struggles to idealize and to unify. It is essentially *vital*, even as all objects (as objects) are essentially fixed and dead.[69]

In characterizing primary imagination as the "prime agent of all human perception," Coleridge means that human beings take in the world through the senses as other animals do, but in a distinctive way. (The emphasis in his remark should fall on the word *human*. Coleridge is here transcribing Kant's theories of apperceptive awareness and of productive imagination as he received them partly by way of Fichte and Schelling.) Somehow, as we grow up out of infancy, our taking in of the world comes to be interfused with a sense of ourselves as subjects, able to conceptualize objects in a variety of ways, not simply to discriminate them. Our sensory awareness, unlike that of other animals, includes both conceptual structure and always available (if implicit) self-awareness. Unlike animals, we can always step back in perception and say not just "this peach is ripe" but also "*I see that* this peach is ripe." Unlike animals, we can conceptualize this object *as* a peach, a fruit, a projectile, a seed, or a favorite of Joan's, as occasion suits. Our capacity to be aware of ourselves and to see the same object in various ways – under various descriptions or aspects – is central to our lives as beings who freely make and live in human culture, not merely under the necessities of nature. Objects *mean* various things to us as subjects. Primary imagination – sensory world intake that is interwoven with conceptualization – is essential for this. Without it we would not be human subjects with a human culture.

Secondary imagination possesses the same kind of agency as primary imagination. It, too, is a free "seeing" of things: an awareness that is not *merely* sensory and not altogether determined by the laws of nature. It is to some extent voluntary, or under the control of the will, and it is devoted to *making*: it dissolves, diffuses, dissipates, *in order to recreate* something that is whole and *vital*. In doing this, it participates in something *like* the

---

[69] Coleridge, *Biographia Literaria*, p. 167.

emergence of subjecthood and self-awareness out of mere sensory awareness. This claim captures our sense that successful creative artists seem
somehow to revert to what Freud calls the material of "primary process" –
the material of the less structured associations of childhood and the unconscious, somehow managing to come away from this reversion with a
newly formed product. They seem to redirect or refocus our capacities of
attention as subjects, teaching us to see this *as* that, and thus to contribute
to the free making of culture, in the hope that it will be a more fit home
for the further exercise of human powers.

Such free makings – the esemplastic arrangement of materials so as to
present a subject matter as a focus for thought and emotional attitude –
are specifically situated, socially and historically. They are typically in one
way or another incomplete, one-sided, sectarian, and imperfect. But it
seems hard to believe that they will not continue nonetheless to be of essential human interest. "We shall not cease from exploration,"[70] T. S. Eliot
wrote, in the effort freely to achieve a fully meaningful human culture,
beyond coercion and the drudgeries of repetition. Original achievements
of the arrangement of materials to form a whole, presenting a subject
matter as a focus for thought distinctively fused to emotional attitude
and the exploration of materials, continue to be possible and valuable. As
Monroe Beardsley sums up the importance of art,

> In aesthetic experience we have experience in which means and ends are
> so closely interrelated that we feel no separation between them. One
> thing leads to the next and finds its place in it; the end is immanent in
> the beginning and the beginning is carried up into the end. Such
> experience allows the least emptiness, monotony, frustration, lack of
> fulfillment, and despair – the qualities that cripple much of human life.
> One of the things that trouble us in our society is, according to some
> philosophers, the wide gap that often exists between means and ends.
> Much of labor is itself uninteresting, mechanical, and spiritually
> deadening, and the laborer has no way of seeing a meaningful
> connection between what he is doing and what the ultimate product
> will be – the way a craftsman making a chair can be guided at every step
> by a vivid realization of its relation to his goal. The means of life lose

---

[70] T. S. Eliot, "Little Gidding," in *Four Quartets*, reprinted in *The Norton Anthology of
English Literature*, ed. Abrams *et al.*, vol. II, p. 2197.

their satisfaction when the end-in-view is entirely distant and remote –
the Saturday night binge, the retirement at sixty-five. But the ends, too,
lose their value by the separation. The binge only becomes a wild
release, followed by headache and remorse. The retirement brings
unutterable boredom and a sense of uselessness. If some of the
satisfyingness of the end could be brought into the means, and the
means at every stage felt as carrying the significance of the end, we
should have in life something more of the quality of aesthetic
experience itself. Meanwhile, such experience holds before us a clue to
what life can be like in its greatest richness and joy.[71]

Original arrangement, freely achieved through shaping imagination and
presenting a subject matter as a focus for thought distinctively fused to
emotional attitude and the exploration of materials, remains a central
aim of artistic making and a principal means for producing such clues to
fully human life.

---

[71] Beardsley, *Aesthetics*, pp. 575–76.

6 Understanding art

Six strategies for understanding art

Consider the following six very broad strategies for understanding Shakespeare's *Hamlet*.

1. *Hamlet* can be seen in light of the conscious preoccupations of a roughly identifiable historical epoch such as Jacobean England, the Renaissance, or early modern Europe. For example, one may see the play as addressing problems of political authority and succession, problems of conscience in the light of the Reformation's resistance to priestly mediation between individuals and God, problems of stagecraft and performance, or some combination of these and other problems. Shakespeare may reasonably be supposed to have known and thought about these problems. To explore *Hamlet* in this light will mean relating the text to varieties of contemporary documents – for example, political treatises, religious tracts, and instruction manuals for actors – that likewise evidently address such problems. Reading will focus on how the action of the play presents characters confronting these problems. *Hamlet* is here seen as a consciously formed document that partakes of the spirit of its times.

2. *Hamlet* can be seen in light of Shakespeare's particular biography. Though location in relation to an epoch may matter here as well, more emphasis will fall on locating the play in the arc of the development of Shakespeare's own œuvre. One will ask: How does this play take up issues of jealousy and trust, or of visionary authority, or of social station that occupied Shakespeare in other plays? How do the plays as a group bear the impress of that particular personality's history of being interested in problems in a distinctive, individual fashion? What is Hamlet's place within this group? Do we have any direct biographical evidence – for example, from journals or letters – that enables us to relate the play to Shakespeare as a distinctive individual agent?

3. *Hamlet* can be seen in light of its fulfillment of nondeliberated intentions. For example, it is written in early modern English, and it was not

Shakespeare's deliberate intention to have early modern English as his native language. Together with having this language may come certain intentions and habits of expression that are *not* objects of conscious deliberation. Perhaps many people who speak a given language and who live in particular times are significantly but unconsciously affected by a variety of continuing subtexts of their concern with public self-presentation. Almost all of us have views that are *not* fully articulated about how to dress, how to hold our bodies, and how to interact with various other sorts of people in conversation. Though we can sometimes *become* aware of these views, we do not always do so. We have largely simply taken them on board from our social surroundings. Continuing subtexts that give shape to *Hamlet* may include such things as the Freudian thematics of the Oedipal crisis, gender anxiety and same sex interest, or class anxiety – anything that people may be supposed significantly to care about covertly in their struggles to form and maintain themselves as subjects in a social setting.

4. *Hamlet* can be seen as an essentially visionary work, the product more of literary language's possession of Shakespeare than his possession of it. That is, one may suppose that Shakespeare came predominantly to *write* out of his spirit, ear, or feel for the language, as used by his literary predecessors and contemporaries, beyond any conscious or unconscious preoccupations of his society and independently of any conscious address to problems. Central to *Hamlet* may be a kind of compulsive making of metaphors and images, cobbled together out of literary examples and contemporary speech in a way that is more inspired than controlled. According to this view, what makes the play what it is as art is this compulsive, visionary meaning-making as a work of inspiration or genius. To understand the play according to this view will centrally require close, attentive tracing of its patterns of metaphor and imagery, and it will require relating those patterns to like patterns in precursors such as the Bible and Spenser, so as to demonstrate their density, extent, and originality.

5. *Hamlet* can be seen as an object to be performed or otherwise to be made use of creatively. It is, among other things, a very long play, and in most performances there will be some cuts to the text. Decisions will have to be made about costuming, lighting, diction, and blocking. Directors and performers will have to settle how to use the stage and how to have the characters interact physically. As a radical extension of this view, one might decide to make use of the characters in other dramatic settings than those presented in the text: for example, to depict Hamlet

as a foil for the doubts of Rosencrantz and Guildenstern, as Tom Stoppard does, rather than the other way around. Or one might write a *Hamlet* suite for viola and string orchestra.

6. *Hamlet* can be seen as an historical artifact – a set of words on particular pages – with rough and disputable boundaries. Historical text editors work very hard to specify the artifact as fully as possible, by looking at variant editions (First Folio [F1, 1623]) vs. Bad Quarto [Q1, 1603]) vs. Second Quarto [Q2, 1604–05]). Which version of the text is closest to Shakespeare's fullest intention? The latest and presumably deliberately revised? Or the earliest one as used in first performances, prior to later corruptions? Which version is most coherent semantically, thematically, and imagistically? Should we even settle as best we can on an "authoritative version," or should we rather publish all versions as themselves independent historical artifacts?

These strategies for understanding are available as well for media of art other than dramatic literature. Beethoven can be seen as a figure of the late Enlightenment, as a tortured soul, as one who covertly furthers masculinist values already in cultural circulation, or as a master of formal relations and through-composition. Themes and motives from his work can be quoted, revised, and refigured by subsequent composers, and music text editors can argue about authoritative texts in relation to shifting performance practices. In a series of anthologies entitled *Masterpieces of Western Painting*,[1] several critics investigate in each volume various ways of understanding a single painting – for example, Titian's *Venus of Urbino*[2] – by considering it formally, sociopolitically, biographically, in relation to gender issues, with attention to issues of physical restoration, and so on.

Each of these strategies for understanding has its own virtues and vices. Interpreting a work by situating it in relation to contemporary issues in religion, politics, and the other arts, as those issues were explicitly articulated, can reveal broad patterns of shared thought, feeling, and interest, but it threatens to devalue individual artists and works by casting them as "typical." Biographical understanding locates the work as a distinctive personal product, but it can sometimes focus on accidents of personal circumstance more than on the work and either its art or history.

---

[1] Published by Cambridge University Press, beginning in 1997.

[2] See *Titian's "Venus of Urbino,"* ed. Rona Goffen (Cambridge: Cambridge University Press, 1997).

To see a work in terms of unconscious or only half-articulated class and gender issues is to see it as giving us *entrée* to the deep, unspoken preoccupations of a people, but it can miss how a work might itself revise such preoccupations. Close formal reading attends aptly to interrelations of elements in the work, but it can devolve into repetitive and predictable dwelling on "balanced paradox" and into the overvaluing of some favored mode of decorum, without sufficient feel for history or meaning. Constructivist appropriations and refigurations of precursor works or elements of precursor works can both issue in valuable new art and cast light on the appropriated precursor, but they run the risk of not in the end really being "about" the precursor work at all. Text editors in music and literature and restorers of paintings, sculptures, buildings, movies, and architecture can do invaluable work, but there are often controversies about where restoration ends and creative interpretation begins. Publishing all variants of a text, say, will not establish an authentic original work, and the ravages of time cannot be unambiguously reversed in restoration. Moreover, it is unclear that textual and restorative labors capture for us what a work may mean.

Is any of these six strategies for understanding a work of art uniquely apt to its objects? Are the claims that are arrived at by pursuing these strategies consistent, or do they contradict one another? For example, does a Freudian reading of *Hamlet* contradict a reading that focuses on its patterns of images? Are these readings even about the same thing? Just what should we do – which strategy or strategies should we centrally practice – in order to understand a work?

The natures of thought and action: Hegel, Baxandall, and others

A remark by Hegel provides a useful clue for addressing these questions. "It must not be imagined," Hegel writes,

> that a human being thinks on the one hand and wills on the other, and that he has thought in one pocket and volition in the other ... [Thought and will] are not two separate faculties; on the contrary, the will is a particular way of thinking – thinking as translating itself into existence, thinking as the drive to give itself existence.[3]

---

[3] Hegel, *Elements of the Philosophy of Right*, ed. Allen W. Wood, trans. H. B. Nisbet (Cambridge: Cambridge University Press, 1991), §4 addition, p. 35.

What Hegel means by this, among other things, is that it is a mistake to regard thinking as primarily and originally a matter of first having an image or other mental object *inside* one's individual mind and then introspecting that image or object. Nor is choosing or willing a matter only of the occurrence of an "inner event" of "mental motion" toward an object. It is true that images and other mental objects may sometimes enter into thinking, and it is true that moments of choice can sometimes be identified. But thinking and willing as processes do not take place originally and only by means of the having of mental images objects and by internal velleity. Thinking and willing are, rather, interrelated achievements, things we learn to do in a certain way. For example, to *think* of a wildebeest (as opposed to having what is in fact a wildebeest within one's field of sensory awareness – something that might happen to or in a sensate but not rational-conceptual animal such as a frog) requires possessing the concept of a wildebeest and applying it. So does choosing to hunt a wildebeest. The animal in question must be recognized under some relevant concept, if genuine thinking and choosing, as opposed to merely being aware and moving, are to take place. Achieving this recognition is something that one learns to do by taking up recognitional strategies (including possibilities of being mistaken) that one learns from others. It does not happen as a result only of events in an individual mind or brain. As Daniel Dennett summarizes this point, "one must be richly informed about, intimately connected with, the world at large, its occupants and properties, in order to be said with any propriety to have beliefs"[4] as opposed to mere sensory awareness.

Recognitional strategies that must be taken up in order for there to be genuine thinking and willing are necessarily shared. We can see this by considering what happens when we encounter a human being who "acts" (as it seems to us) altogether incoherently, without employing any strategy for action or communication that we or anyone else can discern or make use of. In such a case, our confidence that that human being is genuinely an agent who has a point of view on things and who is engaged in genuine action, communicative or otherwise, lapses. We see the human being in question as mad, uninterpretable, not really a thinker or subject. Perhaps such a human being can become a thinker or subject. Infants can grow into common thought and language, and therapy can sometimes help the

---

[4] Daniel Dennett, "Beyond Belief," in *Thought and Object*, ed. A. Woodfield (Oxford: Oxford University Press, 1982), p. 23.

insane. There is good reason to regard human beings, no matter what their failures to think and act coherently over a given stretch of time, as having one and all the dignity of at least potential agents. But thinking and acting remain things that one must grow into by taking up one or another set of recognitional strategies that are necessarily shared to some extent.[5]

Two closely related points about the nature of thought and action as they are objects of understanding or interpretation, including the understanding or interpretation of art, immediately follow. First, there is no unique, isolated, "inner" thought that occurs as a private event prior to the making of the work. It is true that inner thoughts, intentions, and plans can precede actual artistic work. But even these inner thoughts, intentions, and plans require the use of shared concepts – shared recognitional strategies – in terms of which they are formulated. Though there can be conceptual innovations and new strategies for recognition of a work (and for making it), these innovations and new strategies must be intelligible outgrowths of shared concepts. They are also inherently open to further specification and revision in the course of the work. Once we realize this, we can become disabused of the idea that a correct understanding of a work of art must capture some fully formed inner something – the occurrence of a fully formed, individual, governing intention or plan for the work that is somehow private or hidden from us. We can capture no such thing, nor need we. Instead, to understand a work is to situate it within a network of concepts or strategies for recognition that are both in principle shareable and necessarily at least partly shared. While agents, including artists, have a certain degree of first-person authority in knowing and reporting (if they wish) their own "inner" thoughts and plans, this first-person authority is not a matter of their having unique, privileged, introspective access to objects that are inherently private or inner. It is rather a function of the fact that mastery of any concept or recognition strategy normally (though not necessarily on every single occasion) carries with it articulable awareness of what one is doing or can do (though on occasion others can know better).[6] Understanding of thought and action, and *eo ipso* understanding of works of art as products of thought and

---

[5] See the more extended discussion of language and thought in Eldridge, *Leading a Human Life*, especially, p. 271inf.

[6] See Donald Davidson, "First Person Authority," "Knowing One's Mind," and "The Myth of the Subjective," all reprinted in Davidson, *Subjective, Intersubjective, Objective*, pp. 3–14, 15–38, 39–52.

action, need not replicate or match any isolated "inner," "private," mental object, plan, intention, or meaning.

Second, actions are normally *overdetermined* by a number of reasons and motives, both conscious and latent but articulable. Why did McEnroe serve a slice serve wide in the ad court? In order to draw his opponent wide, to force a difficult return, to win the point, to even the match, to win Wimbledon, to acquire the number one ranking, to win the admiration and respect of others, to make money, to exhibit a certain stylistic flair, because for a left-hander it is the most comfortable serve that is effective in that situation, because Borg has had trouble with that serve all day, because the position of the sun makes the toss for that serve the most reliable one available. All of these may reasonably be regarded as among McEnroe's reasons for serving as he did, insofar as he forms his intentions and plans and carries out his action within a larger institutional, social, and conceptual framework. Though none of these reasons need occur to him explicitly in the moment of action, any of them could, depending on the context in question, be acknowledged by him as a reason for doing what he did. While McEnroe has a certain first-person authority as a master of the conceptual repertoire of English (and of tennis) in reporting his own reasons for action, there is often not any single, decisive, governing reason occurring in consciousness to be reported, but rather an indefinite set of considerations that can help us to understand or make sense of his action, depending on the context of questioning. With less isolatable, more complex, and temporally sustained actions, the overdetermination of actions by reasons only increases. Why does one have children, or buy one house rather than another, or practice the cello?

These complexities of overdetermination by reasons apply also to the making of art. Shakespeare may be reasonably taken to have done many things for many reasons in writing *Hamlet*: to work out his thoughts about modern individualism, to give expression to his ear for language, to develop a successful play and make some money, to depict interactions between men and women, to please James I, and so on. When we undertake to understand what Shakespeare did, we may turn to any one of a number of reasons – publicly intelligible and available *strategies* in a problem context – that Shakespeare may be supposed either to have entertained explicitly or to be capable of accepting as characterizations of his enterprise. We need not worry over which is the single, governing, decisive, occurrent reason in his private mind for his (complex) action, for there is none.

Michael Baxandall has usefully developed in detail an account of intentions and reasons for action that are at work in the making of pictures. He notes that both R. G. Collingwood and Karl Popper, in considering historical understanding, "talk of the *reconstruction* of the process of thought,"[7] differing only in that Collingwood regards this reconstruction as recapturing occurrent events in the mind of the agent interpreted, while Popper regards the reconstruction as *our* idealized story about what might have gone on. Baxandall himself deliberately suppresses the ontological question about the status of our "reconstruction" of plans and intentions, in favor of sticking to "the procedural pattern of problems and situations and solutions"[8] on which any reconstruction of plan and intention must be based, as both Collingwood and Popper agree. Here Baxandall's ontological modesty is the path of wisdom and insight. When we undertake to understand the plans, intentions, thoughts, and actions of another agent, then what we develop is "a representation of reflection or rationality purposefully at work on circumstances...and we derive a sense of the agent's quiddity by relating to these circumstances the solution [the poem or painting, sonata or building, as may be] he actually arrived at."[9] Since problem situations, and especially problem situations of artistic work, can be complex, since the action of artistic making is frequently temporally extended, and since the thoughts, reasons, plans, intentions, and so forth of the agent are formed out of publicly intelligible strategies, some articulated and some not, we need not and should not linger on worries about any single "real intentional cause" of the artist's action. Any story that cogently relates details of the work and of collateral historical evidence where available to any aspect of the artist's complex problem situation may be regarded as a story that tells *a* truth about the work – about what it is as a product of action and about what it means.

Pluralism and constraint in interpretation: Abrams, Fish, and Derrida

With this conception of the nature of an artist-agent's reasons for action and of the nature of articulation (ours or the agent's own) of those reasons in place, we can address a number of vexed issues. Different strategies for

---

[7] Baxandall, *Patterns of Intention*, p. 14, emphasis added.
[8] *ibid.*   [9] *ibid.*, p. 36.

understanding can yield widely varying interpretive claims that can be both about the same artistic object and consistent with one another, for the object is itself complexly overdetermined by multiple reasons, is itself a complex solution to multiple problems. We can talk all at once – and co-herently – of Shakespeare's attitudes toward modern individualism, of his depiction of gender roles and gender anxieties, of his concern for stage-craft, and of his power of metaphorical imagination, for thoughts about each of these things may reasonably be supposed to have entered into his complex artistic making. If the story we tell about what Shakespeare did – about his reasons for action in a problem situation – departs too far from anything that Shakespeare himself might, if queried, have acknowledged as pertinent, then the story can be rejected as fanciful projection rather than an understanding of the work. For example, Shakespeare cannot have had thoughts about either synthetic polymers or spark plugs that entered in any way into his reasons for action. But thoughts about religion, poli-tics, language, gender, stagecraft, profit, and fun may all be taken to have entered into what he did.

We can also make sense of some recent controversies about determi-nacy of literary and other artistic meaning, where there is, in the end, more heat than light. In a series of essays in the late 1970s, the emi-nent literary historian and critic M. H. Abrams criticized a number of figures, whom he dubbed Newreaders, who rejected the idea that literary texts have determinate meanings: J. Hillis Miller, Roland Barthes, Jacques Derrida, Stanley Fish, and Harold Bloom. Though these figures each de-ploy quite different arguments and favor distinct interpretive protocols, each of them, according to Abrams, undertakes "a systematic dehuman-izing of all aspects of the traditional view about how a work of literature comes into being, what it is, how it is read, and what it means."[10] They all propose "that reading should free itself from illusory linguistic con-straints in order to become liberated, producing the meanings that it makes rather than discovers."[11] Instead of seeing works of literature as generally scrutable human communications, we should, the Newreaders hold, see literary texts as free-floating instances of self-proliferating *écriture*:

---

[10] M. H. Abrams, "How to do Things with Texts," *Partisan Review* 46 (1979), pp. 566–88, reprinted in M. H. Abrams, *Doing Things with Texts: Essays in Criticism and Critical Theory*, ed. Michael Fischer (New York: W. W. Norton, 1989), pp. 269–96 at p. 269.
[11] *ibid.*, p. 272.

self-proliferating writing without any agentive origin, without any stable message, and without any stable reader or hearer capable of receiving it whole. Stanley Fish seems to embrace such a characterization of his own theoretical stance when he mentions "people like me who push the instability of the text and the unavailability of determinate meaning."[12]

According to Abrams, this view is outrageous. It denies the obvious truth that "the author [of a literary work] actualizes and records in words what he undertakes to signify of human beings and actions and about matters of human concern, addressing himself to those readers who are competent to understand what he has written."[13] Abrams takes care, however, *not* to adopt the Cartesian stance that the literary message is wholly and specifically preformed in the mind of the author as a governing intention, prior to the production of the text. People come to mean what they do in speaking and in writing, not by having thoughts in mind prior to an acquaintance with language, but instead by taking through training to a course of fluid linguistic social practice. They form their messages by taking up the shared and fluid linguistic tools that are available in practice, revising, reforming, and making that message more specific in the course of writing. Conceptual consciousness, explicit linguistic ability, and the ability progressively to formulate coherent messages through the use of shared linguistic tools are all coemergent. As Abrams summarizes his view,

> We are born into a community of speakers and writers who have already acquired this skill [of "knowing a language"], and we in turn acquire it by interplay with those others, in which we learn how to say what we mean and how to understand what others have said by a continual process of self-correction and refinement, based on what are often very subtle indications of when and in what way we have gone wrong...The use and understanding of language...depends on tacit consensual regularities which are multiplex and fluid; except in very gross ways, these regularities are uncodified, and probably uncodifiable.[14]

---

[12] Stanley Fish, "Is there a Text in this Class?," in Fish, *Is there a Text in this Class* (Cambridge, MA: Harvard University Press, 1980), reprinted in *Critical Theory Since 1965*, ed. Adams and Searle, pp. 525–33 at p. 525A.
[13] Abrams, "How to do Things with Texts," p. 269.   [14] *ibid.*, pp. 293–94.

Through tactful engagement with these regularities, we roughly and mostly manage to understand one another, as speaker-writers and auditor-readers.

These claims are unexceptionable. Allowing for some differences of idiom and emphasis, however, they are all endorsed by Fish as well. Fish's central point is that the linguistic norms on which understanding depends *are* tacit, consensual, fluid, significantly uncodified, and connected with the existence of common practical purposes and background experiences. In talking about the instability of the text, Fish is not insisting that understanding never takes place; he is rather arguing that it cannot be arrived at by any sort of detached, purpose-independent, quasi-scientific procedure of attending to language as a well-bounded and exact formal calculus. There is no way simply to hear a sound pattern or see a mark and *then* in a neutral way, independent of shared purposes and background and via a process of calculation, simply to "read off" an intended message. As Fish puts it,

> Public and constituting norms...are not embedded in the language (where they may be read out by anyone with sufficiently clear, that is, unbiased, eyes) but inhere in institutional structures within which one hears utterances as already organized with reference to certain assumed purposes and goals...What constrains [us in understanding] are the understood practices and assumptions of the institution and not the rules and fixed meanings of a language system.[15]

Fish and Abrams agree, then, that literary texts are produced and understood by writers and readers making use of fluid linguistic tools, where the availability and developing use of these tools constitutes the meaning, as opposed to having a preformed "mental meaning" translated into language. Hence they agree that there is no possibility of finding a determinate meaning preformed in the mind of the author prior to the text, and they agree that there is no need to do so. They agree that when there are sufficiently shared backgrounds of linguistic practice and of expectations about the communication situation, then author and readers can be expected roughly to agree on construals of the text, and they agree that nothing deeper than or apart from such shared backgrounds makes communication possible.

---

[15] Fish, "Is there a Text in this Class?," p. 526A.

There are to be sure differences of emphasis within their agreements. Fish, for example, uses the phrase "institutional structures" prominently. In doing so, he points to the possibility and interest of strategies for understanding that see shared linguistic practices as interwoven with shared but largely unarticulated political stances. Hence Fish's own strategy in critical practice for understanding a text often involves noting such political commitments – for example, about who is naturally assumed to possess legitimate political authority: a sovereign over subjects, or men over women – that are tacitly encoded in the text as part of the large background of assumptions that tacitly inform both authorial consciousness and the text. He is particularly interested in variations in political stances across different groups of subjects and in how these variations may enter into both the making and understanding of art. In taking this direction, Fish's strategy resembles the more explicitly political strategies for understanding that have been developed by figures such as Foucault and Said.

Derrida, in contrast, is interested in the ungovernability by any single consciousness of the fluidity of language, of the openness of language to figuration and reconstrual, even against the grain, sometimes, of an acknowledged overt message. His work is strongest when he is himself criticizing the efforts of critics – for example, Jean Starobinski on Rousseau or Jean-Pierre Richard on Mallarmé – who have attempted to establish a single, definitive, unambiguous stance, meaning, or message for a single text or for an author's œuvre. Against them, Derrida emphasizes that the very words Rousseau or Mallarmé use in central figurative passages are multivalent or polysemic. For example, Rousseau construes (human, propositional) imagination as a self-proliferating, excessive, and uncontrollable power in us that casts us forever outside of mere naturalness, insofar as we can fantasize, envy, desire, and remember, but he also construes imagination as open to the acceptance of its own natural limits, so that we might come to fantasize about and desire only that which is reasonably within our power and live "according to nature."[16] Hence it is a mistake to read Rousseau as either exclusively relentlessly aware of how our identities are necessarily caught up in antagonisms that run through civilization or as exclusively simply urging a return from civilization to

---

[16] See Jacques Derrida, *Of Grammatology*, trans. Gayatri Chakravorty Spivak (Baltimore, MD: Johns Hopkins University Press, 1974), pp. 186–87.

pastoral naturalness. Read carefully, his texts incorporate both views. In practicing this kind of close reading, Derrida is, as Abrams notes, a kind of hyperformalist who does manage to "open our eyes to the play of figuration in a literary text"[17] and who emphasizes our possession by language and visionary imagination against our ability always to control language instrumentally. The use of this strategy for understanding need not deny – though Derrida himself in excessive moments sometimes seems to do so – that we can also sometimes control some bits of language instrumentally and use them to encode a definite message. Derrida's animuses against determinacy and control can effectively remind us, however, of how emergent within fluid linguistic and cultural practices our own distinctively conceptual-propositional consciousness is. In reminding us of this, Derrida can further usefully prod and provoke us toward both new readings and new artistic work, against the grain of any master scheme for the control of culture and cultural expression. His stance here is not so far from Cleanth Brooks' emphasis on accomplished poems as structures of paradox: readable, but dense and self-revising, more dramatic than doctrinal. The poet, as Brooks puts it, "must work by contradiction and qualification."[18]

Abrams himself is somewhat closer to the humanist stances of Spirit of the Age understanding and of biographical understanding. His attention is drawn more to large patterns of plot and imagery that are shared within a historical period and forcefully present within a single author's œuvre. He emphasizes successes in what he calls "a transaction [in plot and imagery] between a human author and his human reader"[19] and how the contents thus transmitted *are* distinctly identifiable in different œuvres and different literary epochs. His *Natural Supernaturalism*[20] is a masterpiece survey of fundamental tropes of plot and imagery in major texts of English Romanticism, especially Wordsworth, and in affiliated contemporary and subsequent writers, from Hegel to Virginia Woolf. There is every reason to think that in tracing these tropes Abrams is doing something spectacularly accurate, apt, and useful, even if he does not always linger either over

---

[17] M. H. Abrams, "A Colloquy on Recent Critical Theories," in Abrams, *Doing Things with Texts*, pp. 333–63 at p. 336.

[18] See Cleanth Brooks, "The Language of Paradox," in Brooks, *Well Wrought Urn*, pp. 3–21 at p. 9.

[19] Abrams, "How to do Things with Texts," p. 269.

[20] M. H. Abrams, *Natural Supernaturalism: Tradition and Revolution in Romantic Literature* (New York: W. W. Norton, 1971).

passages of less controlled, more ambivalent figuration or over less artic-ulated matters of the politics of culture.

Given the complex nature of the artistic object, all six broad strategies for understanding art can yield useful, accurate, and consistent results. Authoritative texts need to be established so far as possible, and single-object, nonmultiple copy works such as paintings and carved sculptures need physical care. Historical understanding of all kinds – Spirit of the Age, biographical, and political-structural – can discern some among the many reasons for which a work may have been produced. Tracing critically the achievement of formal arrangements that present a subject matter as a focus for thought and emotion, fused to the exploration of the material, illuminates success within the enterprise of art. Even "free" appropriative refiguring, reuse, rewriting, or other response to a work by subsequent creative artists can count as a form of understanding the work, insofar as it exercises the same sort of creative powers manifested in the work in relation to some of the same themes, motives, characters, or formal elements, though it may drift quite far from explication or paraphrase. In each case whether the critical understanding that is offered is apt will depend on care, comprehensiveness, subtlety, and insight in discerning and deploying relevant evidence; whether the critical understanding is useful may depend on the prior reception history of the work. A history of close formal explication of a given work or set of works may, for example, need to be balanced by more explicitly historical forms of criticism, if the work's full range of themes is to be recovered, while historical criticism may need to be balanced with more formal explication, if the singularly successful density and complexity of arrangement of a particular work are to be kept in view.

In recent years controversies about how to understand art, inspired significantly by the general conceptions of how to understand literary texts put forward by formalists, humanists, structuralists, poststructural-ists, feminists, and neo-Marxists, have spread throughout the disciplines of teaching and writing about the other media of art. Joseph Kerman called in 1985 for a new, more historical, less exclusively formal criticism of music, on the model of the newer political-structural forms of histor-ical understanding developed for literature.[21] That call was soon taken

---

[21] Joseph Kerman, *Contemplating Music* (Cambridge, MA: Harvard University Press, 1985).

up by music critics who are also accomplished in philosophy, sociology, and literary theory, such as Susan McClary[22] and Lawrence Kramer.[23] At the same time, close formal analysis and explication of works of music does not go away, and McClary and Kramer typically include such analyses within their broader readings.[24] In painting, studies of iconography and iconology in the style of Panofsky are balanced by the historically informed but more formally focused readings of Michael Fried and the formally sophisticated but more sociopolitically focused readings of T. J. Clark.

In general, knowledge of the personal, cultural, and social conditions of production of a work (including knowledge of sociopolitical antagonisms under which that production takes place) provides useful knowledge of just what artists are doing and why. As Dewey observes[25] and as Walton and Danto have aptly argued,[26] we need to know the cultural and political situation and the artistic tradition of a work in order to discern what is represented and expressed in it.

The special importance of elucidation of formal-semantic elements

Among the strategies considered for the understanding of art, however, the close elucidation (making use of relevant historical knowledge) of the formal arrangement of the elements of the work so as to bring out what it represents and expresses in a distinctive way is especially pertinent to the understanding of art as art. As Dewey puts it, "Knowledge of social conditions of production is, when it is really knowledge, of genuine value. But it is no substitute for understanding of the object in its own qualities and relations."[27] Many artifacts – industrial or commercial or legal, for

---

[22] See Susan McClary, *Feminine Endings: Music, Gender, and Sexuality* (Minneapolis, MN: University of Minnesota Press, 1991).

[23] Kramer, *Classical Music and Postmodern Knowledge*.

[24] For one example of a spectacularly successful integration of formal analysis with broader historical and sociopolitical reading, see Rose Rosengard Subotnik, "How Could Chopin's A-Major Prelude be Deconstructed?," in R. R. Subotnik, *Deconstructive Variations: Music and Reason in Western Society* (Minneapolis, MN: University of Minnesota Press, 1996), pp. 39–147.

[25] Dewey, *Art as Experience*, pp. 310–11.

[26] See the discussion of their criticisms of formalism in chapter 3 above.

[27] Dewey, *Art as Experience*, p. 316.

example – can be understood as coming into existence for a variety of complex cultural, personal, and political reasons. But they will typically not sustain continuing imaginative exploration of their formal arrangements as distinctive ways of presenting a subject matter as a focus for thought and emotion. If and when they do, then we are tempted to think of the work in question as itself a new form of art.

Close elucidation and what can be called critical understanding (as opposed to broader, historical understanding) involves a particular kind of attention to the art object. It involves dwelling on just why these elements are put here, in these relations to one another, as a way of inviting and sustaining imaginative exploration of the work. In describing critical attention to literature, Beardsley mentions the determination of "the contextual meaning of a group of words"[28] and thematic interpretation of how a unified but complex idea controls a work.[29] Brooks emphasizes the importance of fields of connotation. In a successful poem "the terms are continually modifying each other, and thus violating their dictionary meanings."[30] The poet "must work by [coherent] contradiction and qualification"[31] to present a qualitatively distinct, singular experience. In general, characteristically elucidatory-critical understanding of the arts is, in Dewey's formulation, both analytic or parts-discriminating and synthetic or overall-organization-discerning. Elucidatory critical attention moves back and forth between attention to discrete elements and the location of elements in an overall arrangement. Here the act of critical understanding "is a function of the creative response of the individual who judges. It is insight. There are no rules that can be laid down for its performance."[32]

As Dewey's talk of insight suggests, elucidatory-critical understanding is *perceptual*, not inductive or deductive. As Arnold Isenberg has cogently argued, similar elements can function very differently in different works. Depending on the overall particular configuration of elements, a falling wavelike contour in one painting may be graceful, in another jarring. A modulation from G major to E minor may be thrilling or uninteresting, depending on the overall context of the work. Accordingly, what the acute critic does, according to Isenberg, is give us "directions for perceiving";

[28] Beardsley, *Aesthetics*, p. 401.   [29] *ibid.*, pp. 401–09.
[30] Brooks, "Language of Paradox," p. 9.   [31] *ibid.*
[32] Dewey, *Art as Experience*, p. 313.

the critic "guides us in the discrimination of details, the organization of parts, the grouping of discrete objects into patterns" and so "gets us to see" for ourselves how the elements work (or fail to work) within a particular overall arrangement.[33]

It is, therefore, a mistake to draw up an inventory of formal elements – words and phrases, plastic forms, motives and modulations, or lines and colors – that always have the same meaning and value in any work. It is tempting nonetheless to try to do so, for if we possessed such an inventory, then we would have rules for making meaningful and successful art and rules for the critical deciphering of meaning and value. Some philosophers, in the grip of an obsession with rules and rule-determined objectivity, have tried to produce such an inventory. In the *Republic*, for example, Socrates claims that the Ionian mode in music is inherently "soft," "relaxed," and suitable for drinking, and he argues that all works in this mode should be banned from the education of the warrior guardians, who must instead be exposed only to the "violent" and "willing" Dorian and Phrygian modes.[34] Here Socrates seems significantly to underestimate the ingenuity of composers in using formal elements – such as melodic organization within a mode – in a variety of ways, with quite different meanings and effects, when combined with other elements such as rhythm, harmony, orchestration, and dynamics. Instead of rules for deciphering meaning or determining value, what we need and can receive from apt elucidatory-critical attention to a work is, in Dewey's phrase, "the reeducation of perception of works of art," where the critic's insights into elements and their arrangement function for us as "an auxiliary in the process, a difficult process, of learning to see and hear."[35] Michael Baxandall notes similarly that when he as a critic offers a description of a picture as having a "firm design," for example, then he is using concepts

> not informatively but demonstratively . . . to point to an aspect of its interest as I see it. The act is one of demonstration: with "design" I direct attention to one element in the picture and with "firm" I propose a characterization of it. I am suggesting that the concept "firm design" be matched with the interest of the picture. You may follow my prompting or not; and if you do follow my prompting you may agree or disagree.[36]

---

[33] Arnold Isenberg, "Critical Communication," *Philosophical Review* 57 (July 1949), pp. 330–44; reprinted in *Philosophy of Art*, ed. Neill and Ridley, pp. 363–73 at p. 367.

[34] Plato, *Republic*, trans. Grube, 3983–3993, pp. 399–400.

[35] Dewey, *Art as Experience*, p. 324.   [36] Baxandall, *Patterns of Intention*, pp. 8, 9.

When things go well with such a demonstration on the part of the critic, then we do agree and so see for ourselves just what this arrangement of elements means *here*.

In exploring a work critically, either altogether on our own or also under the guidance of critical-elucidatory writing about it, imagination is specially involved in perception and in understanding. When we analyze a work, we frequently imagine variations of it, asking ourselves such questions as: "What if this word were replaced by a close synonym?," "What if this figure were moved slightly up and to the left?," "What if the arrival at the tonic were delayed here by a suspension?," or "What if a wide angle shot were used here instead of a closeup?" By imagining these things, we explore contrastively what has been done in the work, in order that it has the expressive and absorptive configuration that it has. Contrasts and comparisons with other works function similarly. We explore the elements-in-configuration through imaginative contrast in order to see or hear their expressive and affective significance in the context of the work. This imaginative exploration aimed at seeing or hearing for oneself is quite different from testing the hypothesis that this painting is serene *because* it is predominantly blue. We rely on no generalizations of the form "All predominantly blue paintings are serene." Instead we look to see for ourselves what is going on – what is represented, what is expressed, and what affect is invited in us – in this particular work. As Roger Scruton puts it in describing the role of imagination in critical understanding,

> In aesthetics you have to see for yourself precisely because what you
> have to "see" is not a property: your knowledge that an aesthetic feature
> is "in" the object is given by the *same* criteria that show that you "see" it.
> To see the sadness in the music and to know that the music is sad are
> one and the same thing. To agree in the judgment that the music is sad
> is not to agree in a belief, but in something more like a response or an
> experience.[37]

This sadness in this piece of music, that is to say, is not a property whose presence can be verified by a sensibility-independent test in the absence of hearing (actual or imaginative). There is no sensibility-independent deductive or inductive route from formal elements to the determination of expressive and affective significance. Seeing the sadness in a piece of music is less like verifying the truth of a proposition through a

---

[37] Scruton, *Art and Imagination*, p. 554.

scientific procedure than it is like seeing an aspect of a *Gestalt* figure.[38] As Isenberg puts it, "the critic's *meaning* is 'filled in,' 'rounded out,' or 'completed' by the act of perception"[39] in a way that is quite different from testing to see whether a hypothesis that formal element X causes experience Y is true. To see formal element X *as having* expressive or affective significance is an act of imaginative perception. Elucidatory-critical understanding both proceeds from and appeals to imaginative exploration of the work as a singular whole. This is what makes it natural to speak of critical *understanding* of a work as opposed to critical *explanation* or critical *science*.

The possibility of agreement in understanding

Agreement in the "seeing" of expressive and affective significance via imaginative exploration of the work, guided by elucidatory criticism, can often be achieved and can reasonably be hoped for. For a number of reasons, however, agreement cannot be readily achieved in every case. Interpretations of expressive and affective features depend upon which genres or categories a work is seen in, and there are multiple and sometimes conflicting criteria for determining genre membership. Kendall Walton notes that the criteria for determining genre membership – a necessary aspect of understanding – include at least (i) that there is a well-established genre of somewhat similar work in the cultural context of production, (ii) that the artist intended the work to be perceived in a given genre, (iii) that the work is more satisfying when perceived in a given genre, and (iv) that the work has a large number of taken-for-granted, noninterpreted features in common with other members of a genre.[40] Though these criteria for determining genre membership may often point in the same direction, they need not always do so. An artist may intend a work to be perceived in an altogether new genre – consider performance art at its inception – and these considerations may cut against generic similarities with another already established genre (e.g. theatre or storytelling), with no clear resolution available. Second, new ranges of comparison and contrast that

---

[38] Both Scruton and Isenberg make this comparison. See Scruton, *Art and Imagination*, pp. 107–08, and Isenberg, "Critical Communication," in *Philosophy of Art*, ed. Neill and Ridley, p. 372.

[39] Isenberg, "Critical Communication," p. 367.

[40] Walton, "Categories of Art," in *Philosophy of Art*, ed. Neill and Ridley, pp. 346.

inform imaginative exploration of the work can become relevant as a result of the other forms of understanding: Spirit-of-the-Age, biographical, sociopolitical-structural, editorial-physical, or artistic-improvisatory. The works of Shakespeare or Wordsworth or Austen can bear different meanings for us – with somewhat altered subject matters fused differently to expressive and affective significances – after we have read Freud or Marx, after we have read Eliot or Larkin, or after we have considered critical readings that invoke further historical facts and new ranges of comparison. Schubert can sound different affectively and expressively after hearing minimalist music or Wagner or after reading Adorno or McClary or Dahlhaus. Just as different interpretations of literature and the visual arts can cast new light on them, so can different performances of musical works do so as well.

Given, again, the complexity of the work and the multiplicity of reasons (articulated and unarticulated) that can sensibly be held to have been at work in its production, there is good reason to think that each of these kinds of interpretation, and associated rereading, reviewing, and rehearing, may capture genuine aspects of a work's meaning, of how it distinctively presents a subject matter as a focus for thought and emotion, fused to the imaginative exploration of material. Cultures past and present evolve and are marked by internal conflict. When we notice cultural evolution and conflict, then we can become aware of the different and shifting kinds of reasons that can enter into the making of a work, thence overdetermining its production. Different sets of these reasons can become of interest and relevance for us at different times. Critical-elucidatory attention to a successful work's distinctive way of arranging its elements so as to present a subject matter as a focus for thought and emotion remains a central and privileged form of understanding of a work *as art*. But exactly how critical-elucidatory interpretation is carried out is reasonably affected by shifts in interest and by changing contexts of comparison.

This may make it seem as though different interpretations, achieved either by following different strategies for understanding or through critical elucidatory attention carried out under the influence of different strategies for understanding, simply talk past one another, or that they are even about different objects: not a single work that two different critics approach, but quite divergent work as seen by reader A and work as seen by reader B. It may sometimes seem that critics are talking *only* about their own experiences of the work and not about the work itself.

Perhaps this in fact happens in some cases. Not everything that is put forward as a piece of critical understanding in fact succeeds in being one. Efforts to understand a work critically can collapse into autobiographical effusions on the part of the critic or one or another form of projection, in such a way that contact with the work is lost. But this seems relatively rare, even considering the range of Freudian versus Marxist versus poststructuralist versus humanist versus formalist styles of critical understanding that are in circulation. As interpretations in these various styles bump up against one another, contending critics will often want to accuse one another of empty projection or reading-in, on the one hand, or of "mere" appreciation and decorous paraphrase, without critical-political historical understanding, on the other. Sometimes these accusations may be well founded, in either direction. More typically, however, we become able ourselves in light of new readings to see particular works both more comprehensively and with more awareness of the multiple significances of details – as long, at least, as the critical readings that guide our exploration of the work do engage with its elements and are not generalized screeds or free fantasias. New critical readings are generally achieved against a background of already shared understandings of what a work of art is as an overdetermined, complex, meaning-bearing object, of what a particular work of art means at the level of immediate paraphrase, and of what its maker and many people of its epoch cared about. As Stanley Fish usefully observes about understanding in general,

> The change from one structure of understanding to another is not a
> rupture but a modification of the interests and concerns that are already
> in place; and because they are already in place, they constrain the
> direction of their own modification...The [hearer, viewer, reader] is
> already in a situation informed by tacitly known purposes and goals,
> and [after encountering a new reading] he ends up in another situation
> whose purposes and goals stand in some elaborated relation (of contrast,
> opposition, expansion, extension) to those they supplant. (The one
> relation in which they could not stand is no relation at all.)[41]

A new reading can help us to see a work in a larger and more comprehensive light, with greater awareness of how its maker's complex

---

[41] Fish, "Is there a Text in this Class?," pp. 530B–531A.

pursuit of multiple artistic, communicative, expressive, and affective interests align and misalign with our own.

Given the standing possibility of new critical understandings, arising out of new strategies that invoke new ranges of relevant comparisons, it can sometimes seem as though we may never "really know" the "full meaning" of any work of art, even of any human utterance or act. But we should, again, reject the Cartesian picture of meaning as consisting in a discrete, preformed, articulated intention in the mind of the maker that is waiting there for us to grasp it, if only we deploy the proper tools. Instead the meaning that a work has – and that an interpretation may capture – is a matter of the multiple, complex reasons – expressive, affective, psychological, social, and economic, among others – that may reasonably be taken to have entered into its production. It is true that what may reasonably be taken to be reasons that are effective in the production of a work may change somewhat, as there are changes in *our* conceptions of what it is worthwhile to be interested in and of what counts as a reason for what. But while there are changes here, and as a result of them new critical readings may always be in order, these changes are not absolute and abrupt. There is enough continuity so that works of art remain, as Dewey puts it, "means by which we enter, through imagination and the emotions they invoke, into other forms of relationship and participation than our own."[42] To understand art critically is to explore it imaginatively, guided by a range of relevant comparisons and conceptions of rational action and focused on how a work presents its subject matter as a focus for thought and emotion. When we thus explore works imaginatively, we can understand them anew, more deeply, and yet in coherent elaboration of our prior understandings, as the complex results of overdetermined human action that they are.

---

[42] Dewey, *Art as Experience*, p. 333.

7 Identifying and evaluating art

Why we go on arguing about which works are good

The identification and evaluation of objects or performances as works of art (as opposed to failures, frauds, or the otherwise meretricious) is a process fraught with passion and difficulty. We care about some favorite works that we regard as successful – certain books or movies or paintings – in the way we care about our friends. They appeal to us both immediately and deeply. We often remember them, revisit them, reread them, or rehear them. We recommend them to others, and we are then pleased if the work engages them and sometimes disappointed or troubled if it does not. Prices in the art market and publishing industry depend on what people respond to, as does support by governments and foundations for work in progress.

We often have trouble, however, saying why we respond to a work in the way we do, especially when we are faced with original work. We worry about being taken in, and we can be hesitant to display our enthusiasms. Yet most of us cannot help giving ourselves over to some objects or performances, even to some new and difficult work. Just how and why are we moved to do this? Are there any procedures for being right (at least more often) about which works genuinely have artistic value? What are the relative roles of feeling (liking) and reason in our responses to art? Does reason even play a role? Are or can there be experts in the identification and evaluation of works of artistic value, authorities whose verdicts deserve our deference?

Sometimes the topic of identifying and evaluating works of art is made the centerpiece of the philosophy of art generally, particularly in the discussion of the objectivity (or lack of it) of judgments of taste. Given the vagaries of the markets in the contemporary arts, both financial and reputational, this is unsurprising. It would help to be able to know what is going on and what ought to go on, as objects come before us for our attention to them as art. Given the further facts that we are emotionally invested in our own responses, as though certain favorite works were friends, and that our responses diverge, even sometimes within our most intimate circles of acquaintance, it would help to be able to sort things out. It would help to know which works are worth teaching or buying, and why.

For a number of reasons, however, it is unlikely that identification of objects and performances as having genuine artistic value will become settled with any sharpness, in accordance with a definite procedure with definite results that everyone can endorse. The experience of being at risk in one's responses to works, including possibilities of trust in and betrayal by some works one favors, may be natural to the experience of art, especially in modernity, where originality is explicitly prized.[1] Identification and evaluation of works cannot properly proceed without understanding them, yet if understanding is open to change, as our sense of the reasons at work in the forming of certain arrangements develops,[2] then our identifications and evaluations will properly be hostage to such changes, at least to some degree. Having a formula that seems to capture something of the nature of art and its value in general – for example, the formula that works of art present a subject matter as a focus for thought and emotional attitude, distinctively fused to the imaginative exploration of material – does not directly help much, for such a formula is so abstract that it might fit many cases in many ways, and disagreement about how it may fit cases is not readily resolvable. What I take to be imaginative and emotional exploration of thematic material you may take to be clichéd or incoherent, and vice versa. Even if one of us is in principle correct, there may be no ready way to settle the matter at the moment.

In many cases, it does not matter much which identifications and evaluations we ourselves or other apprehenders settle on. Here it is useful to compare the term *art* to the term *educated person*. In different cultural and historical settings, as different skills are valued and taught, it will be natural to call different sorts of persons educated. Though by no means valueless, fluency in Greek is less central to being well educated than it once was, and some acquaintance with the differential calculus is more central. People can be well educated to various degrees and to various

---

[1] On trustworthiness and fraudulence as unavoidable possibilities in the experience of modern art, not wholly to be avoided by any neutral procedures for reliable evaluation, see Stanley Cavell, "Music Discomposed," in Cavell, *Must We Mean What We Say?*, pp. 180–212.

[2] See chapter 6 above.

degrees in various domains, with no sharp, single boundary between the altogether uneducated and near-universal polymaths. Fuzzy, intermediate education in this or that is the norm. Yet we have good enough reasons for taking certain persons to be paradigms of the well educated and for trusting in the job of education that is done by certain educational institutions, especially where peer review and openness to public scrutiny are valued. Progressive performance on many exercises, in many conversations, examinations, and essays, is part of an open-ended process of becoming more educated, where there is no need or point – apart from ceremony and professional or economic credentialization – to settle on any one moment in that process as the single, decisive moment of becoming educated. Given the complexity and specialized character of knowledge, no one will be an expert in assessing whether anyone whosoever is well educated in any domain whatsoever.

The case is similar with "art." Like "educated person," "art" is a status concept. Artistic value can be exemplified to various degrees in many different domains. Becoming accomplished at making art and at understanding art requires practice on many exercises. No one will be fully expert in works in all media and traditions of art. Practice works and experiments in artistic making can and should be accepted as having a degree of artistic value without worrying over their status as masterpieces or failures, as long as the aims in view in making and for audiences are those that define the practice of art. There is no reason not to regard the paintings of children, students, and Sunday painters – however less distinctive and absorbing they may be than the paintings of Hockney or Matisse – as genuine works of art, as long as the work of making them is done within an acknowledged medium of art and with some attention to its aims, as is generally the case. Dewey is surely right to deplore what he calls "the blundering ineptness…of judicial criticism"[3] that seeks sharp boundaries in every case and to recommend instead the enterprise of critical understanding. We have reason enough to think that the status of certain exemplary works – most denizens of most museums of fine art, most Pulitzer or Booker prize-winning novels, and so forth – is reliably well settled.

Given, however, the emotional, reputational, and financial stakes that attach to the identification and evaluation of some objects and

---

[3] Dewey, *Art as Experience*, p. 304.

performances as successful art, it is unlikely that audiences in general will be able to sustain relaxed attitudes toward candidate works on all occasions. Outrage that anyone could take *that* seriously, on the one hand, and frustrated incomprehension that anyone could fail to respond to *this*, on the other, are likely to continue to occur for some audiences with respect to some works. Even if we cannot specify procedures that will yield exhaustive classifications with sharp boundaries, it would be nice to know just how we are coming to identify and evaluate things, on the basis of which feelings and reasons, and with what hope, if any, of convergence over time. Just what do we do, and how do we and should we do it?

Subjectivism and the sociology of taste: Smith and Bourdieu

Views about the answers to these questions range over a considerable spectrum running from subjectivism or the view that identifications and evaluations are nothing but individual preferences, with no possible basis in reasons, to objectivism or the view that identifications are full-bloodedly true or false: anyone issuing any verdict will be getting something right or wrong (perhaps provably so; perhaps not); there is a fact of the matter about the status of any given object or performance as art.

Toward the subjective side of the spectrum, Barbara Herrnstein Smith has argued that all value, including artistic value, is projected variably on to things by human beings on the basis of contingent, changing needs and interests. "All value," she claims, "is radically contingent, being neither a fixed attribute, an inherent quality, or an objective property of things but, rather, an effect of multiple, continuously changing, and continuously interacting variables."[4] That is, there is neither anything awaiting discovery in any object that might ground our attributions of value to it, nor can there be consensus about such attributions founded on common human interests and powers, for no interests and powers are fully shared. Though there may be certain measures of local and temporary agreement, in the long run and over larger populations we just disagree in attributing artistic value. "The traditional discourse of value," which takes value judgments to be objective matters involving either discovery of properties or answerability to shared interests and powers, reflects, Smith claims,

---

[4] Barbara Herrnstein Smith, *Contingencies of Value: Alternative Perspectives for Critical Theory* (Cambridge, MA: Harvard University Press, 1988), p. 30.

"an arbitrary arresting, segmentation, and hypostatization of the contin-uous process of our interactions with our environments...[The terms of this discourse]...obscure the dynamics of value and reinforce dubious concepts of noncontingency."[5]

Instead, therefore, of undertaking to describe the logic or justificatory basis of judgments of taste, all that there is left for theorists of art to do is to "describe the dynamics of [the] system of [artistic valuing] and to re-late its operations to everything else we know about human behavior and culture."[6] Smith insists that her position does not amount to a quietist, obscurantist, and self-refuting relativism. There is, she argues, plenty left for theorists to do, and there remain many ways to intervene effectively in situations of contested evaluations. The value attributions of any single agent are themselves formed as that agent is formed, via immersion in larger "conjoined systems (biological, cultural, ideological, institutional, and so forth)."[7] As a result, agents formed under the same contingent historical systems of social organization are likely to agree on consid-erable ranges of value attribution. The operations such as socialization, ideological training, institutional reward and punishment, and biological prompting that continue these systems and determine attributions can be studied. One can take "an interest in the subtler, more diffuse, and longer-range consequences of [one's] actions and the actions of others"[8] as opposed to being motivated only by immediate self-interest. When there is disagreement in value attributions in which one has a stake, then one can intervene – rhetorically or violently – from one's own valuational stance (as a woman, as a classical cellist, as a Brazilian, or whatever), and one can seek to understand one's opponent's valuations historically.[9] But what we cannot do, even with infinite stores of time, patience, and goodwill, is to argue any opponent whatsoever, independent of that opponent's own background formation, into valuations that are correct, just by reference to either properties of things or fully shared human interests, for there are none. At bottom, radically, *de gustisbus non disputandum est*.

In a pluralist world, Smith's position has immediate plausibility and appeal. As a matter of practice, it is enormously difficult to resolve many disagreements in evaluation, and it is not clear that the course of wisdom is always to seek to resolve them. It is possible to study valuational stances

---

[5] *ibid.*, p. 31.   [6] *ibid.*, p. 16.   [7] *ibid.*, p. 183.   [8] *ibid.*, p. 161.
[9] See *ibid.*, pp. 154–55 on how one might "answer the Nazi."

as matters of immersion in larger systems of social organization. Pierre Bourdieu, for example, has established by means of questionnaires that, when asked to choose three favorites among sixteen musical works, craftsmen and shopkeepers prefer Verdi's *La Traviata* (30%), Khachaturian's *Sabre Dance* (26%), and Liszt's *Hungarian Rhapsodies* (34%), while secondary and higher-ed teachers and artistic producers prefer Mozart's *Eine Kleine Nachtmusik* (51%), Vivaldi's *Four Seasons* (51%), and Bach's *Well-Tempered Clavier* (32%).[10] On the basis of this and other results, Bourdieu argues that "aesthetic choices belong to the set of ethical choices which constitutes a lifestyle."[11] Differences in judgments of taste are matters of the different cultural capitals – ways of displaying interest and personality that are interwoven with socioeconomic position – that members of different groups bring to bear in the act of evaluative judgment. Differences in lifestyle can be studied empirically, and between them there is, often, not much to be said about who is right.

It would be foolish to fail to recognize, along with Smith and Bourdieu, the existence of such differences and their weight for the judgments of taste that people actually make. There are genuine large patterns of judgment that the sociology of art and taste can usefully study. It may indeed be useful in practice very often to approach such differences with scholarly detachment and to intervene rhetorically where one can, rather than insisting on standards.

Yet it remains unclear how much these results actually affect the activity of arriving at artistic identifications and evaluations in specific contexts of consideration. To begin with, the patterns that Bourdieu has discovered are only statistical correlations, and they are not in every case as striking as in the case of musical preferences. For example, Renoir and Van Gogh are by a considerable margin the preferred painters for every class of respondents Bourdieu surveyed.[12] Statistical generalizations about preferences in populations in any case do not amount to exceptionless laws that determine response. The planets are causally determined to move in ellipses by the law of gravitational attraction operating over initial conditions, but individuals within a given population are free to judge contrary to the majority of their class, and they frequently do so.

---

[10] Pierre Bourdieu, *Distinction: A Social Critique of the Judgement of Taste*, trans. Richard Nice (Cambridge, MA: Harvard University Press, 1984), table A3, p. 529.
[11] *ibid.*, p. 283.   [12] *ibid.*, table A2, p. 527.

Bourdieu's results are also simply aggregations of immediate and uncon-sidered preferences, as elicited by questionnaires. They do not reflect rea-sons that anyone from any group might offer in favor of their verdicts, nor do they consider the phenomenon of elucidatory critical understanding and conversation. One way or another, one might come to "see" through critical understanding the value of many different kinds of work with which one had previously been unfamiliar. Preference shifts need not always be brute and unreasoned, and judgments of taste need not only be matters of mere or brute preference. Understanding can enter into them. Smith simply ignores these possibilities by fiat in talking of valuation as a piece of "behavior,"[13] implying that it is always at bottom a conditioned re-sponse, rather than part of any rational activity of discernment through critical understanding. Even if we are wise to attend to differences in identification and evaluation across populations and not to hold to "strict standards" for judgment in every case, we need not and ought not follow her in this. Sometimes there is learning to see and thence to value things with greater understanding.[14] Smith's sociologically oriented metatheory of artistic value as a function of ungovernable subjective-social valuings expresses in the end boredom, impatience, and exhaustion with critical conversation about art.

Dickie's institutional theory

Similarly concerned to avoid any tendency to conflate art in general with good art or with masterpieces, George Dickie has developed an institu-tional theory of art and of artistic identification. That is, Dickie is con-cerned to keep separate what he calls the evaluative and classificatory senses of "work of art"[15] and to show how to identify works of art – how to classify them – in a detached way, without entering into any contro-versies about value. The classificatory sense of "work of art" alone is his primary focus. In developing his theory, Dickie too is at least open to the thought that evaluation might be a less reasoned, more subjective affair than identification. There is, after all, bad art that is nonetheless art. How, then, do we classify something as art, independently of considerations of value?

---

[13] See Smith, *Contingencies of Value*, p. 20.   [14] See chapter 6 above.
[15] Dickie, *Art and the Aesthetic*, pp. 25–27.

Dickie proposes initially that

> A work of art in the classificatory sense is (1) an artifact (2) a set of the aspects of which has had conferred upon it the status of candidate for appreciation by some person or persons acting on behalf of a certain social institution (the art world).[16]

Not all things dubbed candidates for appreciation, however, need be appreciated (much or even at all). There is, again, bad art. What matters is the conferring of candidacy, not winning the election.

Difficulties remain, however, about just what is going on in conferring. What is the art world? How does anyone manage to act "on behalf of it"? Is the opportunity to do so open to anyone, or must one be trained as a curator, painter, dealer, composer, writer, critic, and so forth in some accredited way? In later work Dickie develops and refines his proposal in order to answer these questions. Following a suggestion by Jeffrey Wieand, he distinguishes between Person-institutions or "organizations which behave as quasi-persons or agents, as, for example, the Catholic Church and General Motors do," and Action-institutions or "types of acts such as promising and the like."[17] In his revised view, conferring the status of candidate for appreciation becomes presenting "an artifact...to an art world public,"[18] and it becomes clear that anyone can do this. Though "museums, foundations, churches, and the like...have relations with art-making," none of them "is essential."[19] Dickie's proposal now clearly focuses on what artists (or other presenters) do when they are putting something forward as art, whether or not they are members of any socially accredited body. His revised proposal consists of five interlocking claims:

1. an artist is a person who participates with understanding in the making of a work of art
2. a work of art is an artifact of a kind created to be presented to an art world public
3. a public is a set of persons the members of which are prepared in some degree to understand an object which is presented to them
4. the art world is the totality of all art world systems
5. an art world system is a framework for the presentation of a work of art by an artist to a public[20]

---

[16] *ibid.*, p. 34.   [17] Dickie, *Art Circle*, p. 52.   [18] *ibid.*, p. 80.   [19] *ibid.*, p. 52.
[20] *ibid.*, pp. 80–82.

Dickie's main point in offering these claims is to capture the fact that making and responding to art are emergent social practices that are distinct from other practices such as the practices of science, politics, child-rearing, food production, and so forth. There is a set of distinctive, interrelated things that makers and audiences do when they are trafficking in art as art[21] – well or badly as may be – as opposed to trafficking in other things.

Theses 1–5 seem true, and it is useful to have highlighted the idea that making and responding to art as art are distinct emergent social practices. Making and responding to art are distinctive social roles into which anyone may enter. It is less clear, however, that theses 1–5 do much to illuminate the nature of these practices and roles. What is an art world system within which such roles are taken up? Dickie might answer this question enumeratively, by listing painting, concert music, drama, and ballet, among others, as such systems. But why do just these systems and some others count as art world systems? What is the criterion for classing these systems and some of their kin as systems of art? If the enumeration of art world systems is closed, then the possibility of new media of art seems mistakenly ruled out by fiat. Movies, installation art, and conceptual art, for example, would not have been regarded as art world systems if the enumeration had been closed at some earlier historical time, and it seems altogether possible that new systems of art should continue to develop. But if the enumeration is open, then we need to know the criteria for adding a new system to the list. What makes a new system a system *of art*?[22]

The underlying difficulty that troubles Dickie's approach is that the identification of art (establishing what is art in the classificatory sense) and the evaluation of art (judging something to be successful or unsuccessful as a work of art) do not readily come apart. The practices of making and responding to art are partly defined by the distinctive kind of value to which they are directed: artistic value as opposed to economic, prudential, cognitive, and so on value. Even if not everything rightly regarded as a

---

[21] Dickie of course accepts that we can and do traffic in art in other ways. Works of art are bought and sold, for example, as part of an economic system. But his own interest is in what makes art objects different from other objects that are bought and sold.

[22] I adopt this line of criticism from Jerrold Levinson's review of *The Art Circle, Philosophical Review* 96, 1 (January 1987), pp. 141–46 at p. 145.

work of art in fact embodies this value – there is bad or unsuccessful art – it is nonetheless the case that the effort to embody artistic value is definitive for the practice of artistic making. Without any characterization of this value as that to which artistic making and responding are directed, we cannot distinguish systems, practices, and roles that have to do with art from systems, practices, and roles that do not.

Historical and narrative identifications: Levinson and Carroll

A similar difficulty troubles so-called historical definitions of art, such as that offered by Jerrold Levinson, and narrative identifications of art, as proposed by Noël Carroll. Levinson argues that an object or performance is a work of art if and only if it is presented by someone having "appropriate proprietary right" over it for "regard-as-a-work-of-art."[23] This may be true enough, and it may usefully highlight the fact that making and responding to art are distinct social roles. But what is "regard-as-a-work-of-art"? Either we must simply offer a closed list of looking at paintings (in the right way), listening to music (in the right way), reading novels (in the right way), and so on as modes of regarding art. Where this list is closed, we may make the mistake of ruling out new media of art. Or if we offer an open list, then we need to say something about what the members of the list have in common and about what "in the right way" amounts to. What kind of value is regard-as-a-work-of-art on the lookout for?

In a spirit similar to Levinson's, Noël Carroll suggests that we can accurately identify works of art, without worrying too much about evaluation, by "accurately narrating the descent of the new work from the tradition."[24] But what are the terms of accurate narration of descent within a tradition of art? It seems hopeless to try to characterize traditions of art without saying something about the values whose pursuit is definitive of these traditions. No doubt narratives of artistic descent will vary considerably for different media of art, and it will often be useful to locate new works against backgrounds of specific prevailing artistic practices, such as moviemaking, painting, lyric-writing, and so on. Carroll's suggestion aptly focuses on the role in identifying art of the kinds of narratives that are

---

[23] Jerrold Levinson, "Defining Art Historically," *British Journal of Aesthetics* 19 (1979), reprinted in *Philosophy of Art*, ed. Weill and Ridley, pp. 223–39 at p. 236.

[24] Carroll, *Philosophy of Art*, p. 258.

often produced by critics, curators, and reviewers to accompany exhibitions, performances, and publications of new works. Such figures do centrally undertake to place the new work narratively in relation to prevailing specific practice. But what makes the specific practices in question practices *of art*, and exactly *how* must a new work relate to its precursors in order to count as art within an evolving specific artistic practice? It will not do to say only that it is made as a commentary on its precursors, since a review or a quip might do that. Rather, the new work must take up, whether successfully or not, the enterprise of undertaking to achieve and embody artistic value, in relation to how it has previously been achieved and embodied within a tradition. Narrativism does not free us from the obligation to say something about the nature of this enterprise and about the nature of artistic value.

All these proposals for identifying art – Dickie's institutional theory, Levinson's historical theory, and Carroll's narrativism – usefully highlight both the fact that making and responding to art is a matter of engaging in one or more large, emergent, and evolving social subpractices of moviemaking and movie watching, of painting and looking at paintings, of composing and performing music and listening to it, and so on, and the fact that engaging in these practices is a matter of taking up one or another available social role. It is true that these subpractices have in some measure their own evolving "inner logics" of development and response to precursors. Someone adept in one of these practices is not necessarily or even frequently adept in another. Without, however, invoking some substantial characterization of the nature of artistic value, none of these proposals can successfully characterize what makes these subpractices into practices *of art*, nor can objects and performances be identified as art without some reference to artistic value, the pursuit of which is definitive of practices of art, even where individual works may fail to achieve it.

In the historicist and social spirit of Dickie, Levinson, Carroll, Bourdieu, and Smith, one might object that talk of artistic value is beside the point. Many national museums of fine art such as the Louvre, the Prado, and the Hermitage evolved out of royal collections that were quite haphazard.[25] Paintings and sculptures shared space not only with pots, but also with gems, headdresses, taxidermic specimens, fans, musical

---

[25] See the useful discussion of the rise of the museum in Freeland, *But is it Art?* pp. 91–93.

instruments, and other curios – anything in which a king might take a passing interest. Somehow, historically and socially, it all gets sorted out, more or less, though without sharp or definite boundaries. Scholars catalogue collections, curators mount shows, and, more latterly, investors finance film productions, and government organizations support performance art. A conception of art with very rough edges is, in the long run, formed simply by accretion. Given this welter of practical activities that are effective, seemingly, for putting forward certain objects and performances as art, do we need to talk of artistic value? Given what Ivan Gaskell has called the multiple "motivating factors – aesthetics, politics, and commerce –"[26] that are at work in interaction with one another within this welter of activities, would it even be accurate to talk of practices and works that aim distinctively at the achievement and embodiment of artistic value?

Yet while this line of thought is appealing and descriptively accurate up to a point, it omits in the end any characterization of the quality of our attention to works of art and of inviting and sustaining this attention as a central aim of artistic making. We do not use works of art only as we use cabbages, cabinets, and capstans, and there are distinctive practices of attending to works of art and of making works of art for the sake of this attention. Even where the making and the identification of art are overdetermined by economic, scientific, religious, practical, or other considerations in addition to artistic ones, artistic considerations exist as a distinct focus of concern, for makers and audiences alike.

Objectivism: Mothersill and Savile

Perhaps, then, we should turn away from talk of identifying works of art as a matter of projection based on subjective needs and social formation and away from attention to systems and institutions in favor, instead, of construing the identification of works of art as centrally a matter of establishing one-by-one that they carry out to some degree the task of achieving and embodying artistic value. Plausibly, what counts as art depends on what works of art, at least some central ones, distinctively do successfully, in the way of inviting and sustaining absorbed attention.

---

[26] Ivan Gaskell, *Vermeer's Wager: Speculations on Art History, Theory, and Museums* (London: Reaktion Books, 2000), p. 171.

Toward the objective side of the spectrum, Mary Mothersill has claimed that it is a common-sense fact that some judgments of taste are "genuine," that is, "either true or false." These judgments actually have a truth-value, as opposed to being mere subjective reactions (such as nausea) in apprehenders; they are "such as to admit testing by anyone who cares to take the trouble," according to "determinate confirmation procedures that can be sketched in advance."[27] Can anyone who pays suitable attention seriously and honestly doubt that Beethoven's Razumovsky Quartet, Op. 59, No. 1, is beautiful?[28] Well, perhaps some people can. Mothersill herself concedes that "there are (or used to be) students forced to read the *Iliad* and they found it boring. They are not *ipso facto* monsters."[29] Her claim is not that everyone will agree in either every case or every important case, but only the weaker claim that any normal human subject who is not disqualified from discussion of art must concede that there is at least "*something* he takes to be beautiful and further that at least one such taking [is] allowed by him to be an aesthetic conviction"[30] (a genuine judgment, as opposed to a mere reaction or sentiment). Even where there is not ready agreement, judgments of taste are genuine, truth-value-bearing judgments – or so, Mothersill claims, we all take for granted in our genuine discussions of art.

But is this right, and, if so, how significant is it? I may have great confidence in my liking for William Gaddis' *JR*. I am prepared to point to features of the novel that inspire my love for it and motivate my attention to it. I regard those who fail to respond to these features as somehow making a mistake. And yet I also know that not everyone will in fact respond to this novel. I know specifically that it is a difficult, hypermodernist work that appeals to university-educated intellectuals (with whom I am likely to have discussions) who find themselves flattered by the thought that making and understanding modern art is an esoteric activity that is at odds with the vulgarities of commerce. So do *I* take *this* judgment of taste that *JR* is artistically valuable to be genuine? I do not take it to be "merely subjective" or a matter of undiscussable brute response, but I am less than fully confident that it falls under "determinate confirmation procedures that can be sketched in advance." This seems to be the case with nearly every judgment of taste, as Mothersill effectively concedes in

---

[27] Mary Mothersill, *Beauty Restored* (Oxford: Clarendon Press, 1984), p. 164.
[28] The example is Mothersill's, *ibid.*   [29] *ibid.*, p. 175.   [30] *ibid.*, p. 176.

admitting that some people will not find the Razumovsky Quartet or the *Iliad* beautiful. Without describing a confirmation procedure and applying it in a convincing way to a very large range of cases, Mothersill's insistence that artistic value is there "in the object" is empty in practice.

In a similar vein, but with more attention to what audiences actually do in arriving at evaluations, Anthony Savile has argued that passing what he calls the test of time is sufficient to ensure that a work is of value. More precisely, Savile argues for the conclusion: "It is reasonable to believe that if a beautiful or deep work of art passes time's test [i.e. "survives in our attention"], it is of stature."[31] As he goes on to explain:

> When a work of beauty or depth survives over time, we must be able to find an explanation of why it does so, and failing any other account of the matter the only reasonable thing to believe is that its survival is rooted in precisely those features of it which make it well placed to survive, that is, in the fact that such works, through their beauty and depth, offer us goods which in our culture it falls largely to the arts to provide.[32]

In short, in the long run we – all of us together, over a long period of time – are very unlikely to be wrong about which works possess artistic value. This view has considerable plausibility, since many of the works that have most persistently survived in our attention are paradigms of the artistically valuable: *Hamlet*, *Don Giovanni*, the *Iliad*, and the *Inferno*, among others. If these works are not artistically valuable, what is?

Yet Savile's account is open to a number of objections. Exactly what is the scope of "us"? First, do contemporary Americans recognize over time the same successes in art as nineteenth-century Frenchmen or as twelfth-century Khmer? Does anything survive in the attentions of enough people over time to establish that judgments of taste are more objective than they are matters of variable cultural habit? If only a few works thus survive, does their survival show anything about the objectivity of judgments of taste in general, in more problematic cases? Second, do we always lack "any other account of the matter"? Perhaps some works survive in our attention because they are hugely expensive to build (the Great Pyramid)

---

[31] Anthony Savile, *The Test of Time: An Essay in Philosophical Aesthetics* (Oxford: Clarendon Press, 1982), p. 224. The interpolated phrase is from p. vii.
[32] *ibid.*, p. 224.

or trashy (the romance novels of Barbara Cartland, Erich Segal's *Love Story*) or sentimental (*Gone With the Wind*) or scandalous (*Fanny Hill*). Savile attempts to meet this latter objection by arguing that a work must be seen "under its canonical understanding."[33] Vulgar, obscene, and sentimental works will, he argues, reveal themselves as such, rather than as beautiful or deep, when interpreted aright. There is, for example, "a tendency of sentimentality to yield before our recognition of it,"[34] so that we are not, in the end, taken in. Apt critical understanding will sort out the vulgar from the beautiful and deep.

This last claim, however, has an air of begging the question. If it is used as a premise in order to meet an objection, then Savile is in some danger of assuming the very point at issue: that judgments of what is artistically valuable (beautiful or deep) are objective, in noting the presence or absence of valuable features that are there or absent in the object, for anyone who aptly pays attention. Savile does offer an analysis of beauty in a work of art as a matter of the work's having recognizable style features that both answer to a problem and cause pleasurable emotional engagement in suitable apprehenders.[35] This might very well be true, but it does not by itself address the question whether all suitable apprehenders can and will recognize and respond to works in any style whatsoever, and that is the point at issue. Just how widely is there consensus about artistic value, and is that consensus – if and where it exists – a matter of objective recognition of problem-solving features? To say that some works that are recognized by many people to have pleasing problem-solving features are (for them) works that are of stature sidesteps this question rather than meeting it. It comes close to saying that beautiful and deep works (for many) are beautiful and deep (for many), without establishing that there is an objective fact of the matter underlying judgments of taste in general. In the end, the strong objectivist views of both Mothersill and Savile express a somewhat peremptory confidence, dismissive of the significance and interest of continuing disagreements, about the accuracy of some judgments of taste to features in an object.

Hume on feeling and judgment

Both strong subjectivist positions such as that of Smith and strong objectivist positions such as those of Mothersill and Savile frequently take

---

[33] *ibid.*, p. 230.   [34] *ibid.*, p. xii.   [35] See *ibid.*, p. 180.

their bearings from a science-oriented model of objects and their properties. Following the lead of science, they take the problem of the nature of judgments of taste to be a version of the problem of discovery versus projection. Either artistic values are simply there in some objects and performances, in ways that can be determined through objective tests, as acidity of a liquid is determined by putting a drop of it on litmus paper, or they are projected on to things from the subjective mind and sentiment of the perceiver, just as one person likes the taste of blackberries while another does not. Instead, however, of attempting to assimilate identifications and evaluations of art to either judgments that record scientific discoveries or mere recordings of subjective reactions, we might do better to pay attention to how we live with both objective and subjective aspects of judgments of taste. Attention to the peculiar status of artistic identifications and evaluations as subjectively objective or objectively subjective is the great project of the two most important works on the nature of judgments of taste, Hume's essay "Of the Standard of Taste" and the transcendental deduction of the intersubjective validity of judgments of taste in Kant's *Critique of the Power of Judgment*.

Hume begins his essay by describing what can be called the paradox of taste: three commonplaces about the identification and evaluation of art that win ready assent but that are inconsistent – any two entail the negation of the third. These three commonplaces are as follows:

1. Judgments of taste are expressions of sentiment. That is, unlike science, where "an explanation of the terms commonly ends the controversy,"[36] in identifying and evaluating works of art different people feel differently, and their divergent feelings of liking and aversion are the basis of their divergent identifications and rankings.
2. "All sentiment is right."[37] That is, an expression of sentiment is a report of a feeling that has occurred in a subject. A sentiment is "always real, wherever a man is conscious of it"; it "has a reference to nothing beyond itself."[38] There is no question of whether the taste of blackberries is genuinely or objectively pleasing. The only question is whether any particular subject is pleased – some are, and some are not – and that question is entirely settled by what the subject feels, not by the nature of blackberries "in themselves."

---

[36] Hume, "Of the Standard of Taste," p. 256.   [37] *ibid.*, p. 257.   [38] *ibid.*

3. Some judgments of taste are objectively true or false; they are gen-
    uine judgments about matters of fact independent of the reports of any
    particular, individual experiencing subject. "Whoever would assert an
    equality of genius and elegance between Ogilby and Milton, or between
    Bunyan and Addison, would be thought to defend no less an extrava-
    gance than if he had maintained a mole-hill to be as high as Teneriffe,
    or a pond as extensive as the ocean."[39] Those judgments are "absurd
    and ridiculous."[40] "No one pays attention to such a taste,"[41] and rightly
    so.

What in the face of this paradox should we do? Should we hold to
(1) and (2), thus accepting some kind of subjectivist or relativist position,
depending on how far overlaps in sentiment may have stable causes? Or
should we hold to (2) and (3), thus adopting an objectivist position, denying
variable sentiment any crucial role in the making of judgments of taste,
so as to see them as more nearly like cognitive judgments?

Hume's own stance is to hold to (1) and (3) and to reject or at least to
qualify (2). "It is," he writes, "natural for us to seek a *Standard of Taste*; a
rule, by which the various sentiments of men may be reconciled; at least, a
decision, afforded, confirming one sentiment and condemning another."[42]
That is, not all sentiments that are expressed in the making of a judgment
of taste are right; only those sentiments (and the judgments that express
them) that accord with the standard of taste are.

But what is this standard? It cannot be "fixed by reasonings *a priori*."[43]
What is beautiful or valuable as art is a matter of which objects and performances are pleasing, and this is a matter for "general observations"[44]
about what people feel, not for obscure, metaphysical remarks about ideal
proportions or unity or clarity. Yet people disagree in what they feel, so
where is the standard for feeling to be found?

Hume's way out of the paradox is *not* to specify a feature of objects
and performances that properly causes artistic pleasure in all suitably attentive apprehenders. In this he explicitly departs from other theorists of
taste who do specify such features, such as Hutcheson, with his talk of
"uniformity amidst variety" as that which properly pleases. That kind
of talk is too vague and tendentiously metaphysical for Hume. Instead,
Hume argues that the standard of taste is established by the "joint

---

[39] *ibid.*, pp. 257–58.   [40] *ibid.*, p. 258.   [41] *ibid.*   [42] *ibid.*, p. 257.
[43] *ibid.*, p. 258.   [44] *ibid.*

verdict" – whether it is a matter of consensus or of a majority is unclear – of acknowledged experts in the identification and evaluation of art. Hume lists five features of character that lead us properly to regard anyone as an expert in the evaluation of art.

> Strong sense, united to delicate sentiment, improved by practice, perfected by comparison, and cleared of all prejudice, can alone entitle critics to this valuable character; and the joint verdict of such, wherever they are to be found, is the true standard of taste and beauty.[45]

Strong sense is a matter of having a feel for what is plausible or implausible in a plot or in another treatment of a subject matter. Delicate sentiment is the ability to discern small-scale elements of a work and to note how their arrangement contributes to its success or failure. Practice in an art and its criticism, comparisons among works, and lack of prejudice are straightforwardly what they seem. It may be difficult to find experts who possess these five features, but it is their joint verdict – not any independently discernible feature that is shared by all genuinely successful works – that sets the standard of taste.

This claim naturally raises problems. If we cannot tell independently of their verdicts that these experts are *getting it right*, then why should we defer to them? In the case of judgments of color, the standard for accuracy in discrimination is aptly set by normal human perceivers, that is, by the discriminatory abilities of a large majority. It is by comparison with this majority that it is sensible to regard a smaller set of people as color-blind and sensible for them to defer to the color judgments of others. But we seem to lack any comparable basis for deference to experts in the judgment of art. As Peter Kivy develops this objection, building on the work of Isabel Hungerland,

> We can reasonably dispute about whether an object is red [in certain cases], but not about whether a certain kind of perceiver is normal. That is why appealing to the normal perceiver settles the question. But in the aesthetic case we are just as likely to be arguing about what kind of perceiver should be recommended or admired as what kind of object.
>
> Should the ideal aesthetic observer be passionate or cold-blooded, emotional, or cerebral? Poet or peasant, of the elite or the masses? In

---

[45] *ibid.*, p. 264.

the ivory tower, or in the ash can? Political or apolitical, moral or immoral? Sensitive to craftsmanship or aesthetic surface, technique or impression? Quick to judge or slow in judgment? All these are questions that have been part and parcel of the evolution of artistic and aesthetic schools, just as much as have questions about the recommended aesthetic properties of works of art... "In the end, Sensibility does not function like Sense!"[46]

According to Kivy, then, Hume's turn away from properties in objects and toward acknowledged experts as the basis of a kind of objectivity for judgments of taste is a failure. It leaves open the very question it was intended to settle. What is the standard of taste? In particular, why should we defer to the verdicts of so-called experts with just these five features, rather than either deferring to others or judging for ourselves?

Here, however, Hume's resolute empiricism affords him something of a reply. It is, Hume claims, a matter of straightforward empirical fact that we *do* acknowledge as experts those who possess the five qualities and that we *do* defer to them. "That such a character is valuable and estimable *will be agreed in* by all mankind...Some men in general, however difficult to be particularly pitched upon, *will be acknowledged* by universal sentiment to have a preference above others."[47] People who have studied the arts (practiced and made comparisons), who are apt in the discernment of elements (delicacy of imagination), who have strong senses of plausibility and significance, and who are free from prejudice are valued by most of us for the abilities to identify and evaluate art. Who would we expect to do better than such people? Surely schools of art and criticism in which people practice and make comparisons cultivate an ability to judge that is esteemed by us.

Against Hume, it might be objected that even if we, or many people, do agree that those who possess the five qualities are authoritative judges, we do so not for any good reason, but only as a result of social conditioning and craven conservatism. Smith and Bourdieu, after all, point to social conditioning as the basis of deference in taste. But Hume can respond by pointing out that no better basis for ascribing critical

---

[46] Kivy, "Recent Scholarship and the British Tradition," p. 639. In the final line Kivy is citing Isabel Hungerland's essay "The Logic of Aesthetic Concepts," *Proceedings and Addresses of the American Philosophical Association* 36 (1962/63), p. 58.

[47] Hume, "Of the Standard of Taste," p. 264; emphases added.

authority is available. When features in an object such as uniformity amidst variety (Hutcheson) or the instancing-imaging of the beautiful (Plato) are suggested as criteria for art, bypassing and correcting the verdicts of authoritative judges, then what really happens is that these object-oriented standards function as props to baseless social authority in teaching art, taste, and social decorum. Plato explicitly appeals to his standard to censor the arts. Hutcheson's work suggests an order of social decorum founded on the authority of the aristocracy, in its pursuit of varied but unthreatening entertainments. Better, according to Hume, to avoid "all distant and high enquiries" into the metaphysical nature of artistic value, together with the baseless social authority in which they are complicit, and to confine ourselves instead "to common life, and to such subjects as fall under daily practice and experience,"[48] including our natural deference to the joint verdict of true judges.

Nor can we do without standards altogether. It is natural for us to seek a standard of taste, and so to defer to the joint verdict of true judges, insofar as works of art provoke strong, unruly emotions, and we may fear ourselves to be mad when in the grip of them. When my attention is held raptly by *Paradise Lost* or by Schubert's *Trout Quintet*, then something can seem to me to be wrong with me. Why am I thus held so raptly? Not everyone is. Is there anything in the work that merits this kind of absorption and so allows me to see it as sane? If I can then turn to the joint verdict of experts, I might feel reassured that the answer is yes, even if neither I nor anyone else can figure out directly any objective, "metaphysical" nature of beauty that is present in all objects that merit absorption.

Hume's position is plausible, deep, and honorable. We do by and large defer to some extent to the authority in identifying and evaluating art of those who have native sense and discrimination, who have trained in the arts and are practiced at judgment, and who are open to artistic achievements in many genres and traditions. We have good reasons for this deference, and these reasons have in part to do with resistance to baseless "metaphysical" cultural authority, with a need for reassurance, and with keeping faith with common humanity. The joint verdict of true judges does help us to negotiate the play of strong emotion and attention, as

---

[48] David Hume, *An Enquiry Concerning Human Understanding*, ed. Eric Steinberg (Indianapolis, IL: Hackett, 1977), p. 112.

they are provoked by objects and performances that are widely divergent. Taking this verdict as a standard helps to maintain sanity, balance, and openness.

It is not clear, however, that Hume has completely captured the nature of our deference to true judges, and he may also have missed the limits of that deference. We do not care only about identifying and ranking works of art in order to reassure ourselves in our responses. We also care about seeing and feeling for ourselves exactly how they are valuable, one by one. True judges *might* help us to do this, and so further deserve our deference, if they produced critical remarks that embodied elucidatory-critical understanding,[49] rather than simply verdicts. But Hume does not dwell on this. His focus remains identification and ranking, not under-standing and thence coming to see and feel for oneself what is of value in a work.

Kant on feeling and judgment

Once we become aware of this further interest in seeing and feeling for ourselves, we can then wonder whether there is any reason to think that our individual seeings and feelings will coincide, when we take the time and trouble to pay careful attention to a work at hand. We look for our-selves to see what is of value, and then we feel pleasure or indifference. Accredited authorities – true judges – may have their uses in establishing a class of favored works. But what happens when we look at or listen to one of these works? Will we agree then in feeling, if we all pay attention in the right way? How can something so personal and apparently subjective as a feeling be the basis for a genuine judgment?

These are the questions that Kant addresses in the transcendental de-duction of the intersubjective validity of judgments of taste in the *Critique of the Power of Judgment*. Kant insists that all subjects must judge for them-selves whether a work is artistically valuable, without deferring to experts. "Taste makes claim merely to autonomy. To make the judgments of oth-ers into the determining ground of one's own would be heteronomy"[50] – a less than praiseworthy (even if not morally blameworthy) failure to act as a full subject in one's own right.

Yet it does not follow that anything one says on one's own is right – "for oneself" as it were. Kant holds that it is possible to make "an erroneous

---

[49] See chapter 6 above.   [50] Kant, *Critique of the Power of Judgment*, §32, p. 163.

judgment of taste."[51] But this does not happen in virtue of disagreeing with a standard (such as the joint verdict of true judges) that is independent of oneself and to which one ought to defer. Rather, one misassesses and misreports what has happened in oneself in attending to a work.

Kant's term for paying attention to a work so as to determine whether it invites and sustains absorptive pleasure is "judging" or "estimation [Beurtheilung]."[52] In estimation, one focuses one's attention on the work, exploring its parts or elements and their interrelations, without settling on any single definite conceptualization of it as wholly explaining what it is.[53] Here imaginative attention plays freely over the work and its parts or elements, without settling on a definite conceptual assessment or classification of it. Kant characterizes this lack of settling on definite classification as our imagination being in "free play" in attending to a work. When we thus attend freely to a work, then sometimes things go well – it is as though it were purposively intelligible to us, even though we are *not* classifying the work or regarding it as intended for any definite use – and we feel pleasure. Sometimes it goes less well, and we do not feel pleasure that sustains our imaginative attention. The estimation or *Beurtheilung* of the object is attending to it in order to see whether or not this happens. If it does, then our cognitive faculties are said to be in harmonious free play, and the work is beautiful (artistically successful or well formed). If it does not, then it is not.

When one makes an erroneous judgment of taste ("ein irriges Geschmacks*urteil*"[54]), then what has happened is that one has misassessed and misreported the causal history of a pleasure one has felt. One has come to "offend against"[55] the conditions for making a judgment (*Urteil*) of taste. Specifically, one has attended to the work in an interested way, with some conceptualization in mind, rather than estimating it freely.

---

[51] *ibid.*, §8, p. 101.

[52] The distinction between estimation (*Beurtheilung*) and overt, linguistic report or judgment that an object is beautiful (*Urteil*) is the topic of §9 of the *Critique of the Power of Judgment*, and Kant observes that it is "key to the critique of taste, and hence worthy of all attention," §9, p. 102.

[53] Here I draw on the explication of what it is to attend to an object in freedom from (definite, explicative) conceptualization that is suggested by Ted Cohen, "Three Problems in Kant's Aesthetics," *British Journal of Aesthetics* 42, 1 (January 2002), pp. 1–12 at p. 3. Cohen reports that he owes this suggestion to Arthur Melnick, in conversation.

[54] Kant, *Kritik der Urteilskraft* (Frankfurt-on-Main: Suhrkamp, 1974), §8, p. 131; emphasis added.

[55] Kant, *Critique of the Power of Judgment*, §8, p. 101.

One has felt pleasure – it is impossible to be mistaken about that; and there are no phenomenal "marks in consciousness" of different kinds of pleasure – but *not* pleasure that is due to the harmonious free play of the cognitive faculties, for one has not freely estimated the work at all. Perhaps one has responded with pleasure because it is a play written by one's child, in the success of whose performances one has an interest; perhaps it is a quartet by a wealthy patron whose favor one courts. In any case, one can feel pleasure and be mistaken about its cause. One can surmise and report that it is a pleasure that occurs through free estimating and yet be wrong. In this way, one comes to make a mistake not by reference to an independent standard, but in relation, as it were, to oneself.

The question then naturally arises whether, if and when we do freely estimate a work, we necessarily feel the same pleasure in genuinely estimating the same objects. If we do, then judgments of taste, even though based on individual felt response to a work, are "intersubjectively valid" – true or false for everyone; if not, then they are not. The transcendental deduction of the intersubjective validity of judgments of taste is Kant's argument that necessarily all human subjects do feel the same pleasures (or indifferences) in estimating the same objects (if and when they genuinely estimate them freely and do not "offend against" the conditions for making a judgment of taste). That argument runs as follows.[56] (Each premise is supposedly known *a priori*, via reflection alone, not through specific empirical investigation.)

> (1) Cognitions (knowledge-claims) are communicable. (Nothing purely internal to and idiosyncratic to oneself could count as knowledge.)
>
> (2) Like effects have like causes.
>
> Therefore (3) The subjective conditions [*Stimmungen*] of cognition – i.e. those states of the subject out of which cognitions are generated – are communicable.
>
> (4) The subjective conditions of cognition = a harmony, accord, or proportion of the cognitive faculties [imagination and understanding cooperating to construct intuitions and to subsume intuitions under concepts in a judgment].

---

[56] The most worked out and plausible version of the argument appears in sections 38 and 39 of the *Critique of the Power of Judgment*, especially in the footnote to §38. I base my presentation closely on Paul Guyer's reconstruction of it in his *Kant and the Claims of Taste* (Cambridge, MA: Harvard University Press, 1979), chapter 9, pp. 308–19.

Therefore (5) This harmony, accord, or proportion of the cognitive faculties that underlies cognition is communicable.

(6) The harmony, accord, or proportion of the cognitive faculties that underlies cognition = the harmony, accord, or proportion of the cognitive faculties in free play (when we are estimating freely).

Therefore (7) The harmony, accord, or proportion of the cognitive faculties in free play is communicable.

(8) Judgments of taste are intersubjectively valid if and only if subjects feel pleasure in the harmonious free play of the cognitive faculties with regard to the same objects (when they are genuinely estimating them or paying free and disinterested attention to them).

Therefore (9) Judgments of taste are intersubjectively valid.

Against this argument it is possible to make a number of reasonable objections.[57] First, premise (1) seems like an empirical claim, not one that is *a priori* knowable. Though the transcendental deduction of the *Critique of Pure Reason* argues that any subject with an apperceptively unified and judgmentally structured consciousnesses is entitled to claim knowledge of causal relations – that is, is able to know some of them – it does not follow that all subjects are able to know the same causal relations or further the same things in general. The empirical claim that we can know the same things – can communicate our cognitions – seems dubitable.

Second, premise (6) likewise seems to be an empirical claim that is dubitable. Why should the subjective conditions that underlie cognition – that is, the states and interrelations of the cognitive faculties through which a cognitive judgment is constructed – be the very same as the subjective conditions that sometimes occur when the cognitive faculties are in harmonious free play? Here it seems either that all objects should be beautiful, since we would feel pleasure in the harmonious working of the cognitive faculties in the construction of any cognition whatsoever, or that there is something special about the cognitive faculties in harmonious *free* play – that a special pleasure attaches to that. But if so, then why should this pleasure – achieved independently of the activity of knowing – occur with regard to the same objects in everyone? As Guyer summarizes the objection, "possession of the subjective conditions of knowledge in general, or what might be regarded as the *minimal* conditions for knowledge [viz. an imagination and understanding that work properly to construct

---

cognitions], does not entail the capacity to become conscious, through pleasure, of the synthesis of manifolds apart from concepts,"[58] let alone that this capacity is the same in everyone.

Against this reconstruction and criticism of the argument, Salim Kemal suggests a number of interesting moves that increase the plausibility of some of its premises and that point toward rich accounts of the roles of art and its criticism in culture.

First Kemal denies that the subjective conditions of the power of judgment ("die subjektiven Bedingungen der Urteilskraft") are properly understood as psychological states of the subject that are causally effective for the construction of a cognition. Rather, Kemal argues that these subjective conditions are best construed as the unity of apperception – the ability to become aware of any act of judgment as one's own act of judgment – that must be part of the formal structure of the consciousness of any judging subject. As Kemal puts it, "the 'I think' embodies the act of judging, and [it] is the subjective formal condition for all judgments [either cognitive or reflective through estimation] because it is the component in any judgment that signals the subject's *act* of judging"[59] as opposed to merely reacting, as in a wince.

Once we see this, Kemal claims, the argument goes through all at once. The claim that cognitions are communicable is fairly weak, but defensible *a priori*. Subjects need not be able to know all the same things; they must simply have the same structural kind of judging consciousness – an apperceptively unified one. This makes them one and all the kinds of being who are capable of using evidence to distinguish objective successions or causally determined sequences of events outside their control from subjective successions. This is all premise (1) claims, and it is *a priori* knowable (if anything in Kant is).

Second, we do not need to use premise (2) to get to premise (3); we do not need to make a causal inference that the relevant subjective conditions in us are similar. That which is required in any subject to make any genuine judgment possible – apperceptive unity – must be in any judging subject. So premise (3) survives as *a priori* knowable without relying on premise (2). As Kemal puts it, "the [necessary, formal] subjective conditions

---

[58] *ibid.*, p. 321.
[59] Salim Kemal, *Kant's Aesthetic Theory: An Introduction* (New York: St. Martin's Press, 1992), p. 82; emphasis added.

for judging must be present in all [judging] subjects."[60] Once we see this, worries about whether our underlying wiring, hence our propensities to feel pleasure when estimating or freely reflecting, might be different, even though we could functionally know the same things, are beside the point. Those worries are aimed at a causal construal of the role in judging of the subjective formal conditions of judging, but that construal is mistaken.

So far Kemal's reconstruction of the argument is both textually faithful to Kant's very compressed presentation of it in sections 38 and 39 and to Kant's theory of judgmental consciousness and judgmental acts in the *Critique of Pure Reason*, and its premises are plausibly knowable *a priori*. But what about the identity claim in premise (6)? Can we have that? Kemal argues that we can. The subjective formal conditions for judging are used *in the very same way* in both cognitive judgments and aesthetic estimations. Subjects must freely pay attention and in doing so discern order. In Kemal's words,

> If we can judge by discerning order and thereby can gain [cognitive]
> experience and communicate knowledge, then we can judge by
> discerning order and can gain a harmony of the faculties [in free play].
> As Kant describes it, our apprehension of the harmony of the faculties
> "occurs by means of a procedure that judgment has to carry out to give
> rise to even the most ordinary experience...[The resulting] pleasure
> must of necessity rest on the same conditions in everyone, because they
> are subjective conditions for the possibility of cognition as such."[61]

In short, same procedure of using the same structure in both cognition and estimation, so same universality. Kant has shown *a priori* "that aesthetic judgments are possible,"[62] that is, that any reflective report [*Urteil*] that one has found pleasure due to the harmonious free play of the cognitive faculties in the estimation [*Beurtheilung*] of the object will be true or false for everyone – intersubjectively valid – though it remains to be established whether any particular such report *is* true or false.

This defense of premise (6) begs the question, however, in Kemal and in Kant. It is true that only creatures who are capable of cognitive judgments are capable of aesthetic judgments. My dog has neither a nose for beauty nor a taste for art. But to some considerable extent, inquiry and aesthetic reflection are different activities. Seeking knowledge and freely estimating

---

[60] ibid.   [61] ibid., p. 86, citing *Critique of the Power of Judgment*, §39.   [62] ibid.

or attentively opening oneself to the uncognized intelligibility of objects are not the same thing. Even if these activities require the use of the same powers of imagination and understanding, it does not follow that these powers are used *in the same way* in these distinct activities. *Contra* Kemal, then, the argument does not go through; premise (6) remains dubitable.

Even if, however, he fails to establish that the transcendental deduction is sound, Kemal does manage to point toward rich accounts of the roles of art and art criticism in culture. After claiming (mistakenly) that the deduction is sound and that Kant has shown that intersubjectively valid judgments of taste "are transcendentally possible,"[63] Kemal further notes that "we do not as yet know how to confirm in any actual instance that ours is an aesthetic judgment."[64] This is exactly right. I can be wrong in claiming (overtly) that I have freely estimated the object. That is, when I report that I have experienced pleasure due to the harmonious free play of the cognitive faculties in my estimation of an object, I may be wrong. I experienced pleasure, but it did not have that cause. I might rather have taken pleasure in the fact that my child made the object or in the fact that it's a poem about philosophy, rather than through finding the object as-it-were intelligible without subsuming it under a kind.

Elsewhere Kemal suggests that the deduction is not complete until confirmation can be secured that I am correct *in some particular cases.* Until I have that confirmation I cannot demand the agreement of others. So far, this is mistaken. What Kant means by *demand (fordern)* is that I *am entitled* to speak as though others must agree with me – must have the same pleasure as I do – assuming for the moment that I am right about my pleasure and its causes. That I am entitled to do this would be entirely established by the deduction as outlined, were it sound. *Demand* here indicates an entitlement possessed in virtue of the underlying similarity of the cognitive faculties of judging subjects. It does not indicate any coercive power to make others agree with this particular judgment. They must judge for themselves, freely, and if I am right, then they must agree in feeling pleasure due to the harmonious free play of the cognitive faculties, if they too estimate freely – or at least so the deduction argues.

But this is not to say that confirmation – getting others to estimate freely and then, after reflecting on their pleasure, to *say* that they agree – does not matter. Here Kemal is on to something deep in Kant, as he

---

[63] *ibid.,* p. 88.   [64] *ibid.*

remarks that "the only way to gain confirmation [that one's report of one's experience of aesthetic pleasure is correct], it seems, is by bringing other subjects to make the same judgment"[65] through their own free estimating. In fact, as Kemal notes, it is not even certain that this will help. Other subjects may likewise experience pleasure (or not), but misreport that they have estimated the object freely. They can be wrong just as I can. If no one can be certain of being right, how can we reassure one another by agreeing?[66]

But perhaps this inability of all and any of us to be sure we are right does not matter so much. When we develop the practice of estimating objects freely, reflecting on our experience of them, and then reporting to other subjects the results of our estimation and reflection, then something interesting and important happens. "Judgments of taste," Kemal writes, "sustain an exploration of the nature and form of the community of subjects. In seeking confirmation, we must address subjects as subjects capable of such... judgments."[67] That is, we must address them freely. We must report what, on reflection, we have felt – when using, we suppose, common human cognitive faculties – and then wait. Others may also then report that their cognitive faculties lead them freely to make sense of the same objects, or they may not. Hence the experiences of art and beauty, together with the further practice of talking about those experiences, is a way of "deepening and enlarging the community"[68] of free subjects. Culture is here the proleptic exploration and enactment of possibilities of free assent. As Kemal puts it, "Judgments of taste celebrate the relation of individual to community, which is ever in process, for the individual's autonomous judgment is always in search of a warrant from the community, which is itself always in a process of development that depends on assent from its members."[69] "The more we... acknowledge [through exploring and confirming our aesthetic responses] that our exclusively private feelings are *not* the only model for subjectivity, the more we will develop [the] moral feeling"[70] of respect for the idea of free community. "In this context culture as discipline is the *emergence of humanity* – of the individual liberated from subjugation to natural impulses and truculent egoism and now considered as a reasoning moral end."[71]

---

[65] *ibid.*, p. 91.   [66] See *ibid.*, pp. 96–97.   [67] *ibid.*, pp. 98–99.   [68] *ibid.*, p. 99.
[69] *ibid.*   [70] *ibid.*, p. 117.   [71] *ibid.*, p. 120.

We have, therefore, good reason to look and judge autonomously, "for ourselves," as best we can. When we do so, we can be wrong, in mistaking the character of our own attention and experience. We have good reason to make our individual verdicts public and to discuss them with others, in the hope of establishing that we can and do freely respond to the same works – even if we cannot prove *a priori* that we must do so on all occasions. Public discussion of identifications and evaluations can sometimes help both to bring us together in response and to make me more confident that I have not misunderstood the basis of my own responses. Public discussion of identifications and evaluations will rightly take the form not of proofs, but of the articulation of elucidatory-critical understanding,[72] as we explore in the work possible foci of our responses, shared or divergent as they may be. Since, however, the articulation of elucidatory-critical understanding is an open-ended activity, where shifts in foci of response may occur as a result of new comparisons with other works and as a result of new, wider, historical-cultural and psychological forms of understanding, the activities of identification and evaluation will likewise be open-ended and subject to shifts.

Personal and/versus discussable: Isenberg, Scruton, and Cohen on taste

Are judgments of taste – identifications and evaluations of works of art – then, in the end objective? Hume is right to emphasize the facts of continuing disagreements in judgments of taste and of shifts in our own personal verdicts over time. He is right that it is both natural, as a means of seeking reassurance about oneself, and reasonable, in light of a command of greater powers of sense and discernment and a greater command of relevant comparisons, sometimes to defer to the verdicts of authorities in criticism, at least to take seriously the possibility that they might be right. Yet Hume is wrong to insist that the joint verdict of acknowledged authorities entirely constitutes a standard of taste. We do not and should not always defer to it. Acknowledged adepts in critical understanding and in identification and evaluation sometimes disagree with one another, and their verdicts – individual and joint – are no more (though no less) stable and shared than their eludicatory-critical understandings. Kant is

---

[72] See chapter 6 above.

right, therefore, to emphasize the importance of looking and seeking for oneself, of exploring the work imaginatively, in pursuit of elucidatory-critical understanding that rightly figures in identification and evaluation. Such exploration of the work, by both novices and the well practiced, can be motivated by the hope of agreement in identification and evaluation. But it cannot be guaranteed through the use of any method or by appeal to any standard that that hope will be fulfilled. Understandings, identi-fications, and evaluations remain reasonably discussable through "point-ing out" features of a work that are relevant to understanding it and to identifying it and evaluating it as art, but not provable independently of exercises of "free" sensibility. As Arnold Isenberg poignantly puts it,

> It is a function of criticism to bring about communication at the level of the senses; that is, to induce a sameness of vision, of experienced content. If this is accomplished, it *may or may not* be followed by agreement, or what is called "communion" – a community of feeling which expresses itself in identical value judgments.[73]

Following the lead of Kant and Isenberg, we can usefully distinguish at some level mere gustatory judgments of personal sensory liking ("I like pistachio ice cream"), aesthetic identifications and evaluations ("Gaddis' *JR* is an important work of twentieth-century art"), and moral judgments ("It is wrong to set cats on fire for fun"). As Roger Scruton characterizes the differences between these kinds of judgment, with mere taste a retreat to "Well, I like it" is always available: no one is blamed for free sensory likings or aversions, and reversion in conversation about them to "Well, I like it" is less a retreat from critical reasoning than it is an apt withdrawal from the impertinent hectoring of another. With at least some moral judgments, no retreat is possible. We are prepared – at least sometimes – to appeal to principles and to argue that anyone who disagrees with the moral verdict in question must be wrong; standing outside certain moral consensuses may disqualify one from having standing in moral conversations at all. With aesthetic identifications and evaluations, retreat to "Well, I like it" is available and relevant, but it is, sometimes, a genuine retreat from further shared exploration of and conversation about the work. "Well, I like it" can function *either* as a withdrawal from hectoring, that is, as a reminder to an impertinent other (and to myself) that my experience of the work

---

[73] Isenberg, "Critical Communication," p. 367.

counts, *or* as a genuine retreat, a disengagement, a withholding of oneself from exploring the work further oneself and with others.[74] Identifications and evaluations of works of art involve, always, a normative "search for agreement...A man with a normative attitude toward X feels that others should recognize the qualities he likes or admires in X, and on this basis come to like X themselves."[75] But the force of one's normative attitude is "a matter of degree,"[76] and, as Isenberg reminds us, even after considerable critical conversation, communion may or may not follow.

Here identifications and evaluations of art resemble our responses to persons. We can, sometimes and with some success, talk about what we like or dislike in a person, and so both bring others to a similar response and feel more confidence that our own liking has a reasonable basis. But not always. There is a residue of free liking. My response to Jones that differs from yours may have to do with differences between me and you, not only with the objective features of Jones. Moreover, we may both see the same or similar features of character in another, but understand them in different contexts and evaluate them differently. What I take in Jones to be resolute patience, concern for craft in intellectual work, and faithfulness to the subject rather than to public whim, you take to be timidity, self-indulgence in private fantasy, and failure to achieve any reputable point of view. It is not clear that we will be able to talk this disagreement out so as to understand and feel about Jones together, no matter how long we go on, though we may each sometimes have something to say. (Both Scruton and Cavell note, against the sharpness and absoluteness of Kant's distinctions, that moral verdicts, including for example judgments of character, are often, perhaps typically, more like aesthetic judgments than they are wholly "objectively" determined by moral principle and unambiguous facts.[77] Nor is it clear that "mere gustatory" judgments are *always* beyond reasonable discussion.)

Thinking, among other things, about the unruly mixture of openness to reasoned critical discussion and of a "sheerly" personal dimension of

---

[74] See Scruton, *Art and Imagination*, pp. 137–38. Compare also Cavell, "Aesthetic Problems of Modern Philosophy," pp. 88–94. Cavell is explicitly taking up and developing Kant's distinctions between judgments of the (merely) agreeable, judgments of the beautiful, and judgments of the morally good in §§3–8 of the *Critique of the Power of Judgment*, pp. 90–101.

[75] Scruton, *Art and Imagination*, p. 139.

[76] *ibid.*   [77] See the references in note 74.

liking and divergent point of view that attaches, always, to identifications and evaluations of art, Ted Cohen reports that

> In some cases I hold out the vain but necessary, beautiful hope that the work will – or at least *could* – reach everyone, that it could be our *entré* into what we desperately wish to be our universal humanity, that it could be what Kant, in all the profound, obtuse, crystalline opacity of the optimism of the Enlightenment thought beauty is, the mark of the "universal substrate of humanity." But in most cases the net of my hopes is cast less widely. This is not a bad or limiting thing: it is essential to my location of myself... Some works connect me with many people, including, sometimes, considerable varieties of people. Thus *The Simpsons* and some Marx brothers movies connect me with both very young people and some widely varying kinds of people my own age and older. And some works connect me with very few people. Thus some stories by I. B. Singer and some by Richard Stern seem to connect me with only a few people, people who are much like me...*Hamlet* and *The Marriage of Figaro* connect me with most of you, I would guess, perhaps all of you. Elaine May's movie *Ishtar*, which I am very fond of, leaves me virtually alone. That's all fine: I need to be with you, and I need to be alone. I need to be like you, and I need to be unlike you. A world in which you and I never connected would be a horror. And so would a world in which we were exactly the same, and therefore connected unfailingly, with every object on every occasion. *The Marriage of Figaro* helps us be us. *Ishtar* helps me be me. Thank God for them both.[78]

As our ongoing agreements and disagreements in identification and evaluation show, works of art are for us crucial sites of the display and testing of both what is deepest and most common among us, including shared capacities of felt response to presentations of a subject matter as a focus for thought and emotional attitude, distinctively fused to the imaginative exploration of material, *and* what is most personal about us, as we seek to sustain distinctive personalities and routes of interest in social life. Identifications and evaluations of works of art are, sometimes, open to reasoned discussion and to reasoned discussion that issues in agreement. Critical authorities sometimes play useful roles in these reasoned

---

[78] Ted Cohen, "High and Low Thinking About High and Low Art," *Journal of Aesthetics and Art Criticism* 51, 2 (spring 1993), pp. 151–56 at pp. 153B–54A, 155B–56A, 156B.

discussions, in which elucidatory critical understanding is cultivated. But sometimes one will see and feel for a work only "for oneself" or in common with a few others. This can be terrifying and isolating, and so we can wish and seek to talk out our responses with others, and sometimes this talk will bring more of us together. But it can also be exhilarating and reassuring, in reminding me that *I* have a point of view and a free personality, rather than being only a fungible functionary of objectivity. No wonder that philosophers (and people in general) argue over the objectivity and subjectivity of judgments of taste, particularly in relation to cases, and no wonder also, and a good thing, that these arguments do not quite come to an end.

8 Art and emotion

Some varieties of emotional response

Consider the following cases:

1. On an April 10, 1982 installment of SATURDAY NIGHT LIVE, the Not-Ready-for-Prime-Time Players threatened to boil a real lobster named "Larry the Lobster" live on the air. As Eddie Murphy informed the audience (speaking quickly): "You want to save Larry the Lobster dial 1-900-720-1808. Then (speaking slowly) "If you want to kill him dial 1-900-720-1809. Now unless you call in to save him, we're going to boil Larry's little butt right here on national television. Now you call in. The phone company is going to charge you fifty cents, but isn't it worth fifty cents to save Larry's life? Or look at it this way: Isn't it worth half a buck to see us boil Larry on TV?" Nearly 500,000 viewers dialed into the program. The final tally? KILL LARRY: 227,452; SAVE LARRY: 239,096.[1]

2. Hand in hand,
   > we've met life's
   >> changes and challenges.
   Side by side,
   > we've shared
   >> our most precious dreams.
   Together
   > we've built a beautiful life.
   > And every year,
   I grow more in love with you
   Happy Birthday![2]

---

[1] Information archived at http://www.tvacres.com/fish_lobsters.htm

[2] Hallmark electronic greeting card, archived at http://www.hallmark.com/hmk/Website/Shopping/Greetings/nfg1770_detail.jsp?BV_SessionID = @@@@0167947399. 1029164712   @@@@&BV_EngineID = dadceldhdijdbedcfchcie.0&fromPage = /Website/

3. A middle-aged, bachelor scholar from Massachusetts travels to Europe
    at the behest of his patron, a wealthy widow, in order to persuade her
    son to abandon Paris, where he has what may be an indelicate attach-
    ment, and to return to run the family business. While in Paris, he enjoys
    the sophisticated conversation and company of an expatriate American
    woman. He comes to see that the young man has been much "improved"
    by Paris and by his "education" at the hands of a somewhat older French-
    woman. Initially unclear about the relationship between this woman
    and the young man, the scholar comes to see that it is fully sexual. He
    nonetheless continues to regard the young man's experience as improv-
    ing for him. The young man tells him he will follow his advice, whatever
    it is. The scholar must then decide whether, as commissioned, to advise
    the young man to return to Massachusetts or to continue life in Paris.
    (If the scholar successfully arranges a return, it is understood that his
    patron will marry him and make his life comfortable.) He must also
    decide whether himself to return to America, either as a success in his
    mission or as a failure. If he stays in Paris, he may continue to enjoy the
    company and further affections of his woman friend, and he may also
    enjoy the company and affections of the son's French lover, with whom
    he is himself perhaps somewhat in love.[3]

Each of these cases solicits an emotional response. Nearly half a million
television viewers were moved to try to affect the fate of Larry, for better
or worse. The birthday greeting card invites gratitude and satisfaction in
shared recognition of the value of time spent together. The narrative (at
least in its full version) generates curiosity, apprehensiveness, a wish that
the protagonist should manage his difficult situation well, and sympathy
with his efforts to move through uncertainties.

But there are important differences as well. While numbers of people
were moved to do something about Larry, it is by no means clear that they
reflected on and became clearer about their emotional responses. Perhaps
numbers of viewers did reflect on their social roles as viewers, on live versus taped performance, and on art versus provocation, but it seems likely
that many, given the time pressure, felt and acted fairly immediately. The

---

Shopping/sh_eg_home.jsp&sku = nfg1770&oid = -102270   &desc = ECards&first = 1&
price = &text = Hand+in+hand,+we've+   met+life's%85&pname = More+In+Love+
With+You&cname = Birthday&page = 1

[3] As I hope is evident, this is a summary (my own) of much of the plot of Henry
James' *The Ambassadors*.

greeting card is formulaic, even clichéd. While it expresses an emotion in one sense of "express" – it gets it out – and invites a response, there is no clarification of that emotion's specific bases and meaning. It is, perhaps, more described and even simulated rather than articulated and clarified. This is not to be scorned; a simulation of an emotion might itself both express a deep and genuine one and invite a deep and genuine response. Perhaps, for example, it is important, for whatever reason, for the parties to relationships in which the exchange of this card might figure to acknowledge and accept the full ordinariness and yet value of their lives together. Yet the card can also seem hollowly sentimental. In the third case, the response that is invited is more a matter of specific engagement and feeling-with, rather than the upsurge of an emotion that is independently describable and apt in its specific development to other occasions. Unlike Larry and either a giver or the writer of the greeting card, the protagonist, Lambert Strether, is a fictional character who does not, in the most obvious sense, exist.

Just what is going on when we are absorbed in and moved by the career and fate of Lambert Strether? How is our being moved related to the fact that we encounter him in an artistic representation, a supreme work of fiction? How do learning and the development of feeling, as opposed both to felt response immediately discharged in action and to formula, figure in an emotional response to art?

The paradox of fiction

To some theorists, emotional responses to fiction seem to pose a special problem that can be summed up in the following paradox developed by Colin Radford.[4]

1. We are moved by the career and fate of Anna Karenina (for example).
2. Anna Karenina does not exist, and we know this.
3. Being moved by the career and fate of a subject requires belief in the real existence of that subject; it is impossible really to care about something that one knows does not exist.

---

[4] Colin Radford, "How can We be Moved by the Fate of Anna Karenina?," *Proceedings of the Aristotelian Society*, supplementary vol. 49 (1975), pp. 67–80. Radford's own conclusion is that "our being moved in certain ways by works of art, though very 'natural' to us and in that way only too intelligible, involves us in inconsistency and so incoherence" (p. 78).

These three claims are paradoxical, since any pair of them entails the negation of the third. Such paradoxes can readily be generated for other media of art as well. Why can, do, or should we care about Cézanne's *Bathers*, for there are no bathers really there, but only blobs of paint? Why should we care whether Luke Skywalker will destroy the Death Star, since there is no real Luke Skywalker, but only beams of light that project an image of an actor? Why care about music, which is nothing but sound that signifies, so it seems, nothing? Perhaps we should say, "well we *do* care about arranged paint, arranged sound, and fictional plots, and any theory of emotional response must take account of these obvious facts." But while this remark may be true, it does not yet explain exactly how or why we care.

One way out of this paradox is to deny (2) and to hold that Anna Karenina, though she does not exist in our actual world, is a fictional subject who exists in some possible world, a fictional world.[5] The novel that bears her name is then regarded as a description of the doings of Anna Karenina and other fictional subjects. In this way, we can, among other things, seemingly explain how certain sentences are true, for example, "Anna Karenina is married to a dull bureaucrat." Though this sentence is not true in our world, it is – so it is held – true in or of some possible world, the nonexistent, fictional, "real" but possible-not-actual world of the novel.

The difficulty with this maneuver is that it displaces rather than answers the difficult question of why we can, do, or should care about Anna's career and fate. First of all, it is unclear what the identity conditions are for possible objects or subjects. How many possible Anna Kareninas are there? Is the possible Anna Karenina with a shorter haircut different from the possible Anna Karenina with a longer one?[6] But even if we overcome our scruples about talk of possibilia, including possible subjects, it remains

---

[5] See, for example, Thomas G. Pavel, *Fictional Worlds* (Cambridge, MA; Harvard University Press, 1986). Broadly speaking, Nelson Goodman's work on all descriptions, including what we take to be scientific descriptions of our actual world, as our inventions that highlight one way of being interested in things rather than neutral recordings of the real, is sympathetic to this approach. See Goodman, *Ways of Worldmaking* (Indianapolis, IN: Hackett, 1978).

[6] This is, of course, Quine's criticism of possibilia-talk in general as unintelligible. See W. V. O. Quine, "On What There Is," in W. V. O. Quine, *From a Logical Point of View*, revised edn (Cambridge, MA: Harvard University Press, 1961), pp. 1–19.

mysterious why we should care about them and their doings. They cannot talk to us, feel pain, or suffer in our presence. We can do nothing to respond to them (other than read, watch, or listen). Our interactions with them are wholly unlike our interactions with actual human subjects, about whom we do care as a matter of course. As Arthur Danto trenchantly comments,

> the sorts of things that philosophy [of this possible-worlds kind] has laid down to connect literature [to us] in order to give it meaning – *Gegenstände*, intensions, fictive worlds – are themselves as much in need of ontological redemption as the beings to whose rescue they were enlisted – Don Quixote, Mr. Pickwick, Gandalf the Grey.[7]

Hume on tragedy

A second, more plausible way out of the paradox is suggested by Hume in his discussion of the problem of tragedy: why do we enjoy the distressing events that a tragedy presents, when we would not enjoy the same events were they to occur in real life? Hume proposes in his moral philosophy that we are by nature sympathetic creatures who tend to take pleasure in the pleasures of others and pain in their pains. This can explain why we are moved to pity by the fate of Anna Karenina: a sad story is a representation of something that is, for us, naturally sadness-inducing. But it does not yet wholly answer the questions why we attend and enjoy tragedies or why we read and enjoy sad novels. This why-question is ambiguous between asking about a *cause* for our feeling as we do and asking for a *reason* why it is apt or appropriate to have such feelings as a part of our (well-founded) practice of making and responding to representations. Hume's account of natural sympathies can answer the first, causal why-question but not the second. At first blush, an account of natural sympathies cannot explain why we deliberately produce, seek out, and enjoy sadness-inducing representations. As Hume puts it,

> It seems an unaccountable pleasure which the spectators of a
> well-written tragedy receive from sorrow, terror, anxiety, and other
> passions that are in themselves disagreeable and uneasy...The whole art

---

[7] Danto, "Philosophy as/and/of Literature," *Grand Street* 3, 3 (spring 1984), pp. 151–76 at p. 159.

of the poet is employed in rousing and supporting the compassion and indignation, the anxiety and resentment, of his audience. They are pleased in proportion as they are afflicted, and never are so happy as when they employ tears, sobs, and cries, to give vent to their sorrow, and relieve their heart, swoln with the tenderest sympathy and compassion.[8]

Since such afflictions are not pleasing in real life away from the theatre, then whence, Hume wonders, "this singular phenomenon."[9]

Hume argues that it will not do to say that a moving tragedy is nothing but an "amusement" that removes us from the "painful situation" of being in a "languid, listless, state of indolence," for "it is certain that the same object of distress, were it really set before us, would give us the most unfeigned uneasiness, though it be then the most effectual cure to languor and indolence."[10] Why, then, does it please on the stage?

Nor will it do to say that we are pleased just because and insofar as the tragedy is a fiction, for moving and pleasing tragedies can present events that really happened. For example, Cicero's "pathetic description of the butchery made by Verres of the Sicilian captains...is a masterpiece"[11] of pleasing and moving dramatic art, but not a fiction. Here Hume is surely right to emphasize that the object of pleasure in otherwise distressing emotion is a made thing, a play or painting or other work of art, not the events or objects recounted or depicted in themselves. With too much sense of the factual reality of the distressing or tragic, our pleasure tends to lapse, as we are overwhelmed by the events themselves.[12] But at least with a certain distance set up by time and art, we can take pleasure in the representation of actual distressing events. It is not necessary that the objects and incidents described be fictional. Hence it must somehow matter that it is a recounting or a depiction in which we take pleasure. But how?

Hume proposes as a solution that

All the passions, [when] excited by eloquence, are agreeable in the highest degree, as well as those which are moved by painting and the theatre...[The] extraordinary effect [pleasure in otherwise distressing

---

[8] Hume, "Of Tragedy," in David Hume, *Essays Moral, Political and Literary* (Oxford: Oxford University Press, 1963), pp. 221–30 at p. 221.

[9] *ibid.*   [10] *ibid.*, p. 22.   [11] *ibid.*, p. 224.

[12] Alex Neill has cogently urged me to remember that not every tragic incident can be pleasingly represented; some are too close to us for that.

emotion] proceeds from that very eloquence with which the melancholy scene is represented. The genius required to paint objects in a lively manner, the art employed in collecting all the pathetic circumstances, the judgment displayed in disposing them; the exercise, I say, of those noble talents, together with the force of expression, and beauty of oratorical numbers, diffuse the highest satisfaction on the audience and excite the most delightful movements. By this means, the uneasiness of the melancholy passions is not only overpowered and effaced by something stronger of an opposite kind, but the whole impulse of those passions is converted into pleasure, and swells the delight which the eloquence raises in us.[13]

In effect, Hume denies (1). Though we *are* moved by the fate of Anna Karenina, it is not that fact by itself that induces us to read about her career. It is only when the sadness we feel at misfortunes is "converted" by eloquence or artfulness into a kind of pleasure that we enjoy sad stories and have a good reason to read them.[14] We are not pleased by the fate of Anna Karenina itself, but by the artfulness with which it is presented.

This answer has some truth in it. Some of our engagement with *Hamlet* is due to the glories of its language; some of our delight in Cézanne's *Bathers* is due to its pleasing arrangement of colors. But it cannot be the whole story. In assimilating pleasure in art entirely to the delights of artfulness of arrangement, Hume is failing to capture the character of our engagement as members of an audience in working through the subject matter of the art. For Hume, it is as though our pleasure in art and in being moved by art were like the pleasure of a warm bath, supposing that that languid pleasure is also enlivened by bracing perfumes or occasional infusions of cold water. For Hume, the surface of our experience matters more – at least for pleasure – than what we explore in the work.

---

[13] *ibid.*

[14] For a detailed reconstruction of Hume's doctrine of the "conversion" of aversion into pleasure, see Alex Neill, "'An Unaccountable Pleasure': Hume on Tragedy and the Passions," *Hume Studies* 24, 2 (November 1998), pp. 335–54. Neill argues, aptly I think, that Hume is not committed to either the view that pleasure simply overpowers aversion or that aversion is itself directly and wholly transformed into pleasure. Rather the "emotions or movements [mental energies?] produced by the negative passions...are appropriated and converted" (p. 347) so that delight in artistry is swelled.

This stance fits well with Hume's suspiciousness toward claims that we have much to learn from tragedies and other works of art. Hume regards such claims as of a piece with the baseless pretensions of religious narratives to afford genuine insight into the workings of nature and humanity. He remarks, for example, that errors concerning religion (what god or gods exist, what we owe them, etc.) are "the most excusable in any compositions of genius" precisely because in general "good sense is not hearkened to in religious matters."[15] That is to say, religion is in general a matter of fantasy, not knowledge. It is only when religious principles do not "remain merely principles"[16] – that is, when they are taken seriously and urged with zealotry in a work (a practice that Hume identifies with Roman Catholicism in particular) – that the work itself is disfigured. This is a way on Hume's part of radically deemphasizing the claims of art to instruct us on any matters of value in human life and of emphasizing instead that art is a matter of pleasure more than of knowledge.

Hence Hume instead casts pleasure in moving art as a function of eloquence, artfulness, and surface, not of insight. But while there is real pleasure in these things, in the end Hume's account is faithless to the depth and detail of our engagement with art. Alex Neill notes that Hume in fact offers no "sustained thought about tragedy. In fact, and despite the essay's title, Hume does not appear to have been particularly interested in tragedy at all."[17] When we think seriously about what it is like to watch or read *Hamlet* or *Oedipus at Colonus* or *The Man with a Flower in his Mouth*, then it is hard to believe that eloquence is the sole or primary focus of our attention. As Colin Lyas rightly remarks, "we are interested in far more than the looks and appearances of art."[18] We are also interested in how a work presents a subject matter as a focus for thought and emotional attitude, distinctively fused to the imaginative exploration of material.

Making-believe and quasi-emotions: Walton, Levinson, and Feagin

Kendall Walton likewise denies (1) but proposes a different explanation of what moves and pleases us in art. "We do not actually pity Willy Loman or

---

[15] Hume, "Of the Standard of Taste," p. 267.   [16] *ibid.*, p. 268.

[17] Alex Neill, "Hume's 'Singular Phenomenon,'" *British Journal of Aesthetics* 39, 2 (April 1999), pp. 112–25 at p. 115.

[18] Lyas, *Aesthetics*, p. 199.

grieve for Anna Karenina or admire Superman...nor do we feel contempt for Iago or worry about Tom Sawyer and Becky lost in the cave."[19] There are, after all, no really existing beings toward whom we might feel such emotions. Instead, Walton proposes, we make-believe that we feel these things. It is "fictional that we feel sorrow or terror."[20] We imagine, pretend, or make-believe that there are these people, and we imagine, pretend, or make-believe feeling appropriate emotions in response to their actions and plights. When we do this, we can frequently feel what Walton calls quasi-emotions, such as quasi-fear or quasi-terror. Feeling these involves having "constellations of sensations or other phenomenological experiences characteristic of real emotions"[21] – the felt quality of terror, say, but without the belief that anyone is in danger. Since we do not feel real emotions, the problem of tragedy collapses: there is no need to explain why we feel full-blooded painful emotions. (Walton notes, by the way, that there can be cases where we do feel full-blooded painful emotions as well as quasi-emotions. For example, we might make-believe in watching Eisenstein's film *Ivan the Terrible* that we are actually seeing people being slaughtered and so have quasi-emotions, but also feel genuine sorrow toward the actual, historical victims of the tyrant.[22] He also notes that being sad or sorrowful is not always in itself an unpleasant experience. Though what we are sad or sorrowful about may be unpleasant, it may be appropriate to feel sadness or sorrow, and one may enjoy feeling appropriately.[23])

As Walton is well aware, however, this way of solving the problem of tragedy immediately raises the questions of why we play such games of imagining, pretending, or making-believe and of what the relation is between the quasi-emotions that occur in the playing of these games and real emotions in daily life. Why do and should we bother to feel even quasi-emotions, since these may themselves be genuinely painful?[24] "What is to be gained from *fictionally* caring?" Walton asks. "What is in it for us? Why

---

[19] Walton, *Mimesis as Make-Believe*, p. 249.   [20] *ibid.*, p. 256.

[21] *ibid.*, p. 251.   [22] *ibid.*, p. 256.   [23] *ibid.*, p. 257.

[24] Alex Neill notes that Walton remains committed to the view that we do actually feel *something* (phenomenologically) in response to some fictional representations. "On [Walton's] view," Neill observes, we can actually be *moved* by works of fiction, but it is make-believe that what we are moved *to* is *fear*." (Alex Neill, "Fear, Fiction, and Make-Believe," *Journal of Aesthetics and Art Criticism* 49, 1 (winter 1991), pp. 47–56 at pp. 49B–50A.)

do we participate?"[25] Among the answers that Walton suggests are that we are trying out skills of emotional response, that we are purging ourselves of emotions, that it is enjoyable to do such things, and, above all, that by game-playing audiences arrive at "deepened awareness of themselves and their situations."[26] All of these suggestions seem apt answers to the first question of why we play such games. But they sidestep the second question: what is the relation between quasi-emotions and genuine emotions? If they are not identical – as Walton surely intends in calling them quasi-emotions – and quasi-emotions are only the phenomenological or felt accompaniments of genuine emotions, then how exactly are skills of responding with genuine emotion trained by experiencing quasi-emotions? How do we arrive by pretending at deepened awareness of which genuine emotions it is appropriate to feel when in daily life? Walton can reply to these questions that fictional or quasi-emotions are not identical with genuine ones, but are "close enough" that practice in response via quasi-emotions "carries over" into training in emotional response in daily life. But if quasi-emotions and genuine emotions are thus brought close together, then the terms *quasi-emotion* and *fictional emotion* seem introduced to solve the problem of tragedy by verbal fiat, for we seem in having quasi-emotions to care a good deal about Anna Karenina, Emma Bovary, King Lear, and so on, and this is what was initially puzzling.

We can see the same dilemma troubling Jerrold Levinson's similar account of emotional response to music. Along Walton's lines, Levinson claims that we feel emotions such as grief and sadness in response to music, but not in a "full-fledged"[27] way. The appropriate object of awareness (something really to be sad *about*) and physiological responses (crying or doing something about it) are largely absent. As a result, it is only "something *very much like* the arousal of negative emotions"[28] that we experience in listening to sad or mournful music. Often we *imagine* ourselves to experience the emotion expressed.[29] Like Walton, Levinson suggests that the benefits of the experience of something *very much like* an emotion or of imagining oneself to experience an emotion include enjoyment, understanding, reassurance that one is capable of powerful feeling,

[25] *ibid.*, p. 272; emphasis added.   [26] *ibid.*, p. 257.
[27] Jerrold Levinson, "Music and Negative Emotion," in *Music and Meaning*, ed. Jenefer Robinson (Ithaca, NY: Cornell University Press, 1997), pp. 215–41 at p. 217.
[28] *ibid.*   [29] See *ibid.*, pp. 234–36.

coherent work-guided development of an emotion, emotional closure, and a sense of oneself as having expressive power. But here too we must ask, are the quasi-emotions or imagined emotions real emotions? If they are quite unlike them, then the significance of experiencing them for our regular emotional life is unclear. If they are quite like them, then we are back with the puzzle of how and why we have *them* in response to "mere sound."

Susan Feagin suggests a solution along Walton's lines in proposing that in reading with feeling we often simulate the emotions and feelings of the characters we encounter. Perhaps what Walton calls the experience of quasi-emotion is better understood as a matter of taking oneself to be or to be in the position of the protagonist of a representation and so "feeling with" that figure. Both in ordinary life and when reading,

> One can shift or slide into a psychological "gear" wherein one uses one's own mind to model what another person does psychologically (the mental activity that person engages in) under certain conditions. This [modeling] activity is crucial to empathizing with actual people, and a similar phenomenon figures importantly in those emotional and affective responses known as empathizing with a fictional character...
> One empathizes with a fictional character, whom I shall call the protagonist, when one "shares" an emotion, feeling, desire, or mood of that character. The "sharing"...is done *through a simulation*, which explains not only what emotion or affect one has but also how one can come to be in the phenomenological state identified with that affect.[30]

As in Walton's account, the problem of how we respond with emotion to the plights of nonexistent characters is dissolved. There are no such actual characters, but we pretend that there are, and we further imagine that we are they. We simulate their doings and feelings, and so come ourselves to feel. The difference from Walton is that what we feel in simulating the mental activities of fictional characters are, according to Feagin, real emotions. Her account seems to capture much of what people mean when

[30] Susan L. Feagin, *Reading with Feeling* (Ithaca, NY: Cornell University Press, 1996), pp. 85–86, 81; emphasis added. Gregory Currie develops a similar simulationist view in "The Moral Psychology of Fiction," *Australasian Journal of Philosophy* 73 (1995), pp. 250–59 and "Realism of Character and the Value of Fiction," in *Aesthetics and Ethics: Essays at the Intersection*, ed. Jerrold Levinson (Cambridge: Cambridge University Press, 1998), pp. 161–81.

they remark that in reading a fiction (or watching a movie or a play) they learn "what it is like" to be another person.

But is Feagin's account of what happens quite right? Do I, for example, feel bitter vengefulness, masking my own feelings of a love I will not myself profess, toward Cordelia, when she refuses to proclaim her love publicly in empty clichés? Lear feels that toward her, and I am intensely interested in Lear and his feelings, and in Cordelia and hers. I typically also imagine what Lear may be thinking and feeling that might lead him to act as he does. But do I *feel his* bitter vengefulness (through simulating his mental activity)? This seems doubtful. As Noël Carroll notes in criticizing simulationism, in reading we typically learn about the thoughts and emotions of characters either because they tell us about them in dialogue or because they are revealed in the commentary of an omniscient narrator. "Character simulation" or oneself imaginatively adopting the viewpoint, thoughts, and emotions of another "is just not as pervasive as the simulation theorist suggests."[31] It seems even more doubtful that we simulate makers' or characters' emotions when we turn to parallel problems of emotional response in other media. Do I myself feel the manic energy and exhilaration that Jackson Pollock may have felt in painting *Blue Poles*? Do I feel either Elizabeth Bennett's embarrassment for her family or Jane Austen's amusement in and charity toward her characters? Carroll suggests not.

Elsewhere Feagin describes other modes of emotional response to fiction, usefully and aptly distinguishing sympathy from empathy. In empathizing, one "*simulates* the mental activity and processes of the one with whom one empathizes."[32] For example, I may imagine myself to be in Luke Skywalker's position and to feel his feelings as he maneuvers to fire the fatal rocket at the Death Star. Movies often invite empathy by using shots that make the point of view of their characters available to us. Lyric poetry similarly offers us a speaking voice with which to identify. In contrast, sympathizing requires only "having feelings or emotions that are in concert with the interests or desires the sympathizer (justifiably) attributes to the protagonist...[The sympathizer has] a desire that the specific interests or desires of the protagonist in question be satisfied."[33] This seems to capture much of the quality of my affective engagement and

---

[31] Noël Carroll, "Art and Ethical Criticism: An Overview of Recent Directions of Research," *Ethics* 110, 2 (January 2000), pp. 350–87 at p. 373.
[32] *ibid.*, p. 113.   [33] *ibid.*, p. 114.

interest in the careers of fictional characters. I desire that the aestheticizing manipulativeness of Adam Verver in *The Golden Bowl* should be exposed, but I do not imagine myself doing this, nor do I imagine myself to have his experiences and attitudes. I was rooting against him. No problem about either my having mere quasi-emotions or about my matching my feelings to his is raised. It is my rooting that makes his exposure satisfying to me. Likewise, in watching *The Graduate* I root for Benjamin Braddock (Dustin Hoffman) to win Elaine Robinson (Katharine Ross) but without imagining that I am Benjamin or that I have his experiences – or so, at least, Feagin's distinction suggests.

But again a fundamental question seems sidestepped. Adam Verver and Benjamin Braddock do not exist as real people. They are fictional characters. How can I come to root against and for such beings? And how are we to account for cases in which we do empathize with fictional characters?

Metaphorical identification: Danto and Cohen

In moving from accounts that emphasize pretending, making-believe, and simulating to an account that emphasizes the importance of sympathy in emotional response, we are coming close to retracting (3) straightforwardly and to holding that we can be directly moved by the career and fate of a fictional subject or a depicted subject matter, even when subject or subject matter have no further existence apart from the work. Why should we not say this? It seems possible for me to care directly about numbers of things that do not exist: say, perfect justice, my own fluent performance of Bach's cello suites, the future of my children. But while this is a start, and (3) is false, it remains puzzling how we come to care about the careers of fictional characters and to respond to representations of nonactual subject matter. When I care about the future of my children, I care about something that will matter to them and to me. They will live through their futures in some measures or absences of happiness and meaningfulness. They will experience them. But just what are the mechanics of the process of coming to care about a fictional protagonist?

Instead of focusing on the products of our engagements with representational art – quasi-emotions, imagined emotions, models, and the like – we might do better to characterize directly just what we do in attending to works of art to which we respond emotionally and affectively. Arthur

Danto endorses what he describes as "Hegel's wonderful thought [that] the work exists for the spectator and not on its own account: it exists, as he says, only for the individual apprehending it, so that the apprehension completes the work and gives it final substance."[34] This is more than a little obscure. In order to unpack this obscurity, Danto suggests that what Hegel has in mind is that

> each work is about the "I" that reads the text, identifying himself...
> with the actual subject of the text in such a way that each work
> becomes a metaphor for each reader: perhaps the same metaphor for
> each...[Though] it is literally false that I am Achilles, or Leopold Bloom,
> or Anna Karenin, or Oedipus or King Lear or Hyacinth Robinson or
> Strether or Lady Glencora; or a man hounded by an abstract bureaucracy
> because of an unspecified or suspected accusation, or the sexual slave O,
> [I become each of these beings metaphorically in the act of reading]. The
> work finds its subject only when read.[35]

The work is, in the end, about me and every other reader, not descriptively, but metaphorically.

Ted Cohen claims similarly that in reading works of imaginative narrative literature we are taking up what he calls "metaphors of personal identification" and so seeing ourselves, more or less, as Lily Bart (in Edith Wharton's *House of Mirth*), Jake Gittes (in Polanski's *Chinatown*), and Marlow (in Conrad's *Heart of Darkness*), just as David recognizes himself as the slayer of the poor man's one ewe lamb in the story told by the prophet Nathan.[36] "How real is this capacity [thus to identify ourselves with others]? How secure?" Cohen wonders.[37] Its mechanics and limits are unclear in both art and life. Yet we do thus identify with others, in both art and life, to some extent through acts of imagination and imaginative attention. Following J. L. Austin, Cohen notes that we do sometimes understand the emotions and thoughts of others, and we do so not via introspecting them, but via an "act of imagination" in which we "entertain...a metaphorical identity."[38] It is, Cohen claims,

---

[34] Danto, "Philosophy as/and/of Literature," p. 170, citing, he says, Hegel, *Aesthetik*, in *Werke*, vol. XV, p. 28.

[35] *ibid.*

[36] See Cohen, "Identifying with Metaphor: Metaphors of Personal Identification," *Journal of Aesthetics and Art Criticism* 57, 4 (fall 1999), pp. 399–409.

[37] *ibid.*, p. 405A.   [38] *ibid.*, p. 408A.

the *same* achievement when we (i) appreciate a fictional narrative by identifying with its characters, (ii) appreciate a work, narrative or not, fictional or not, by identifying with its artist, where this requires imagining oneself to be making those marks, or writing those words, or sounding that music, and (iii) engage in genuine moral exchange, where this requires getting a sense of things as felt by one's opponent.[39]

Against this talk of metaphorical identification, Walton, Levinson, and Feagin can reply that their own talk of making-believe, quasi-emotion, and simulation provides a deeper analysis of what is going on. Danto describes the *apprehension* of oneself *as* Anna Karenina or Lambert Strether in the text, and Cohen describes metaphorical identification as an imaginative act. Walton, Levinson, and Feagin can plausibly be understood to be specifying what such apprehensions and imaginative acts consist in, that is, to be explaining exactly what and how we are doing when we do them. These explanations are appealing. But just why do we feel ourselves to need them? Perhaps it is because at bottom Walton, Levinson, and Feagin each take the paradigm, central case of understanding something to be the recognitive perception of an object present to the senses. They perhaps feel an urge to explain in detail how we identify with and understand fictional texts (and paintings and works of music and movies) in part because the understanding of these works seems so much less clear to them than telling a hawk from a handsaw. Something like the imaginative processing of information taken from the mere physical marks or sounds out of which a work is constituted must be going on, and it seems reasonable to try to say what that processing-in-imagination is.

Danto and Cohen perhaps feel this urge less strongly. They are less oriented toward recognitive perception as the central cognitive act, and they are struck by the primitive mystery and wonder of the fact that we sometimes do manage, somehow and to some degree, to understand another person in real life. To them, it seems more apt and useful to compare the imaginative understanding of art to this primitive, mysterious, and wonderful understanding of another. We have no account of the mechanisms of processing through which we do this, and any account that might be offered of these mechanisms seems likely to miss or betray the content of what we understand about another. For them, seeing oneself as another, in an act of imaginative, metaphorical identification, is a mysteriously

---

[39] *ibid.*

emergent and unanalyzable human ability. Our feeling with and about another then attaches directly to apt exercises of this ability.

Aristotle on catharsis

Even if, however, we cannot aptly specify the mechanics of imaginative metaphorical identification and attendant emotional response, we might nonetheless wonder *what* we tend most persistently and strongly to identify with in others, in art and in life, when we see ourselves "in" them. In the *Poetics* Aristotle takes up this question, as he argues that the function of tragedy is to accomplish "by means of pity and terror the catharsis of such emotions."[40] Just what does Aristotle mean by pity (*eleos*) and terror (*deos*; fear), and how is feeling these emotions toward protagonists in tragedy an aspect of metaphorical identification with them?

In the *Rhetoric* Aristotle defines pity as

> a feeling of pain caused by the sight of some evil, destructive or painful, which befalls one who does not deserve it, and which we might expect to befall ourselves or some friend of ours, and moreover, to befall us soon. In order to feel pity, we must obviously be capable of supposing that some evil may happen to us or some friend of ours ... What we fear for ourselves excites our pity when it happens to others.[41]

"Fear," he tells us,

> is caused by whatever we feel has great power of destroying us, or of harming us in ways that tend to cause us great pain ... Fear is felt by those who believe that something is likely to happen to them, at the hands of a particular person, in a particular form, and at a particular time ... Consequently, when it is advisable that the audience should be frightened, the orator must make them feel that they really are in danger of something, pointing out that it has happened to others who were stronger than they are, and is happening, or has happened, to

---

[40] Aristotle, *Poetics*, p. 7.

[41] Aristotle, *Rhetoric*, trans. W. Rhys Roberts, in *The Basic Works of Aristotle*, ed. Richard McKeon (New York: Random House, 1941), pp. 1325–451, Book II, ch. 8, 1385b, 1386a, pp. 1396, 1398. I thank my colleague, Grace Ledbetter, for directing me toward Aristotle's discussions of pity and fear in the *Rhetoric*.

people like themselves, at the hands of unexpected people, in an unexpected form, and at an unexpected time.[42]

These definitions make it clear that pitying another and fearing for another involve seeing *oneself* as in the same or similar situations as another – facing the same or similar problems, subject to the same or similar misfortunes and losses. If something is utterly unlike ourselves, then we cannot pity it or fear for it. Pity and fear get no foothold for us with a rock or a distant star. If we manage to pity or fear for the fly struggling in the spider's web, that is because we take ourselves, rightly or wrongly, to share a sensate life with it, and we see ourselves in it. To pity and fear for another involves both sympathy and apprehensiveness: feeling with another that an undeserved misfortune of the kind we ourselves might suffer is imminent. The same structure of seeing oneself in another and feeling with another is part also of the inverses of pity and fear: admiration and exhilaration. We admire another who accomplishes what we too think worth accomplishing or wish to accomplish; we are exhilarated in imagining ourselves doing likewise. Openness to emotions of this kind that involve seeing oneself in another is part of the human form of life from very early ages on.[43] The structure of these emotions allows us to make some sense of the claims of Danto and Cohen that metaphorical identification is a natural human ability that can be exercised in both life and art, without recourse to quasi-emotions or to make-believe. In sympathizing, being apprehensive, fearing, and pitying, and also in admiring and being exhilarated, we see ourselves as Anna Karenina or Luke Skywalker, in that we take ourselves immediately to share with them a common humanity, with all its liabilities and prospects. The kind of thing that happens to them might happen to us. In reading or viewing their careers, we have the sense not so much that we *are* them or are simulating their point of view, but rather that a common humanity with common liabilities and

---

[42] *ibid.*, Book II, ch. 5, 1382a, 1382b, 1383a, pp. 1389, 1390–391, 1391.

[43] On the basis of fieldwork with great apes and with children, Michael Tomasello argues that seeing others as having a point of view, being able to identify with them, being able to imagine oneself having that point of view are abilities that are unique to human beings. These abilities have a biological basis, but they then emerge explicitly only through socialization progressively from the age of six months to into the third year. See Tomasello, *Cultural Origins of Human Cognition*. These are also leading ideas of Wittgenstein's in *Philosophical Investigations*.

prospects is distributed among us, audiences and fictional protagonists alike.

To have our emotions subjected to catharsis[44] is then to have these emotions clarified: to have it made clear to one the kinds of things – actions, events, incidents, characters, gestures – that are properly pitiable, fearful, admirable, exhilarating, and so on – for human beings such as we are. In dwelling reflectively at length on the details of particular cases, it can become evident that emotions are partly matters of immediate fellow-feeling but partly also matters of rational understanding of and response to shared human problems, possibilities, and liabilities. As Aristotle and Walton both hold, the work of the catharsis of emotion makes our emotions both more stable and more reasonably apt to their objects in life as well as in art.

Many more things are pitiable, fearful, admirable, and exhilarating, however, and properly so, than Aristotle supposed. *Contra* Aristotle, we do not care only or centrally about well-being (*eudaimonia*) and its achievement or inhibition.[45] We have a greater sense than Aristotle that any achievement of well-being is fragile, uncertain, and housed within social structures in which that achievement is not readily open to everyone. We think that the struggle to achieve well-being, reciprocity, and expressive freedom[46] never quite comes to an unambiguously successful end.

Artistic making and the "working through" of emotion

Yet we continue to pity the pitiable, fear the fearful, and admire the admirable in life and in art, and in successful art the nature of these objects of emotion is worked through and clarified. This is the difference, in the end, between the story of Lambert Strether, on the one hand, and the greeting card and the skit with Larry the Lobster, on the other. Soliciting and working through emotional response occur as well in media of art that are not narrative. Recall Cohen's observation that it is "the *same* achievement when we (i) appreciate a fictional narrative by identifying with its characters, (ii) appreciate a work, narrative or not, fictional or not, by identifying with its artist, where this requires imagining oneself

---

[44] See the discussion of the catharsis of emotions in chapter 2 above.
[45] See Eldridge, "How can Tragedy Matter for Us?" and chapter 2 above.
[46] See chapter 1 above.

to be making those marks, or writing those words, or sounding that music." We can identify with the patient, attentive rendering and faithfulness to an object that are present in a Cézanne still life or landscape, and we can feel the emotions of stillness, attentiveness, and success in rendering that we imagine to inhabit Cézanne's own working of his materials. We can experience the shifts of space and the relations of abstract form to human figure that we may suppose to have occupied Anthony Caro's attention in forming his sculptures. These sculptures have what Michael Fried usefully describes as a syntax[47] – a structure that shapes an order of experience and that invites and sustains attention and emotion in relation to one's embodied self. William Rubin notes that "In Caro's work, scale is not just a matter of internal aesthetic relations, but is fixed by the height of the human being and relates to his size in a literal way ... Caro's works are fixed in rapport to the height of the eye and the viewer's perception of the floor."[48] In forming his sculptures, Caro is himself is working through visual experiences of surprise, order, coherence, and wit; in viewing them we follow him and participate in the emotions that attend these visual experiences. Or in music we can follow and imaginatively participate in the working of motivic material as dramatic tension is developed and resolved.

The reason why identifications with artists and imaginative participation in experiences and emotions are available to us is that works of art are made things, products or instances of human action. To understand an action, including actions of artistic making, is to understand its suitable motivation by reasons in contexts. (If there are no reasons available to us that motivate an action, our sense that what is in question is an *action* lapses, and we tend to see what occurs as mere reaction or happenstance.) Actions of artistic making, including the making of both narrative art and nonnarrative art, are concerned with the shaping of materials to hold attention on a presented subject matter. (In abstract work, the presented subject matters are often centrally the perception and gestural action of the artist and the possibility of the audience's imaginative participation in that perception and gestural action.) Whatever emotions

---

[47] See Michael Fried, "Anthony Caro's Table Sculptures, 1966–77," in M. Fried, *Art and Objecthood: Essays and Reviews* (Chicago, IL: University of Chicago Press, 1998), pp. 202–09.

[48] William Rubin, *Anthony Caro* (Boston, MA: New York Graphic Society, 1975), cited *ibid.*, p. 204.

figure in attention to this subject matter are emotions that members of the audience are solicited to experience and explore, as they participate in the attention that is embodied in the work.[49]

As Frank Palmer notes, "understanding human action" – including actions of artistic making and presentation – "is saturated with moral concepts."[50] When someone does something, either in the plot of a narrative work or in the making and presenting of art in general, wherein a subject matter is presented as a focus for thought and emotion, then we see that doing as variously attentive, lazy, guilty, kind, cruel, affectionate, melancholic, forgiving, remorseful, exhilarated, and so on. The attitudes that can be expressed toward a subject matter in the artistic working of materials are as various as the attitudes that we can have toward the phenomena of human life, and they are always present. When we follow the work as an instance or product of human action, then we follow and participate in the emotional attitudes that are expressed in it. In this way, as Palmer puts it, the work "gets us to see something and not merely to know"[51] it descriptively or at second hand; we "dwell in the experience"[52] of attending to the subject matter that the work presents. If the work is less successful, then attention to the subject matter is incoherent, halting, or interrupted. The unsuccessful work will seem to us to be determined in its form not by coherent attention, but by shifting personal needs that are not worked through, or by market forces and a wish to pander to an audience or provoke a scene, or by sentimentality, in which the emotion

---

[49] Here I am close to Richard Shusterman's suggestion that all works of art, as products of action, have an implicit dramatic structure, in "working through" an emotion related to a subject matter. See Richard Shusterman, "Art as Dramatization," *Journal of Aesthetics and Art Criticism* 59, 4 (fall 2001), pp. 363–72, especially p. 370A inf., where Shusterman describes the "knot of productive tension that binds art's heightened experience to its formal staging." See also my own earlier suggestion that fiction makes possible the comparatively free exploration of the dramatic structure of emotions in relation to their proper objects in Eldridge, *On Moral Personhood*, pp. 11–12.

[50] Frank Palmer, *Literature and Moral Understanding* (Oxford: Clarendon Press, 1992), p. 2.

[51] *ibid.*, p. 193.

[52] *ibid.*, p. 203, taking this phrase from David Pole, *Aesthetics, Form and Emotion*, ed. G. Roberts (New York: St. Martin's Press, 1983), p. 11.

is prepackaged rather than worked through in an act of attention.[53] If the work is successful, then we participate in a coherent emotional attitude toward its subject matter, and that emotional attitude is clarified in an act of full attention that is expressed in the work. We sense and feel that it is apt to feel pity and terror (toward the situation and prospects of a shared humanity) toward this developing action in a plot, or we sense and feel that it is apt to feel admiration and exhilaration and this interplay of intelligence and wit, or we sense and feel that it is apt to feel a majestic elegiac calm at this landscape or developing musical phrase.

Collingwood describes a kind of lightening and easing of mind that occurs in the successful act of artistic expression.[54] A helpless and oppressive sense of feeling we know not what is converted into "the same emotion...accompanied by a new feeling of alleviation or easement."[55] The feeling of alleviation or easement that attaches to the same emotion thus transfigured is due to the achieved sense that it is natural and apt to feel just this emotion, in full and coherent attention to the subject matter presented. This explains, among other things, why Walton is right to say that we do not always find the experience of being sad to be painful. Sometimes in feeling sad we have an achieved sense also that it is apt to feel just this sadness toward just these subject matters, and that achieved sense has its own satisfactions.

We do feel infinitely graded mixtures of pity, fear, remorse, exhilaration, delight, awe, calm, and many other emotions toward the phenomena of life – including toward such things as experiences of space, landscape, and gestural action, not only toward the kinds of subject matters that are presented in plots in narrative art. Artists express these emotions, thus

---

[53] Rick Anthony Furtak provides a nice account of sentimentality as a form of evasiveness and a failure to engage with reality in "Poetics of Sentimentality," *Philosophy and Literature* 26, 1 (April 2002), pp. 207–15. In commenting on this essay during a conference presentation at the 2001 meeting of the American Society for Aesthetics in Minneapolis, Alex Neill noted that it is possible to distinguish two different senses of "sentimentality": indulgence in tender feelings (with which there is nothing *per se* wrong); and indulgence in evasive, inappropriate feelings (which is to be deplored). One might add that a connection between these two senses is that often (though not always or necessarily) tender feelings *are* indulged in as a way of escaping from life and clear-sightedness into mawkishness.

[54] Collingwood, *Principles of Art*, pp. 109–10.   [55] *ibid.*, p. 117.

transfiguring and easing them in a kind of clarification of their specific aptness to their specific subject matters, in acts of full attention to the subject matter, which acts are themselves achieved in the working of the materials of a medium of art. In following that working of materials, we participate in the artist's attention, emotion, and expression. How and why we respond with feeling needs no more explanation than this.

9 Art and morality

Some controversial cases: Mapplethorpe, Serrano, Finley, and others

In 1989 national protests erupted in response to a decision by the US-government-funded National Endowment for the Arts to support exhibitions featuring Robert Mapplethorpe, whose work included homoerotic photographs, and Andres Serrano, whose work included *Piss Christ*, a 5 foot by 3 foot photograph of a wood and plastic crucifix floating suspended in the artist's urine. In response to the protests, Congress enacted a law directing the NEA to "take into consideration general standards of decency and respect for the diverse beliefs and values of the American public" in awarding grants.[1]

In June 1990 NEA chairman John Frohnmayer, citing this law and describing their work as "indecent," then vetoed awards to four artists – Karen Finley, Holly Hughes, Tim Miller, and John Fleck – that had been recommended by a NEA peer review panel. Hughes, Miller, and Fleck are gay and deal with homosexual issues in their work.[2] Finley's most notorious work is her 1989 performance piece *We Keep Our Victims Ready*, inspired by the case of Tawana Brawley, a 15-year-old girl who was found on November 28, 1987 alive near her home in upstate New York, covered with feces and wearing only a Hefty trash bag. Ms. Brawley claimed to have been abducted and assaulted by three or six white police officers. After several weeks of investigation, a grand jury concluded "there is nothing in regard to Tawana Brawley's appearance on November 28 that is inconsistent with this condition having been self-inflicted."[3] In her performance piece, Finley asks about Brawley's staging of her abduction and discovery:

---

[1] Information archived at http://eclipse.barnard.columbia.edu/~sg280/.

[2] Information archived at http://www.thefileroom.org/FileRoom/documents/Cases/338neafour.html

[3] A full account of the Brawley case is archived at http://www.courttv.com/legaldocs/newsmakers/tawana/index.html

"Was this the best choice? What was the worst choice? What was the other choice? All of us have that moment where puttin' the shit on us is the best choice we have." At the end of the piece, after smearing herself with feces-symbolic chocolate, Finley covers herself with tinsel because, she says, "no matter how bad a woman is treated, she still knows how to get dressed for dinner."[4]

Finley, Hughes, Miller, and Fleck – the so-called NEA Four – sued the NEA for unconstitutionally restricting their freedom of speech. In 1996 the United States Court of Appeals for the ninth circuit ruled that the phrase "decency and respect for the diverse beliefs and values" was un-constitutionally vague. The Justice Department then appealed the case to the Supreme Court. In an 8-to-1 decision, the court ruled to uphold the statute.[5]

What are we to make of these cases? Do the works of Mapplethorpe and Serrano and of the NEA Four contribute to moral understanding? They each seem designed to make some point about values; they are not only exercises in decoration or form, even where formal arrangement is a con-sideration in the work. But how, then, are they works of art and different from theoretical moral argument? Or are they, as detractors urged and as Frohnmayer apparently agreed, indecent polemics that do not deserve government support? Perhaps artists should even be prohibited from ex-hibiting work that – so it is argued – undermines "public morality." Should such works be defended – if one is inclined to defend them – by establish-ing that they instead offer genuine moral insight, on the one hand, or by establishing that they are, as art, "above morality," in having autonomous and independent artistic value, on the other? What, if anything, does art have to do with morality?

These works are the latest and most widely discussed ones in the art and morality controversy, but the controversy itself is far from new. Plato urged that artists should be prohibited from producing or performing work that undermined public order and the stability of the ideally just government, if it should ever come to exist. Tolstoy admitted that any works that are emotionally infectious by means of color, line, and form count as art but held that the very best works that excel in both formal expressiveness and subject matter must express "the religious perception

---

[4] Finley discussed her piece in a lecture at Harvard, reported in the Harvard Gazette and archived at http://www.news.harvard.edu/gazette/2002/02.14/06-finley.html

[5] Information on the court cases is archived at http://eclipse.barnard.columbia.edu/~sg280/

of our time,"[6] particularly as exemplified in the Christian Gospel. The novelist John Gardner criticized the nihilism, absurdism, and avant-gardism of contemporary art and urged a return to moral fiction that investigates the conditions of human fulfillment.[7] Representations, artistic and otherwise, are widely thought to have some effect on the sensibility and behavior of those who view or read them. Access to adult movies is regulated in order to prevent harm to minors. In a 1973 obscenity case, Chief Justice Burger based his verdict in favor of community regulation of the distribution of films and magazines in part on the "assumption that commerce in obscene books, or public exhibitions focused on obscene conduct, have a tendency to exert a corrupt and debasing impact leading to antisocial behavior."[8] Parents pay considerable attention to what their children read and view, whether or not it is art, and parents and teachers alike often seek to influence the development of sensibility, judgment, and behavior in the young by putting what they take to be elevating representations before them. Clearly, when artists make a work they are doing something. Should not what they do be subject to moral assessment along with all other actions? Perhaps much art is morally innocent, perhaps some is praiseworthy, and perhaps some is dangerous. Why not look and see?

Autonomism and experimentalism

Yet exactly what the effects of reading or viewing works of art are is unclear. As Anne Sheppard notes, the Williams Report on Obscenity and Film Censorship in Britain found that "the psychological research which has been done on the effects of obscene or violent visual material has produced only inconclusive results."[9] Noël Carroll observes that "rates of violence [are] lower in Japan than in the United States, despite the fact that Japanese programming is much more graphic in its depiction of gore and mayhem than American programming."[10]

The effects of representations on audiences seem even more unclear in the case of art. Richard Posner argues that "great literature somehow

---

[6] Tolstoy, *What is Art?*, p. 145.

[7] John Gardner, *On Moral Fiction* (New York: Harper Collins, 1978).

[8] US Supreme Court 413 US 49 (1973), cited in Karen Hanson, "How Bad Can Good Art Be?," in *Aesthetics and Ethics*, ed. Levinson, pp. 204–26 at p. 213.

[9] Sheppard, *Aesthetics*, p. 140.

[10] Noël Carroll, "Morality and Aesthetics: Historical and Conceptual Overview," in *Encyclopedia of Aesthetics*, ed. Kelly, vol. III, pp. 279–82 at p. 280A.

causes the reader to suspend moral judgments,"[11] as though works of literary art presented a self-contained imaginary world that is altogether insulated from our own. Developing this line of reasoning more fully, Monroe Beardsley notes that the writer of a work of fiction "does not make an assertion, at least on the Report level."[12] Nothing is urged on anyone. The literary work "is not a 'message,' and not in the ordinary sense a 'communication,' since it is not an assertion and therefore claims to convey no information."[13] At best ideas are entertained or suggested, and there is little risk of harm in gazing on self-contained imaginative products from without.

> Of course literary works cannot be understood apart from their language; of course they have social roots and fruits; of course their enjoyment requires in the reader an elaborate set of previous adjustments in belief and feeling; of course the themes and theses of literary works are taken from, or contributed to, the whole life of man. But what makes literature literature, in part, must be some withdrawal from the world about it, an unusual degree of self-containedness and self-sufficiency that makes it capable of being contemplated with satisfaction in itself. And the secret of this detachment seems to lie in its capacity to play with, and to swallow up in its design, all the vast array of human experiences, including beliefs, without that personal allegiance and behavioral commitment to them that constitutes assertion in the fullest sense.[14]

Withdrawal from the world into self-containedness seems to apply even more fully to abstract paintings and works of pure instrumental music, which seem, as Carroll puts it, to "have no moral dimension" such that "it is just conceptually confused to attempt to assess them morally."[15]

It is tempting, then, to conclude that art is its own practice with its own distinct values. William Gass, for example, claims that "artistic quality depends upon a work's internal, formal, organic character, upon its inner system of relations, upon its style and structure, and not upon the morality it is presumed to recommend."[16] Or, as Oscar Wilde notoriously

---

[11] Richard Posner, "Against Ethical Criticism," *Philosophy and Literature* 21, 1 (April 1997), pp. 1–27 at p. 7.

[12] Beardsley, *Aesthetics*, p. 421.   [13] *ibid.*, p. 423.   [14] *ibid*, pp. 436–37.

[15] Carroll, "Morality and Aesthetics," p. 280A.

[16] William Gass, "Goodness Knows Nothing of Beauty: On the Distance Between

remarks even more sharply, "There is no such thing as a moral or an immoral book. Books are well written or badly written. That is all... The only excuse for making a useless thing is that one admires it intensely. All art is quite useless."[17]

Carroll dubs positions of this kind *autonomism*, and he notes that it comes in two forms. Extreme autonomism holds that no work of art ever has any moral value, good or bad, as Wilde's remark suggests.[18] Moderate autonomism holds that while some (but not all) works of art are morally worthwhile or morally pernicious, their moral value has nothing to do with their value as art. Morality and artistic value are two independent dimensions of assessment; moral evaluation "is never aesthetic evaluation."[19] Posner, Beardsley, and Gass are all closer to this version of autonomism.

A third position likewise sharply rejects didacticism and emphasizes the obtuseness of censorship and the folly of worrying about the moral consequences of the experience of art. This third position accepts, however, that works of art often, perhaps typically, have moral value, but embraces an open-ended moral experimentalism. Works of art, especially works of imaginative literature, are means of marking out new eligible paths of life and of enlarging sensibilities that are all too prone to impoverishment. Outright cruelty apart, nearly anything goes, in life and in art. Even what counts as cruelty may be unclear, especially between consenting adults. J. S. Mill's harm principle that no one is justified in interfering with another for that other's own good is frequently cited in order to justify this position. As Mill himself puts it,

> The only purpose for which power can be rightfully exercised over any member of a civilised community, against his will, is to prevent harm to others. His own good, either physical or moral, is not a sufficient warrant. He cannot rightfully be compelled to do or forbear because it will be better for him to do so, because it will make him happier,

---

Morality and Art," in *Reflecting on Art*, ed. John Fisher (Mountain View, CA: Mayfield Press, 1993), p. 115.

[17] Oscar Wilde, "Preface," *The Picture of Dorian Gray*, ed. Peter Ackroyd (Harmondsworth: Penguin, 1982), p. 5.

[18] See Carroll, "Morality and Aesthetics," p. 280B and Noël Carroll, "Moderate Moralism," *British Journal of Aesthetics* 36, 3 (1996), pp. 223–37.

[19] Carroll, "Morality and Aesthetics," p. 281B.

because in the opinions of others, to do so would be wise, or even right. These are good reasons for remonstrating with him, or reasoning with him, or persuading him, or entreating him, but not for compelling him, or visiting him with any evil in case he do otherwise. To justify that, the conduct from which it is desired to deter him must be calculated to produce evil to some one else. The only part of the conduct of any one, for which he is amenable to society, is that which concerns others. In the part which merely concerns himself, his independence is, of right, absolute. Over himself, over his own body and mind, the individual is sovereign.[20]

This is, for Mill, explicitly and exclusively a political principle. Others *may* be reasoned with, persuaded, and entreated, if not compelled. But Mill's position does explicitly rule out almost all censorship, unless it can be shown ("calculated") that direct harm to others does result from the production and circulation of certain works of art. When the harm principle is politically established and censorship is loosened, then it is natural to let a thousand flowers bloom and a hundred schools of thought contend. Let each individual judge what artistic works and moral values he or she favors, without worrying so much about moral education. Friedrich Schlegel favored this kind of artistic and moral experimentalism in arguing that "the will of the poet can tolerate no law above itself."[21] John Dewey argues similarly that

> It belongs to the very character of the creative mind to reach out and seize any material that stirs it so that the value of the material may be pressed out and become the matter of a new experience...One of the functions of art is precisely to sap the moralistic timidity that causes the mind to shy away from some materials and to refuse to admit them into the clear and purifying light of perceptive consciousness.[22]

In a Deweyan experimentalist spirit and citing Nietzsche as a further precursor, Richard Rorty urges us to follow strong poets, to embrace life and

---

[20] J. S. Mill, "On Liberty," in J. S. Mill, *Utilitarianism; On Liberty; Essay on Bentham*, ed. Mary Warnock (New York: New American Library, 1974), pp. 126–250 at p. 135.

[21] Friedrich Schlegel, "Athenaeum Fragments 116," in Friedrich Schlegel, *Philosophical Fragments*, trans. Peter Firchow (Minneapolis, MN: University of Minnesota Press, 1991), p. 32.

[22] Dewey, *Art and Experience*, p. 189.

libidinal energy, and to overcome our tendencies to small-mindedness and fearfulness.[23] Engaging with imaginative art of all kinds is, Rorty argues, likely to nurture such efforts. Defenders of experimentalism often recommend Kleist's *The Marquise of O* and the Marquis de Sade's *Juliette* as morally unconventional works of art that might help to widen our sensibilities.

Controversial works are frequently defended by invoking both autonomism and experimentalism. The art critic Lucy Lippard makes a case for the significance and value of Serrano's *Piss Christ* by arguing that it "is a darkly beautiful photographic image ... the small wood and plastic crucifix becomes virtually monumental as it floats, photographically enlarged, in a deep rosy glow that is both ominous and glorious."[24] Here Lippard appeals to a formal value – beauty – the instancing of which in artifacts is taken to be a central function of art, distinct from other functions fulfilled within other practices and capable, perhaps, of overriding other meanings. But Lippard also characterizes *Piss Christ* as offering unfamiliar insights and so provoking the enlargement of sensibility. Serrano, according to Lippard, is concerned to denounce cheapened and commercial religious institutions and to present genuine religious commitment as incorporating, at least sometimes, an ecstatic acceptance of the human body, including every aspect of its flesh and fluids.[25]

In reaction to such appeals to formal values and provocative meanings, some viewers of the work are likely to feel puzzled or outraged. Surely *Piss Christ* is neither beautiful nor insightfully provocative just because Serrano or Lippard says it is. In 1975, well before the wide notoriety of Serrano, Finley, bodily performance art, and other forms of avant-gardism, Tom Wolfe already worried that avant-gardism had degenerated into a stale, repetitive, formally and cognitively insignificant game of "*épatez le bourgeoisie*, shock the middle class,"[26] driven only by adolescent rebelliousness and commercialism rather than by any genuine concern for art. But then

---

[23] See especially Richard Rorty, "The Contingency of Selfhood," in R. Rorty, *Contingency, Irony, and Solidarity* (Cambridge: Cambridge University Press, 1989), pp. 23–43.

[24] Lucy Lippard, "The Spirit and the Letter," *Art in America* 80, 4 (April 1990), pp. 238–45 at p. 239. I base my account of Lippard's defense of Serrano on Cynthia Freeland's discussion of it in her *But is it Art?*, pp. 18–26.

[25] See the discussion of Lippard's defense of the meritorious thematic content or meaning of Serrano's work in Freeland, *But is it Art?*, pp. 20–21.

[26] See Wolfe, *Painted Word*, p. 14.

this is as it may be, depending on the historical reasons that can be discerned to figure in the production of avant-garde work and on the critical elucidations of an avant-garde work's formal and cognitive significance that can be constructed.[27] Stravinsky, Joyce, and Courbet scandalized taste in their time, yet their works prove to have lasting formal and cognitive value.

Historically, varieties of autonomism or aestheticism, urging the practice of "art for art's sake," may well have arisen, as Carroll has suggested, as "an art world maneuver to protect artworks from censorship...in response to Plato and his puritanical descendants" and as a defensive response against the spread of bourgeois culture and philistine instrumentalism: "aestheticism attempted to seal off art hermetically from the surrounding bourgeois and mass cultures by declaring art to be autonomous,"[28] separating high art by fiat from commerce, entertainment, and kitsch. Against these developments, Carroll is himself concerned to maintain connections between art and life, among other things by endorsing the moral and cognitive interest of mass art, including such genres as the detective story and the horror film.[29]

Moral experimentalism in the styles of Schlegel, Mill, Nietzsche, Dewey, and Rorty has even deeper roots in cultural developments than aestheticism does. Advances in technology have made more possibilities of life, including more material satisfactions, available to more people. While these advances may well have significant ecological limits, and while the material satisfactions they enable are, though widespread, still largely limited to the middle and upper classes of industrialized societies, the pursuit of material satisfactions of many kinds seems unlikely to lapse significantly. Modern mathematical-physical science typically (even if not necessarily) depends on and helps to articulate a materialist metaphysics that puts pressure on religious understandings of human nature and its fit expression. (Schlegel, Mill, Nietzsche, Dewey, and Rorty all knew themselves to be opponents of the great bulk of organized religion.) As a result,

---

[27] See chapter 6 in this book.

[28] Carroll, "Art and Ethical Criticism," pp. 351, 352.

[29] See Noël Carroll, *The Philosophy of Horror, or Paradoxes of the Heart* (London: Routledge, 1990) and Noël Carroll, *A Philosophy of Mass Art* (Oxford: Clarendon Press, 1998). Carroll describes his motivation to connect art with life explicitly in the introduction to *Beyond Aesthetics: Philosophical Essays* (Cambridge: Cambridge University Press, 2001).

a fairly free moral experimentalism seems likely for the foreseeable future to remain the norm in both art and life, with the consequence that wide varieties of artistic avant-gardism will continue to be practiced, tolerated, and largely encouraged. Making and engaging with experimentalist art seem likely to continue to be regarded as activities that are insulated – both in fact and for good reason – to some extent from the political incursions of limiting moralisms, and this is, on the whole, a good thing. Controversies about the value of artistically experimental works that function as vehicles of moral experimentalism are likely to persist, with competing remonstrations, persuasions, and entreaties on all sides, within an institutional setting of political openness, and properly so.

Against extreme autonomism, extreme aestheticism, or "art for art's sake," Carroll notes that historically "art is impure" in mixing "freely and naturally with other realms of human practice,"[30] such as religion, education, the cultivation of social solidarity, and the display of wealth and power. Attempts to specify an essence of art as a matter of having "purely aesthetic interest" have foundered, Carroll argues, in the face of works such as John Cage's 4′ 33″ that have little formal interest,[31] while talk of art as intended to afford an experience "valuable for its own sake" is countered by works that have liturgical, devotional, political, or utilitarian uses, such as altarpieces, tribal masks, and drinking bowls.[32]

One might, then, revert to moderate autonomism – the position of Posner and Gass – and hold that artistic value is independent of any other uses and values a work may have. While any bowl may be intended for drinking, whether it is a work of art will depend only on its shaping and decoration, say. While any hymn may be intended for use as a vehicle of devotion, whether it is art will depend only on its melodic, harmonic, and rhythmic structure and on the skill employed in setting its text. As Gass puts it, the artistic value of a work depends on its "internal, formal, organic character" alone. But this too cannot be right, Carroll argues, for "sometimes a moral defect in an artwork can figure in a negative *aesthetic* evaluation" of it; "there are some cases where a moral defect in a work amounts to an aesthetic defect."[33] For example, a play that presents the historical Hitler as someone to pity and with whom to sympathize will

---

[30] Carroll, "Morality and Aesthetics," p. 281A.
[31] Carroll, "Art and Ethical Criticism," p. 358.
[32] *ibid.*, p. 359.   [33] Carroll, "Morality and Aesthetics," p. 281B, 282A.

be "an aesthetic failure."[34] "A novel that calls upon audiences to deliver the moral sentiment of admiration for a sadistic colonizer who cruelly and relentlessly tortures every Indian he encounters" will fail artistically, in that the emotional response it prescribes will, rightly, not be felt.[35] In such cases the moral significance and the aesthetic value of the work cannot be separated. They are artistically flawed *because* of their moral import.

Moralism and the clarification of thought and feeling

Given the difficulties that trouble both extreme and moderate autonomism, given the desire to connect art with life, and given the frequent efforts of artists themselves to make moral and political statements, Carroll adopts a position he calls *moderate moralism*. Some but not all works of art have moral value. (Works of pure instrumental music and pure visual design, according to Carroll, do not.[36]) Sometimes but not always moral defects and virtues imply artistic defects and virtues.[37] Here Carroll distinguishes his position from what he calls *ethicism*, the view that moral defects and virtues in a work *always* imply artistic defects and virtues in it. Matthew Kieran and Berys Gaut each advocate this stronger view. Kieran argues that

> Art can widen, develop, and deepen our imaginative understandings of
> ourselves, others, and our world. Good artworks will do so for most
> people, across time and cultures, far better than mediocre ones. Great
> artworks are those which may promote the imaginative understanding
> of many people, across many times and cultures.[38]

Gaut claims that "if a work manifests ethically reprehensible attitudes, it is to that extent aesthetically defective, and if a work manifests ethically commendable attitudes, it is to that extent aesthetically meritorious."[39] According to both Kieran and Gaut, then, it is a central function of art

---

[34] *ibid.*, p. 282A.   [35] Carroll, "Art and Ethical Criticism," p. 377.

[36] Carroll, "Morality and Aesthetics," p. 280A.

[37] Carroll, "Art and Ethical Criticism," p. 377.

[38] Matthew Kieran, "Art, Imagination, and the Cultivation of Morals," *Journal of Aesthetics and Art Criticism* 54, 4 (fall 1996), pp. 337–51 at p. 348B.

[39] Berys Gaut, "The Ethical Criticism of Art," in *Aesthetics and Ethics*, ed. Levinson, p. 182.

not simply to be decorative or entertaining, but to promote imaginative understanding of people, their styles of interest, and their successes and failures in pursuing their interests – just as Karen Finley, Andres Serrano, and writers of narrative fictions typically undertake to do. It does this by engaging and clarifying – as Aristotle saw – the emotions of audiences toward both the subject matter presented and the artist's manipulations of the materials of a medium.[40] If a work succeeds in such engagement and clarification, then it is, according to Kieran and Gaut, to that extent always artistically better; if it fails, it is to that extent always artistically worse.

Carroll regards his own position as more moderate than the ethicism that Kieran and Gaut advocate. In fact, however, Carroll does not show against them that failures in the engagement and clarification of ethically significant attitudes and emotions are ever either artistic virtues or artistically neutral. What he shows is that "artworks can be immensely subtle in terms of their moral commitments";[41] an artwork may prescribe a genuinely morally reprehensible attitude toward a character and course of action but do so incidentally, on a very small scale, such that it is scarcely noticeable, all within a framework of overall artistic success. There may indeed be such cases. But they do not show that the morally reprehensible attitude that such a work invites and prescribes in fact counts itself as either an artistic virtue or as artistically neutral. Once it is noticed, it will, as Kieran and Gaut claim, reasonably count against a sense that the work is artistically successful. Leni Riefenstahl's *The Triumph of the Will* is frequently cited as a work that is artistically successful despite being morally flawed in prescribing admiration for Hitler and the racial project of national socialism. But as Carroll himself notes, it is at least "problematic" that *The Triumph of the Will* is "an aesthetically good film": "seen in its entirety and not in the edited versions that are usually screened, it is immensely boring, full of tedious Nazi party speeches."[42]

It is important, also, that there are complex, hard cases. A work may plausibly invite, prescribe, and clarify a number of conflicting attitudes toward the same character and course of action. We may feel that Hamlet in his delay is both immaturely self-indulgent and appropriately deeply troubled about the claims of conscience and the exercise of power. Lester

---

[40] See chapter 8 above.
[41] Carroll, "Art and Ethical Criticism," p. 378.   [42] *ibid.*, p. 380.

Burnham, the Kevin Spacey character in the film *American Beauty*, is both adolescently escapist and concerned to resist the staleness and lack of life that surrounds him in the suburbs, while being prepared to find beauty in the smallest corner of it. Karen Finley and Andres Serrano can strike us both as mere publicity-seeking provocateurs and as paying attention to social phenomena and attitudes toward them that most of us shirk and that are badly in need of clarification. Such complex cases may suggest at first blush that moral defects and virtues are not always artistic defects and virtues, since we do not know quite what coherently to think and feel in the face of them. Their moral import seems unclear, and their artistic success seems, at least in some cases, evident. In fact, however, their artistic success is better described as the achievement of inviting and clarifying complex emotional attitudes toward complex human characters and projects, where it is difficult to reduce these complex attitudes to any single and simple moral message. The achievement of the clarification of complex emotional-ethical attitudes remains, however, as such an artistic achievement, not something that is artistically neutral, even where, and perhaps especially where, it is difficult to sum up the work of clarification in a formula of moral thought.

Carroll, Gaut, and Kieran, along with other theorists such as Wordsworth, Tolstoy, and Collingwood, and Wayne Booth, Martha Nussbaum, and me, among many others, regard the ethical significance of art as a matter of the clarification of what it is appropriate to think and feel, in relation to specific, interesting, and difficult cases that are held before our attention by the work of art. Amy Mullin has usefully distinguished the successful work of art's invitation of what she calls "morally significant imagining" from the didactic purveying of a sound moral message.[43] Kieran emphasizes the importance of "imaginative understanding and its cultivation of moral insight" into particular cases, not simply coming away from a work with a moral philosophy in one's mind or pocket.[44] Carroll calls his position on this issue *clarificationism*. He distinguishes between the acquisition of new propositional moral *knowledge*, which should not happen and typically does not happen in our encounter with a successful work, and the deepening of moral *understanding*, which is a central

---

[43] Amy Mullin, "Evaluating Art: Morally Significant Imagining Versus Moral Soundness," *Journal of Aesthetics and Art Criticism* 60, 2 (spring 2002), pp. 137–48.

[44] Kieran, "Art, Imagination, and the Cultivation of Morals," p. 348A.

function of art.[45] Understanding is, among other things, connected with particulars; it involves "a capacity to see."[46] Evolving understanding, including the exploration and clarification of emotion and attitude, is an aspect of engagement with a work, not a consequence of it.[47] Wayne Booth observes that we engage with values in reading "by *experiencing* them in an immeasurably rich context."[48] Adapting a phrase from Henry James, Martha Nussbaum claims that reading complex works of narrative literature can make us "finely aware and richly responsible."[49] As James himself puts it, "the effort really to see and really to represent is no idle business in face of the constant force that makes for muddlement."[50] I have described the importance of "attention to cases" and "reading through particulars."[51] In each case the emphasis falls on the interest of exploring complex moral attitudes and emotions that are invited by wide ranges of difficult, particular cases, not on didactic moralizing in the manner of Aesop's fables.

When narrative literature and other forms of art direct attention toward the complex details of particular cases, then there is some danger of arriving at moral particularism. Nussbaum suggested in earlier work that there might be "irreconcilable visions" of human life put forward by particularist literature and generalizing moral philosophy.[52] The arts might be taken to show that many different and divergent characters and

---

[45] Noël Carroll, "Art, Narrative, and Moral Understanding," in *Aesthetics and Ethics*, ed. Levinson, pp. 126–60 at pp. 142–44. See also Noël Carroll, "The Wheel of Virtue: Art, Literature, and Moral Knowledge," *Journal of Aesthetics and Art Criticism* 60, 1 (winter 2002).

[46] Carroll, "Art, Narrative," p. 145.

[47] *ibid.*, p. 145.

[48] Wayne C. Booth, *The Company We Keep: An Ethics of Fiction* (Berkeley, CA: University of California Press, 1988), p. 70.

[49] Martha C. Nussbaum, "'Finely Aware and Richly Responsible': Literature and the Moral Imagination," in *Literature and the Question of Philosophy*, ed. Anthony J. Cascardi (Baltimore: Johns Hopkins University Press, 1987), pp. 169–91, reprinted in Martha Nussbaum, *Love's Knowledge: Essays on Philosophy and Literature* (Oxford: Oxford University Press, 1990), pp. 148–67 at p. 148.

[50] Henry James, *The Art of the Novel* (New York: 1907), p. 149, cited in Nussbaum, *Love's Knowledge*, p. 148.

[51] Eldridge, *On Moral Personhood*, pp. 20, 21.

[52] Martha C. Nussbaum, "Perceptive Equilibrium: Literary Theory and Ethical Theory," in Nussbaum, *Love's Knowledge*, pp. 168–94 at p. 190.

actions are appropriately pitied, envied, despised, admired, respected, and so on, in many fine shades of feeling, at the expense of commitment to any settled moral principles. Art such as Finley's that undertakes to show what it might be like to feel compelled to cover oneself with feces in order to fake a horrible abduction might, for example, be thought to illustrate human reality at the expense of the moral judgment that it is wrong or degrading to do this. Such art might be thought to aim at showing that nothing human is alien to us and that we are capable of nearly anything, while forgetting to consider what it might be right or wrong to do. Or, more weakly, some art might aim at showing that many different things might count as virtues and vices in different contexts, foregoing any general account of the natures of virtue and vice. So-called virtue ethics,[53] developed initially by Bernard Williams,[54] Philippa Foot,[55] and (with qualifications) Alasdair MacIntyre[56] in the mid 1970s to early 1980s argued that it is impossible to cultivate all the genuine virtues simultaneously. In at least some cases, spontaneity competes with integrity, foresightedness competes with generosity, moral uprightness competes with sympathy and love, and courage competes with prudence; some relationships may have to be sacrificed for the sake of others. Against this background of thinking about ethics, a turn to literary accounts of complexities of particular actions-in-contexts seemed natural. Nussbaum did her initial, influential work on literature and moral philosophy explicitly under the influence of Williams' thought that tragedy, resulting from having to make hard choices in cases in which the cultivation of one virtue must lead to the suppression of another, might be inevitable in human life.[57]

---

[53] For a general survey of the rise of virtue ethics, prefacing selection of major essays in this area, see *Virtue Ethics*, ed. Roger Crisp and Michael Slote (Oxford: Oxford University Press, 1997). For a survey of the influence of these theories on thinking about the value of art, see Richard Eldridge, "Aesthetics and Ethics," in *The Oxford Handbook to Aesthetics*, ed. Jerrold Levinson (Oxford: Oxford University Press, 2003).

[54] See Bernard Williams, *Moral Luck: Philosophical Papers, 1973–1980* (Cambridge: Cambridge University Press, 1981) and Bernard Williams, *Ethics and the Limits of Philosophy* (Cambridge, MA: Harvard University Press, 1985).

[55] See Philippa Foot, *Virtues and Vices and Other Essays in Moral Philosophy* (Berkeley, CA: University of California Press, 1978).

[56] See Alasdair MacIntyre, *After Virtue: A Study in Moral Theory* (Notre Dame, IN: Notre Dame University Press, 1981).

[57] See Nussbaum's discussion of the work of Williams in her *The Fragility of Goodness: Luck and Ethics in Greek Tragedy and Philosophy* (Cambridge: Cambridge University Press, 1986), pp. 18–20.

The trouble with moral particularism, despite its insights into the complexities of hard cases, is that it threatens to underplay the thought that there are some values, such as justice, that might command our allegiance, however difficult it is to cultivate them. Worried about this threat, Kieran complains that "moral particularism ends up implausibly and uncritically exempting received ways of carrying on from reflective inquiry and criticism."[58] Gaut criticizes the tendency of moral particularism to "den[y] the existence of any general and informative moral principles."[59]

In fact, however, those who have developed a clarificationist stance have generally not been full-blooded moral particularists. Rather, they accept the thought urged by Kieran that "it is perfectly compatible with foregrounding the rich particularities of certain cases to allow that there is a symbiotic interplay between moral principles and judgment."[60] Thus Nussbaum argues that "perception without responsibility is dangerously free-floating, even as duty without perception is blunt and blind. The right 'basis' for action is found in the loving dialogue of the two."[61] She has gone on to articulate a multidimensional neo-Aristotelian theory of the good, arguing in detail that complex works of literature offer us insight into the difficulties and possibilities of furthering values that do command our allegiance. Rich, complex, and plausibly developed novels do not just offer perceptions of the particular; they also "shape, in their reader, certain evaluative judgments that lie at the heart of certain emotions."[62] And these judgments may be tested by and integrated into a general moral theory that "contains the potential to organize and transform perceptions on a large scale, in a way that may be crucial for political change and individual self-criticism."[63] Literature and ethical theory can be, as she puts it in a recent essay, allies and not adversaries.[64] I have argued explicitly that

---

[58] Kieran, "Art, Imagination, and the Cultivation of Morals," p. 340B.

[59] Gaut, "Ethical Criticism of Art," p. 191.

[60] Kieran, "Art, Imagination, and the Cultivation of Morals," p. 340B.

[61] Nussbaum, "'Finely Aware and Richly Responsible,'" p. 155.

[62] Martha C. Nussbaum, "Exactly and Responsibly: A Defense of Ethical Criticism," *Philosophy and Literature* 22, 2 (October 1998), pp. 343–65 at p. 353.

[63] Martha C. Nussbaum, "Review of *Making Sense of Humanity and Other Philosophical Essays* by Bernard Williams," *Ethics* 107, 3 (April 1997), p. 529.

[64] See Nussbaum, "Literature and Ethical Theory," pp. 5–16. For a full description and evaluation of Nussbaum's ways of opposing and allying literature and moral philosophy, see Eldridge, "Reading for and Against the Plot: On Nussbaum's Integration of

the richest narrative texts are best understood as "allegories of the possibilities of human freedom and morality and self-understanding in the
world,"[65] as understood in Kantian terms. Kantian moral philosophy accepts the standing presence of complexity and tragedy in human life and
yet sees complexities and tragedies as in principle (if not always availably
in practice) problems to be worked through as we cultivate our powers of
meaning-making in and through present antagonisms.[66] Complex narratives, including tragic ones, naturally complement this thought.

The idea put forward by Carroll that works of art *prescribe* the emotions
and attitudes that they clarify may initially suggest moral didacticism,
thus classing works of art with propaganda, advertising, and pornography, in which emotional responses are likewise prescribed and expected.
Some viewers may see Finley's *We Keep Our Victims Ready* as prescribing and
inviting predictable and moralistic liberal sympathy, just as some viewers
may see the paintings of Norman Rockwell as prescribing and inviting
predictable nostalgia for an idyllic middle-class Americanism now lost.
These judgments might be justified. Each work seems perhaps too overtly
to argue didactically for a certain moral-political stance, though everything will depend on how in detail the work may be aptly understood to
work through and clarify the responses it prescribes, rather than simply
provoking them for the sake of some moral or political action or stance.
(Compare Collingwood's distinction between art, where a singular, object-
specific emotion is articulated and clarified, and magic, including propaganda, where a general emotion is evoked for the sake of action.[67]) Mullin
accuses both Carroll and Gaut, in talking of prescribed emotion in art, of
undervaluing the improvisatory imaginative exploration of emotion, and
she notes that they both "often make references to rather predictable genres in attempting to explain their positions."[68] I have complained similarly
that Nussbaum, particularly in discussing literature and politics, tends to
focus on "conventionally realist novels" – E. M. Forster's *Maurice*, Richard

---

Literature and Moral Philosophy," in *One World: Essays on Martha Nussbaum on Literature
and Philosophy*, ed. Leonard Ferry (Albany, NY: SUNY Press, forthcoming).

[65] Richard Eldridge, "How is the Kantian Moral Criticism of Literature Possible?,"
in Eldridge, *Persistence of Romanticism*, pp. 71–84 at p. 77. See also Eldridge, *On Moral
Personhood*, p. 63.

[66] See Richard Eldridge, "How Can Tragedy Matter for Us?," in Eldridge, *Persistence of
Romanticism*, pp. 145–64, especially pp. 162–64.

[67] Collingwood, *Principles of Art*, p. 32.   [68] Mullin, "Evaluating Art," p. 144A.

Wright's *Native Son*, and Dickens' *Hard Times* – "that are fairly far from the more protean imaginative and linguistic efforts of William Faulkner or Gabriel Garcia Marquez or Toni Morrison,"[69] and I have suggested that Kantianism, with its emphasis on perfectionist moral experimentalism, within the limits of justice and under conditions of social antagonism, may be friendlier to a wider, somewhat less moralized conception of artistic imagination and its moral significance.

In reply, Carroll has charged that in emphasizing experimentalism I fall, along with Bernard Harrison,[70] Hilary Putnam,[71] and Herbert Marcuse,[72] among others into what he calls "the subversion approach,"[73] according to which genuine art "is always on the side of the angels," just because genuine works of art inherently unsettle conventional expectations and "show that the world can be otherwise."[74] Against the subversion approach, Carroll objects that it is biased in favor of "radical works," where "most artworks, including most fictions, are not morally radical. A great many artworks, notably fictions, operate within established moral frameworks and are not morally pernicious, though they may yet possess an ethical dimension."[75] The thought that genuine art should always be liberating because improvisatory and experimental is, Carroll argues, "nothing but a pious, deeply sanctimonious wish-fulfillment fantasy" that rests on making "art a category of commendation rather than of classification."[76]

Despite the sharpness and the plausibility of the criticism in each direction – experimentalist-subversionist versus realist-didactic – there may in the end be less disagreement than agreement. Carroll emphasizes that the successful work of art must carry out some clarification of the appropriateness of an emotion to its presented object, rather than just

---

[69] Eldridge, "Review of *Poetic Justice* by Martha Nussbaum," *Journal of Philosophy* 94, 8 (August 1997), pp. 431–34 at p. 434.

[70] Bernard Harrison, *Inconvenient Fictions: Literature and the Limits of Theory* (New Haven, CT: Yale University Press, 1991).

[71] Hilary Putnam, "Literature, Science, and Reflection," in H. Putnam, *Meaning and the Moral Sciences* (London: Routledge & Kegan Paul, 1978), pp. 83–96.

[72] Herbert Marcuse, *The Aesthetic Dimension: Toward A Critique of Marxist Aesthetics*, trans. Erica Sherover (Boston, MA: Beacon Press, 1977).

[73] Carroll, "Art and Ethical Criticism," p. 364.

[74] Carroll, "Art, Narrative, and Moral Understanding," p. 129.

[75] Carroll, "Art and Ethical Criticism," p. 366.

[76] Carroll, "Art, Narrative, and Moral Understanding," p. 132.

propagandizing. I emphasize that successful experimental-improvisatory works must not be arbitrary and nonsensical, but must rather address a human problem of human expressiveness and fluency that is shared to some degree. In each case the successful work of art is conceived as involving the "working through" of an emotion toward an effort – either happily successful or tragically failed or compromised – to achieve a valuable human action or life.

Art, propaganda, advertising, and cliché

The art critic John Berger distinguishes between the banal artistic image, all too easily assimilable to and by advertising, and the exceptional artistic image, in which the "extraordinary particularity"[77] of the presented subject is focused on. Artworks in general may be said properly to aim at the achievement of the exceptional. They seek to achieve and embody a full act of thematic and emotional attention to a subject matter in the working of materials in a medium and to make this act of full attention available to an audience, in the face of tendencies to revert to cliché and half-attention. Finley and Serrano may be plausibly understood at least to have attempted such an act of attention.

There are degrees of success in this enterprise of attention, and it is fully reasonable to call *art* both partial successes and any efforts within a medium of art that have this aim in view, even if it is unachieved or less than wholly achieved. As a result, it is difficult to draw a sharp line between commendatory and classificatory uses of the term *art*, even while some distinction between these two uses seems pertinent to our experiences of different works.[78] It is fully reasonable to class as art both practice or student works and works that aim as much at entertainment as at art. Attention, even when closely focused on a particular subject matter, may well include discerning features that it shares with other subjects, so that it is natural that there should be some more "realist" genres that draw on standardized ways of structuring an image or presenting a plot in painting, photography, literature, music, and the other arts. The achievement of attention and the clarification of an emotion can take place, sometimes and for some subject matters, both through pushing experimentally

---

[77] John Berger, *Ways of Seeing* (Harmondsworth: Penguin, 1972), p. 61. Berger develops the contrast between the banal and the exceptional from pp. 57–64.

[78] See chapter 7 above.

against the boundaries of a genre and within a more realist genre through exceptional mastery of details and effects in a medium. All that must be resisted is cliché, inattentiveness, and predictable propagandist rhetorizing.

As we think about the moral significance via clarification that art aims to achieve, it is important to keep in mind two things. First, the making of a work of art is a human action. It is, hence, unlike a mere reaction (such as a wince) or a behavior (such as breathing), necessarily to some extent informed by and assessable in terms of reasons. We can ask why an artist has done just that. If the answer is "In order simply to shock, propagandize, make a reputation, or sentimentalize," then we will tend to conclude that the action in question is not (genuinely or fully) that of making art, but rather that of seeking some other kind of reward or effect than the clarification that art centrally seeks to offer. This is a plausible diagnosis in, for example, the case of the Chilean painter and sculptor Antonio Becerra, who with government arts funding exhibited the taxidermically preserved and painted corpses of dogs that had been hit by cars, in what he calls "a mix of butchery, sculpture, and nursing, because I have found dogs on the highway that are half-dead and I have had to help them."[79] Of the corpses exhibited, one "bears an oil painting of Pope John Paul II and a cross on its flank. Another is spotted with blue and orange butterflies on its white fur. A small brown dog, its back arched like a cat, has a row of sharp metal spikes inserted down the length of its spine."[80] Whatever actions of making and exhibition are in question here, they are not centrally actions of art, and they are appropriate objects of moral condemnation and even – supposing they violate health or animal treatment laws – of criminal prosecution. Works such as those by Finley and Serrano are controversial, but they have clarification much more clearly in view as an aim, even if (some may judge) not wholly successfully, and they do not involve otherwise violating criminal law. Works such as paintings by Norman Rockwell and Thomas Kinkade are made within a recognized medium of art but predominantly as a commercial enterprise, not a clarificatory one.

---

[79] Antonio Becerra, quoted in "Dead dogs exhibited as artworks," a report on his work by Gabriela Donoso, Reuters, printed in *Philadelphia Inquirer*, August 27, 2002, section E, p. 7.
[80] *ibid.*

Second, the making of a work of art as a clarificatory enterprise is overdetermined by a combination of communicative and formal reasons, as an artist undertakes to present a subject matter as a focus for thought and emotional attitude, distinctively fused to the imaginative exploration of material. Formal considerations of arrangement to appeal to the eye and ear will interact with considerations of emotional attitude and thematic intent. As Marcia Eaton aptly notes, "human experience – including the experiences of making and attending to art – is not segregated into the moral, the aesthetic, the religious, the political, and so on. Aesthetic experience is special, but that does not imply that it is separate from the rest of one's life."[81] In developing this thought, Eaton further notes that philosophers such as Cora Diamond, R. W. Hepburn, and Iris Murdoch, who have urged that the making of art is a moral enterprise of clarification, have widened the sense of "the ethical" away from moralizing about right and duty and toward the enterprise of reflecting, in Diamond's phrase, on one's "texture of being."[82] Ted Cohen has argued similarly that there is no clear distinction to be drawn between so-called "aesthetic" and "nonaesthetic" (including moral) terms.[83] When we praise James for his subtle discrimination, condemn Dickens for his sometime sentimentality, admire the scope and detail of Beethoven's formal organization, laugh at Beckett's absurd yet idiomatic humor, or are exhilarated by the cathartic quality of Stravinsky's *Firebird*, are we responding aesthetically, morally, or otherwise? Cohen's answer is "aesthetically, morally, and humanly" all at once, as we follow and participate in the work's action of clarification.

---

[81] Marcia Eaton, "Morality and Ethics: Contemporary Aesthetics and Ethics," in *Encyclopedia of Philosophy*, ed. Kelly, vol. III, pp. 282–285 at p. 284A.

[82] Eaton, *ibid.*, p. 284B, citing Cora Diamond, "Having a Rough Story about what Moral Philosophy is."

[83] See Ted Cohen, "Aesthetic/non-Aesthetic and the Concept of Taste: A Critique of Sibley's Position," *Theoria* 29 (1973), pp. 113–52; reprinted in *Aesthetics*, ed. Dickie and Sclafani, pp. 838–66. Against Cohen, Monroe Beardsley suggests that we should distinguish not between aesthetic and nonaesthetic terms but between terms used in an aesthetic sense and terms used in a nonaesthetic sense. He claims that "restful" has a clear nonaesthetic sense in "I had a restful vacation" but a clear aesthetic sense in "Kandinsky's painting *At Rest* has a restful character" (*Aesthetics*, p. xxvii). I see no difference in sense or meaning here, but only a difference in the kind of object to which the term is applied, and the examples mentioned in the text seem to me still not to sort readily into aesthetic versus nonaesthetic uses or senses of the terms deployed.

Ethical understanding and working through puzzlement

Once we see that works of art are products of human action or themselves performances that aim at thematizing subject matters and clarifying emotional attitudes toward them, in and through the working of materials in a medium, and once we see further that there is no sharp distinction to be drawn between aesthetic and nonaesthetic experience, then Carroll's moderate moralism (some works have moral significance and some do not; sometimes moral defects are aesthetic defects, sometimes not) seems less plausible than either what Carroll calls extreme variable moralism (all works are morally good or bad to some degree or other), if we are relaxed about classification, or utopianism (all art is clarifying and liberating), if we focus only on cases of distinct success as art.[84] Yet the utopianism of art – if that is quite the right word for it – that is, its contribution when it is distinctly successful to human moral understanding, is neither exclusively experimentalist-subversivist nor didactic-moralistic. It involves instead the working through in an action of artistic making of possibilities of full attention to a subject matter, including the clarification of emotion toward the subject, via the working of materials in a medium. When this attention and clarification are achieved, then what is further achieved will be an expressively free attention to the subject, as opposed to a clichéd, inattentive, half-hearted, conditioned reaction. (Robert Pippin has argued eloquently along similar lines that Henry James' effort as a writer "really to see"[85] is an investigation of the interest, importance, and continuing difficulty of what it would be "to live freely" in and through specific social circumstances.[86])

---

[84] See Carroll, "Morality and Aesthetics," for the most compact presentation of his taxonomy of types of positions; this taxonomy also appears in both "Art and Ethical Criticism" and "Art, Narrative, and Moral Understanding."

[85] James, Art of the Novel, p. 149, cited in Nussbaum, Love's Knowledge, p. 148.

[86] See Robert B. Pippin, Henry James and Modern Moral Life (Cambridge: Cambridge University Press, 2000). Pippin's picture of free life as a human project is largely inspired by Hegel, so that living freely includes, among other things, some concern for mutuality and reciprocity. One difficulty in the way Pippin describes this project in which, he argues, James took an interest and we have an interest, is that he represents it as contingently historically emergent, perhaps optional. I would argue that commitment to this project comes rather with our possession of Kantian practical reason or conscience or, in Nietzsche's terms, with our being "interesting animals" capable of repression and self-formation, though this project may take a long

The special pertinence of this artistic achievement is that human life continually presents materials about which we do not know exactly how to feel and judge. Patient domesticity in human life can be an appropriate object of both pity and fear *and* exhilaration and admiration; so can heroic unconventionalism. It all depends on the details of the case, and these details may often accumulate in ways that leave us puzzled and divided with ourselves, not knowing quite what to feel or think. We can feel puzzled and divided with ourselves about Tawana Brawley as victim versus Tawana Brawley as fraudulent exploiter of racial antagonism; we can feel puzzled and divided at religion as an ordered but pale social institution versus religion as a thing of blood and mystery. We can wish to have our puzzlement worked through and clarified, and successful art will do this, in a way that does not resolve the puzzlement into a dogmatic moral, but which clarifies its complex particularities in relation to its object.

One good example of the working through of divided emotions and attitudes is Irvine Welsh's novel *Glue*.[87] *Glue* traces the lives of four boys growing up in the Edinburgh housing projects as "schemies," from their first days at school in about 1970 to the present, as they are in their mid-thirties. In many ways, Edinburgh housing project life is straightforwardly awful and in need of more than a little reform based on sound ethical reflection and understanding. There is brutal casual sex, without much regard for consequences, escapism via Ecstasy and heroin and rock music, not so petty housebreaking and thievery, and omnipresent violence, including knife fights and football brawling for fun. One of the four central characters commits suicide by jumping from a bridge. Another shoots an acquaintance through the throat with a crossbow. None of them achieves a stable sexual relationship with anyone. Growing into their forties and beyond – if the remaining three make it – will not be easy for them.

Yet, apart from a much smaller number of passages of third-person narrative and the voices of a few outsiders, the novel is written in the heavy dialect voices of Terry, Billy, Carl, and Andrew. Their experiences and voices have their own peculiar sublimity, a sublimity that effectively solicits the reader's iconoclastic estrangement and yet sympathy. Here is

---

time to come into articulate awareness and in some circumstances may never quite do so.

[87] Irvine Welsh, *Glue* (New York: W. W. Norton, 2001). The following paragraphs on *Glue* are taken from Eldridge, "Reading for and Against the Plot."

just one passage, in Andrew's voice, giving some thoughts about women, and then modulating into a football-related brawl.

> – Caroline Urquhart… she's a fucking stuck-up wee hing-oot, Terry sais tae ays.
>
> – You'd ride her if you goat the chance, ah tells um.
>
> Ah'd fuckin ride her n a minute, Marty Gentleman goes. – Bit ah'd shag that Amy Connor first.
>
> Gentleman could probably bag oaf wi Amy Connor, cause eh looks aulder n eh's a big hard cunt. No wi Caroline Urquhart but, shes' mair snobby, well, ah widnae say snobby, but likesay classier. But ah'm thinkin aboot this, aboot who's the biggest shag between the two. Dozo's aw irritated but. Eh's noddin ower some *Sash*-singing cunts. We up our pace n faw in behind thum. Thir's aboot five boys, drapped in Union Jacks. One's goat ARDROSSAN LOYAL in white letters oan it. Eh's wearin nine-inch Docs. Dozo boots this one in the heel n one leg wraps roond another n eh crashes ontae the cobblestones. Gent boots the cunt on the deck n shouts in a Glesgay accent, – Briktin Derry! Naebody starts *The Sash* 'cept us!
>
> It works a treat! They back off, n one nashes right ower the road. The rest aw go quiet. Aw the other groups ay Huns look confused but dinnae make a move. If we'd hud the colours oan, we'd be stomped. They'll tear anything apart in green, but they think this is jist Hun v Hun, a civil war. Now the other cunts dinnae want tae ken! It's working, that plan wi agreed! Isolate the cunts, even up the odds by makin it personal, us against thaim, instead ay fitba, Hibs against Rangers.[88]

For most middle-class speakers of "standard" English, this language is difficult. The thoughts and incidents that it describes are at best unattractive, at worst repellent. Yet – as even this small excerpt from a 469-page book shows – there is something absorbing about it. Partly this is a function of the sheer difficulty and pleasure of working through the language. But it is also in part a function of *an* attraction of the way of life thus presented. The novel itself offers an explanation of what about this way of life is thus absorbing in a crucial passage recording the thoughts of Kathryn Joyner, a declining American pop singer who has fallen in with

---

[88] Welsh, *Glue*, p. 82.

Terry and a few of his acquaintances for a day or two. In thinking about them, she notices that

> They were nice enough, that was the problem, they always were, but dependency on others and, conversely, theirs on you, just had to stop. They'd shown her something though, something useful and important, during those last few days of drug-addled nonsense. Strange as it was, they cared. They weren't world-weary or blasé. They cared about things; often stupid, trivial things, but they cared. And they cared because they were engaged in a world outside the constructed world of the media and show business. You couldn't care about that world, not really, because it wasn't yours and it never could be. It was sophisticated commerce, and it just chugged on.[89]

The schemie way of life is, despite its violence, sexism, and poverty, not a world that just chugs on in sophisticated commerce. It includes spontaneity, genuine sexual adventurism, fun, enthusiasm, and care, despite including in the very same actions callousness, disrespect, crassness, escapism, and violence. All this comes out in the language and the thoughts of its principal figures.

What are we to do in response to this world? How are we to feel about it? Do Terry and Andrew and Carl and Billy live well? Irvine Welsh, *Glue*'s author, does not, I think, know. We are estranged by the experience of this book – we middle-class readers – from "our" ordinary way of life. We are drawn into this novel's sublimities of both language and experience, as well as into its crudities. We see that gratitude for their lives is something that is possible for some of these protagonists, at some moments, in certain ways, and we can, for a moment, share in that gratitude. Yet their futures are uncertain; their virtues are inseparable from their vices, at least as far as any immediate course of action is concerned. Their culture and way of life are what they are: both like ours and yet desperately different. And so we are to do or feel what? How are we to improve our ethical understanding and reflective deliberation based on our experience of this text?

My sense is that this novel is not one that calls for and contributes to ethical understanding, where ethical understanding is conceived of as having an articulate sense of how to pursue human fulfillment. But we see and feel in this closely attentive realist novel something of ethical

---

[89] *ibid.*, p. 433.

significance: that here is a way of life with rich, interrelated virtues and vices, presenting problems that we feel ourselves to share (caring intensely but fleetingly and self-indulgently vs. routine decency) and that are to be worked out, yet we know not how.

This kind of clarification of complexities in human life and of emotional response to them, yet without arriving at any directly guiding moral conclusion or plan for action, is what Amy Mullin has in mind in suggesting that works of art may enable "morally significant imagining"[90] without definitely prescribing anything. I have argued that any exemplary achievement of human value, in art and in life, "remains marked by particularity"[91] and one-sidedness, given the complexities of any form of social life and the antagonisms that run through it. As a result, the pursuit of specifically detailed self-understanding within the framework of a given social context "must be an activity, not a body of knowledge."[92] The clarifying imaginative work of art is a central aspect of this ongoing activity, as we attempt to work through our situation and prospects, attempting to bring standing moral commitment and principle to its fullest and fittest expression within complex and antagonized situations in which recipes alone will not avail us. The working-through that successful art accomplishes is both humanly significant and not a matter of direct theoretical argument for or against either a moral formula or a specific course of action. This explains why it strikes us, rightly, as all at once different from moral theorizing, insulated from "the rest of life" where action must be taken, and relevant to life. Karen Hanson eloquently describes both the practical moral difficulties that artistic imagining addresses and how it addresses them as artistic imagining, not theory.

> We in fact cannot, in our conduct, honor all the moral ideals that may, in abstract thought and even in the lives of others, seem worthy, admirable, or in some way attractive. This is not because – or not alone because – of pervasive weakness of the will. The more fundamental problem is the practical incompatibility of, the friction between, a wide variety of recognized, or tempting, ideals...Art's capacity to keep alive certain moral perspectives, even if these views diverge radically from our own present moral outlook, can help us remain alert to life's possibilities and our own potentialities. This is a benefit that is neither merely aesthetic, nor solely moral: it is both at once.[93]

[90] Mullin, "Evaluating Art," p. 137A. [91] Eldridge, *On Moral Personhood*, p. 182.
[92] *ibid.*, p. 188. [93] Hanson, "How Bad Can Good Art Be?," p. 222.

That art helps us to honor in our imagination commanding moral ideals that we cannot wholly honor in our present conduct is a way, even the central way, of keeping alive our full humanity in its complex directedness toward and by those ideals. Without art morality becomes either emptily abstract or conventionalistically rigoristic; with art morality becomes legible as fundamental to the complex texture of our human lives.

10 Art and society: some contemporary practices of art

The reproduction of social life *vis-à-vis* "infinite satisfaction"

Presenting a subject matter as a focus for thought and emotional attitude, distinctively fused to the imaginative exploration of material is, whatever else it is, a social practice. As Dewey aptly notes, artistic making was originally not directed toward galleries, museums, pedestals, or free readers. Rather it was

> part of the significant life of an organized community...Domestic
> utensils, furnishings of tent and house, rugs, mats, jars, pots, bows,
> spears were wrought with such delighted care that today we hunt them
> out and give them places of honor in our art museums. Yet in their own
> time and place, such things were enhancements of the processes of
> everyday life. Instead of being elevated to a niche apart, they belonged to
> a display of prowess, the manifestation of group and clan membership,
> worship of gods, feasting and fasting, fighting, hunting, and all the
> rhythmic crises that punctuate the stream of living.[1]

What we now call works of art were used within religious and clan rituals, or they were elements of buildings, or parts of communal festivals involving athletics along with song and ritual. However much care was devoted to their making and however much attention was devoted to form and distinctive expression, the objects and texts that were produced were used within the circuits of the reproduction of social life.

Yet human social life is not always and only a matter of the continuing reproduction of the same. As Hegel observes, production – in hunting, cooking, building, and dressing the body, as well as in art – takes

---

[1] Dewey, *Art as Experience*, pp. 6–7. Here Dewey echoes Hegel's treatment of art in chapter 7 of *Phenomenology of Spirit*, where art is understood as initially bound up with religion, ritual, the cultivation of social solidarity, and athletics. See Hegel, *Phenomenology of Spirit*, trans. A. V. Miller (Oxford: Clarendon Press, 1977), chapter 7, section B, "Religion in the Form of Art," pp. 424–53.

place in the service not only of standing needs, but also in the service of recognition.[2] Human beings are creatures not only of need (*Bedurfnis, besoin*), but also of desire (*Begierde, désir*). Plato makes a similar point in having Socrates accede to the demand of Glaucon that they together imagine an ideal city with "cooked dishes," "seasonings," and luxuries that is thereby fit for men, rather than being a "city of pigs."[3] Human beings are creatures, Plato acknowledges, of *eros*, not simply of pastoral reproduction of the same form of life, day after day. They are articulately aware of or have a conception of what they are doing in making something, and they are aware of alternatives that present themselves either in the course of making or among objects to be made. In their making they seek not only to satisfy needs by making useful objects, but also to display their personalities and talents in ways that win approval, from others and from themselves. They seek not simply to use what they have made, but also to look on what they have done and to see for themselves and with others that it is good, whether they are cooking, building, adorning the body, chanting, plowing, preparing for war, marking the passing of the seasons, or practicing fertility rites.

It is unclear how and why this is so. Hegel notoriously argues that the existence of desiring, self-conscious, recognition-seeking human beings is a logical requirement for the development of Spirit to full self-consciousness. Spirit will come to recognize itself in and through their most richly developed and reasonably sustainable doings, in something like the way we may sometimes recognize ourselves in our artistic works and other doings. This may be so with Spirit, but it is a distinctly theological, even salvationist view of our condition that it is difficult to support with proof or to ground in unambiguous evidence. Hölderlin has a similar sense of the human condition, but he is substantially more cautious about its causes and cure. As he writes in a fragment that may be a letter/essay/response to Hegel:

> You ask me why, even though the people, following their nature, elevate themselves above necessity and thus exist in a more manifold and

---

[2] The *locus classicus* for these points is Hegel's discussion of recognition in chapter 4 of *Phenomenology of Spirit*, centering around the claim that "Self-consciousness is Desire in general" (p. 105). For explication of this gnomic claim, see Eldridge, *Leading a Human Life*, pp. 29–32.

[3] Plato, *Republic*, Book II, 372c, 372d, p. 42.

intimate relation with their world [than do other animals], even though, to the extent that they elevate themselves above physical and moral needs, they always live a – in human terms – higher life, so that between them and their world there be a higher [and] more than mechanical *interrelation*, a higher destiny, even though this higher relation be truly the most sacred for them because within it they themselves feel united with their world and everything which they are [and] possess, you ask me why exactly they *represent* the relation between them and their world, why they have to form an idea or image of their destiny which, strictly speaking, can neither be properly thought nor does it lie before our senses?

You ask me, and I can answer you only so much: that man also elevates himself above need in that he can *remember* his destiny, in that he can and may be grateful for his life, that he also senses more continuously his sustained relation with the element in which he moves, that by elevating himself above necessity in his efficiency and the experience connected to it, he experiences a more infinite [and] continuous satisfaction than is the satisfaction of basic needs, provided that, on the one hand, his activity is of the right kind, is not too far-reaching for him, for his strength and skill, that he is not too restless, too restricted, too controlled. However, if man approaches it in the right way, then there exists, in every sphere that is proper to him, a more than necessity-based, infinite satisfaction.[4]

Whatever may be the causes and cures (in infinite satisfaction, beyond the satisfaction of biological needs) of human self-consciousness and desire, the fact remains that social life is marked and altered by the pursuit of recognition and of infinite satisfaction, set up by the agency of desire in us.

Art and modernity: Schiller and others

Once upon a time it may have been possible to achieve recognition and infinite satisfaction to a significant extent in acting so as to rebind everyone to common ways of social life. This kind of rebinding is a central function of epics such as the poems of Homer, primeval biblical history,

---

[4] Hölderlin, "On Religion," in *Essays and Letters on Theory*, ed. Pfau, p. 90.

or the Icelandic sagas that recount the myth-shrouded history of a people. Perhaps priests carrying out rituals in intimate relation with a public
once enjoyed significant recognition and satisfaction. With the advent of
modernity, however – and perhaps well before that, as soon as there is
a significant differentiation of social roles – recognition and satisfaction
achieved in intimate relation to a public are not so readily found. Dewey
notes that with the development of "modern industry and commerce"
and the intensification of the division of labor, "artists find it incumbent
upon them to betake themselves to their work as an isolated means of 'self-
expression'...[T]hey often feel obliged to exaggerate their separateness to
the point of eccentricity."[5]

Works of art are no longer bound up so immediately with rituals,
uses, the cultivation of social solidarity, and daily life. They instead begin
to function, with increasing division of labor and social stratification, as
vehicles of the display of individual temperament, talent, and interest,
against the grain of standardized manufactured objects. Works of art become loci of the impress of distinctive personality, interest, and emotion
in sensuous material. Commitment to the integrity and interest of the individual work may increase for the artist and a circle of those with similar
personality and interests, but at the cost of the widespread communicative
function of art in relation to ritual and the cultivation of social solidarity.
Works of art become things to be made in order to display one's distinctive
personality, temperament, and powers, in differentiation from others, and
they come to be collected as means of self-display, rather than used. In a famous article, Stanley Cavell describes what he calls "aesthetic problems of
modern philosophy," suggesting not only that there are certain problems
about the function and meaning of works that arise distinctively together
with modernity, but that these problems have to do with the repression or
loss of sensuous aesthetic production as a widely shared practice of social
meaning-making.[6] Makers of art are aware of their freedom in modern
artistic making from the demands of liturgical or social use, and they

---

[5] Dewey, *Art as Experience*, p. 9.

[6] Cavell, "Aesthetic Problems of Modern Philosophy," pp. 73–96. For a full elaboration of how the specific problems Cavell discusses are, according to him, problems
of modernity and its philosophy that involve the repression of artistic-aesthetic work
as a practice of meaning-making, see J. M. Bernstein, "Aesthetics, Modernism, Literature: Cavell's Transformations of Philosophy," in *Stanley Cavell*, ed. Richard Eldridge,
(Cambridge: Cambridge University Press, 2003).

value it and insist on its continuance. But they are also aware of the loss of the widespread social communicative function that once accompanied artistic making when it was more firmly embedded in contexts of liturgy and ritual.

One of the fullest discussions of this development, with attention to both gains and losses, occurs in Friedrich Schiller's essay "On Naïve and Sentimental Poetry." Schiller argues there that what we love in nature – in "a modest flower, a stream, a mossy stone, the chirping of birds, the humming of bees, and the like" as well as "in children" and "in the customs of country folk" – is "the silent creativity of life in them, the fact that they act serenely on their own, being there according to their own laws; we cherish that inner necessity, that eternal oneness with themselves."[7] For us, creatures who grow up within richly articulated social systems with intense division of labor, and hence with opposed social roles that are relatively opaque to one another, it is different. We are aware of living not just as a human being naturally lives, but within one or another specific social role, against a wide background of possibilities, where it is not always clear why that role exists, what its value is, or how to fulfill it well. Anxiety about one's social role, its basis, and its value is especially likely for creative artists who have "betaken themselves to their work as an isolated means of 'self-expression'" without clear social function. Where once the making of art was an integral part of knowing and worshipping and reproducing social life from generation to generation, it is now optional – freely, gloriously, and individually so, but also freighted with anxiety. How is anyone to achieve oneness with oneself or at-homeness within a social role, so as to act "serenely" and with "inner necessity"? In particular, how might artists do this, where they directly confront the problem of making individual works that have sensuous expressive meaning, rather than manufacturing fungible commodities? It may well be an expression of modern social anxiety that we *represent* or *imagine* the lives of children and primitive peoples to be natural, serene, and dominated by inner necessity, like the chirping of birds. Perhaps technologically more primitive human lives and the lives of children were never quite like that. Yet our imagination or representation that they were so indicates the intensity of our longing for fuller sensuous meaningfulness and at-homeness within

---

[7] Schiller, "On Naïve and Sentimental Poetry," trans. Daniel O. Dahlstrom, in Schiller, *Essays*, pp. 180, 179.

our roles, our longing for "serenity" and "inner necessity." It is from this longing that we project this serene condition on to them. For us, Schiller claims,

> They *are* what we *were*; they are what we *should become* once more. We were nature like them, and our culture should lead us along the path of reason and freedom back to nature. Thus they depict…our lost childhood, something that remains ever dearest to us, and for this reason they fill us with a certain melancholy.[8]

But for us – freighted with self-consciousness and aware of our lives as subjects within social roles, whose functioning and value not everyone can readily endorse and wherein work takes place apart from immersion in nature and ritual – there is no ready way to achieve serenity and at-homeness. We represent this serenity as an ideal to be achieved rather than as participating in it as a lived fact.

> Once the human being has entered into the condition characteristic of culture and art has laid its hands on him, that *sensuous* harmony within him is overcome, and he can only express himself as a *moral* unity, that is to say, as someone striving for unity. The agreement between his feeling and thinking, something that *actually* took place in the original condition, now exists only *ideally*. It is no longer in him, but rather outside him, as an idea that must be realized in his work, no longer as a fact of his life.[9]

Poetry – and by implication art in general – aims, Schiller claims, at "giving humanity its most complete possible expression."[10] In modern times, this requires not the depiction of lived meaningfulness, which is lost, "but the elevation of actuality to the ideal or, what comes to the same, the portrayal of the ideal is what necessarily makes the poet."[11]

But how is the ideal to be portrayed? Through a free, personal fantasy of meaningful life or of a utopia? That runs the risk of being *ad hoc* and irrelevant to our condition and to any realistic prospects we might have. Or as a realistic description of the actual? That runs the risk of failing to express our possibilities completely, in portraying us as always caught up in an antagonized present social actuality with which we cannot become wholly reconciled.

Modern poetry and art, Schiller suggests, have found a partial solution to this dilemma – the only possible solution – in that the modern poet

---

[8] *ibid.*, pp. 180–81.   [9] *ibid.*, p. 201.   [10] *ibid.*   [11] *ibid.*

"reflects on the impression that the objects [including the objects of both the natural and the social world] make upon him and only on the basis of that reflection is the emotion founded, into which he is transported and into which he transports us."[12] Reflection is here the mental action of holding together in thought awareness of present actuality with a sense of the nonactualized possibilities of lived meaningfulness.

> The object [represented] here is related to an idea [of how we might live meaningfully], and [modern or sentimental] poetic power rests solely upon this relation. The [modern, sentimental] poet thus always has to deal with two conflicting images and feelings, with the actual world as a limit and with his idea as something infinite.[13]

The product of poetic and artistic reflection will then take on one of two basic forms depending on how the contrast and relation between the actual and the ideal is presented, as Schiller puts it; depending on whether the poet or artist "dwells more on the actual or on the ideal."[14] If actuality is the predominant focus in presenting a subject matter, then the work will be satirical in a special, broad sense of this term. It will represent actuality as falling short of the ideal, either tragically and with pathos or comically and with a sense of absurdity.[15] Alternatively, if the poet or artist dwells more on the ideal and on satisfaction within it, then the work will be elegiac, again in a special broad sense, and again divided into two subclasses.

> Either nature and the ideal are objects of mourning, when the former is presented as something lost, the latter as something unattained, or both are objects of joy, because they are represented as something actual. The first [sub]class yields the elegy in the narrow sense, the second [sub]class the idyll in the broadest sense.[16]

No matter, however, whether the poet or artist works in satire (tragedy or comedy) or elegy (idyll or elegy in the narrow sense), perfect success in artistic making remains elusive. "The [modern] sentimental poet does not complete his task, but his task is an infinite one...The sentimental poet will always make us feel, at least temporarily, out of tune with actual

---

[12] *ibid.*, p. 204.   [13] *ibid.*   [14] *ibid.*, p. 205.   [15] See *ibid.*, pp. 205–09.
[16] *ibid.*, p. 211.

life,"[17] as the modern work of art presents in one way or another a lack of fit between actuality and the ideal.

Schiller's taxonomy of modern poetry yields an astonishingly accurate and insightful account both of the modes of always less than perfect success in artistic making that are open to us (tragedy, comedy, idyll [ideal, beautiful form], and elegy strictly so-called) and of the predominant modes of failure to achieve the aims of art. Exhaustion in the effort to present the ideal in plausible relation to actuality, where this effort can never wholly succeed, is all too likely to occur. The attentions of both artists and audiences are likely to drift toward entertainments and decorative, escapist forms that fail to engage with the actual.

> The state of mind of most people is a matter of stressful and exhausting work, on the one hand, and the kind of indulgence that works like a sedative, on the other...[Exhausted by work, many people seek to be] relieved at once [by art] of the burden of thinking and, in this relaxed state, such natures may indulge themselves in the blissful pleasure of nothingness, on a soft pillow of platitudes. In the temple of Thalia and Melpomene, as it is cultivated among us, the beloved goddess is enthroned and receives in her ample bosom the stupid savant and the exhausted businessman. Rekindling their numbed senses with her warmth and swaying the imagination to a sweet motion, she rocks the mind to sleep, gently mesmerizing it.[18]

There is no doubt that many people – perhaps all of us at least some of the time – bring such expectations to the experience of art. It is natural for makers of artistic representations sometimes to cater to such expectations with an offer of beautiful form or the ideal unmixed with attention to reality, in the form of a predictable happily-ever-after story or a pleasing play of shapes. Art's some-time indulgence of these expectations is what leads people who think of themselves as serious about work and knowledge to scorn it or to reserve it for idle moments of reverie and recovery.

Alternatively, critical thought in relation to actuality may become strident and insistent. Insistence on presenting a message – a thought about the imperfections of the actual – may take the shape of outright experimentalist provocation that challenges any form of settled social life and advocates bohemianism, relentless iconoclasm, or nomadism. The result is

---

[17] *ibid.*, p. 234.   [18] *ibid*, pp. 245, 246.

a kind of soulless, technical avant-gardism, full of assertive self-importance but empty of any expressive clarification of emotion in relation to the actual. Art made from this technically avant-gardist, provocative stance is too confident in its own rectitude in indicting social actuality skeptically rather than constructively.[19] Or it may take the shape of political art, in presenting one or another didactic but implausible recipe for fulfillment in social actuality: in the closed society of Stalinism, for example, a boy-meets-tractor story; in the Gilded Age of 1890s rapaciously expansionist America, a Horatio Alger story; in the present a parable of the preeminence of the virtues of niceness and self-respect. These shapes of almost-art are likewise unlikely to win art many friends.

Lukács, Marcuse, and Adorno

Beginning from what he calls Schiller's "correct and profound insights" into the infinite task of modern art in relation to social actuality, Georg Lukács provides a powerful and plausible account of how a number of artistic movements have confronted and then fled from the problem of genuine artistic making.[20] In the early nineteenth century, perhaps most exemplarily in the works of Jane Austen and Honoré de Balzac, it seemed that the infinite task of art as Schiller conceived it might be satisfied. Realist attention to social actuality might be combined with an account of deeper longings for a sensuously meaningful social life. It was possible to conceive of a plot – ending, typically, in a happy marriage, albeit with qualification – that might both be realistic and yet present deeper longing as largely satisfied. (Marcuse remarks aptly here that "the [unmixed] happy ending is 'the other' of art...Authentic works of art are aware of this; they reject the promise made too easily; they refuse the unburdened happy end...Where it nevertheless appears...it seems to be denied by the work as a whole."[21] That is to say, happy endings in authentic works of art will leave Malvolio in his dungeon at the end of *Twelfth Night* unjustly unintegrated into social life, or the marriage of Darcy and Elizabeth in *Pride and Prejudice* will remain shadowed by the second-best, grim happiness of

---

[19] Compare Marcuse's criticism of merely technical avant-garde art that lacks "authenticity and truth" in Marcuse, *Aesthetic Dimension*, p. x.

[20] Georg Lukács, "Art and Objective Truth," (1954), reprinted in *Critical Theory Since 1965*, ed. Adams and Searle, pp. 791–807.

[21] Marcuse, *Aesthetic Dimension*, p. 47.

Charlotte Lucas alone in her room upstairs from Mr. Collins, by the failures of reciprocity between Mr. and Mrs. Bennett, and by implication in the
roots of enabling wealth in exploitation.) Throughout the nineteenth century, however, as the social division of labor intensifies and manufacturing
becomes increasingly industrialized, it becomes more and more difficult
to imagine even a qualified authentic reconciliation of inner longing for
the ideal with social actuality. Realism drifts toward a documentarian
"false objectivism," as realist writers such as Zola

> isolate objectivity [in representation] from practice, eliminate all motion
> and vitality and set it in crass, fatalistic, romantic opposition to an
> equally isolated subjectivity…A scrap of reality is to be reproduced
> mechanically and thus with a false objectivity, and is to become poetic
> by being viewed in light of the observer's subjectivity, a subjectivity
> divorced from practice and from interaction with practice.[22]

Alternatively, there can result a "false subjectivism" as, first, in impres-
sionism (in painting and in literature) and, second, in moves toward abstract art (in painting, in literature – for example in the *nouveau roman* of
the 1950s – and in music, in its increasing rejection of the vernacular).
These movements reflect an "ever-intensifying subjectivization in artistic
practice"[23] that amounts to a flight from social actuality.

Yet Lukács holds out hope that false objectivism and false subjectivism
can be avoided and that the infinite task of art in relation to social actuality, as Schiller describes it, can be taken up with some degree of effec-
tiveness.

> Within [the] richness and subtlety [of "life," of "ordinary experience,"
> and of longings struggling for expression within these spheres] the artist
> [must] introduce a new order of things which displaces or modifies the
> old abstractions…[The work of art must be made through] a process in
> which from the outset the order within the new phenomena
> manifesting the subtlety of life is sensed and emerges in the course of
> the artistic climaxing ever more sharply and clearly.[24]

To say this is to hope that what Marcuse calls "aesthetic affirmation"[25]
is still possible, through this kind of artistic making, where the artist
engages with both social actuality and subjective aspiration.

---

[22] Lukács, "Art and Objective Truth," p. 794B.   [23] *ibid.*, p. 795A.
[24] *ibid.*, pp. 797B, 798A.   [25] See Marcuse, *Aesthetic Dimension*, p. 22.

But exactly how both false objectivism and false subjectivism are to be avoided and aesthetic affirmation is to be achieved remains a problem that no recipe or formula can address. Lukács himself tends to favor a somewhat more objectivist-representationalist stance, in taking Balzac's *Père Goriot* and Gerhart Hauptmann's *Weavers* as exemplars of artistic success.[26] Adorno, in contrast, favors the more modernist-formalist works of Joyce, Beckett, and Brecht, and he argues that a certain subjectivism and tendency toward abstraction are necessary in order for art to maintain a critical distance on social actuality, indicting its failure to satisfy deep subjective longings for satisfaction. For Adorno, art has become and must remain "an enigma" in comparison with either a commodity or a social sermon; "it achieves meaning by forming its emphatic absence of meaning" (as a coherent plot of social achievement).[27] Genuine modern art manifests a "double character as both autonomous [through being driven toward abstraction, in the face of the weight of social actuality] and fait social"; in modern art "the unsolved antagonisms of reality return as immanent problems of form."[28] In any case, whether predominantly formal-abstract-subjectivist or predominantly realist-objectivist-representationalist-vernacular, art will remain surrounded with penumbrae – including kitsch, entertainment, decoration, propaganda, pornography, narcissicist self-display – from which it will be difficult to distinguish it with sharpness in every single case. Just how to blend attention to social actuality with incorporation of deep, subjective longing remains a standing problem. And yet aesthetic affirmation, in the form of sensuous gesture that presents a subject matter as a focus for thought and emotional attitude, distinctively fused to the imaginative exploration of material, remains possible.

Structuralism and structural opposition in social life: Lévi Strauss and Althusser

For the past thirty-five or so years and centrally under the influence of structuralism and poststructuralism, thinking about the task of art as aesthetic affirmation – in a line of thinking that runs from Kant and Schiller through Collingwood, Dewey, Adorno, and Marcuse – has come to a number of theorists to seem naïve. How is aesthetic affirmation possible? Aesthetic affirmation undertakes to investigate possibilities of an ideally

---

[26] Lukács, "Art and Objective Truth," p. 802A–B.
[27] Adorno, *Aesthetic Theory*, p. 127.   [28] *ibid.*, pp. 5, 6.

meaningful life that are latent in social actuality. But if social actuality
remains always marked by structural oppositions between opposed classes
and ways of life, so that it always fall short of the ideal (as Kant, Schiller,
and Marcuse explicitly concede), then can aesthetic affirmations that hold
the attentions and advance the interests of everyone really exist? Perhaps
art is a weapon in a social struggle more than a means of imagining its
ideal resolution.

This line of thinking that is hostile to aesthetic affirmation begins
to take shape in the claim of Claude Lévi-Strauss that "myths operate in
men's minds without their being aware of the fact."[29] These myths take the
form of a *code* formed of certain terms that are defined in terms of their
opposition to one another: *raw–cooked, youth–elder, man–woman, light–dark,
hunter–gatherer,* and so on. In any myth, indeed in any cultural product of
mind, there will be a "pattern of basic and universal laws."[30] These laws
are laws of structure, not laws of development. They describe the necessity of defining certain central concepts in terms of a range of competitor
concepts, just as, according to Fernand de Saussure, any language contains meaningful words only by marking certain phonemic contrasts as
significant.[31] For example, in English *bat* is a different word from *pat* and a
different sound from the nonword *bnat* because the contrast between the
phonemes *b* (voiced labial) and *p* (unvoiced labial) is marked in English,
while *bn* is not in use. This system of phonemic and semantic contrasts
precedes and informs the thought and speech of any individual. Language
is, according to Saussure "outside the individual who can never create or
modify it by himself."[32] Thought and speech are possible only by coming
to make use of some system of this kind. Applying Saussure's account of
structural opposition in language comprehensively to language, thought,

[29] Claude Lévi-Strauss, *The Raw and the Cooked: Introduction to a Science of Mythology,*
volume I, trans. John Weightman and Doreen Weightman (New York: Harper & Row,
1969), p. 12.

[30] *ibid.,* p. 11.

[31] See Fernand de Saussure, *Course in General Linguistics,* trans. Wade Baskin (New York:
McGraw Hill, 1959), p. 59: "The science of sounds becomes invaluable only when two
or more elements are involved in a relationship based upon their inner dependence,
for the variations of each element are limited by the variations of the other element
or elements; the single fact that there are two elements calls for a relationship and
a rule – and this is quite different from a simple statement."

[32] *ibid.,* p. 14.

and forms of social life, Lévi-Strauss then arrives at the view that "the pattern of those conditions [structural opposition] takes on the character of an autonomous object, independent of any subject."[33] Our myths, our dreams, our theories, and our forms of significant social life refigure and reinstance a basic pattern of opposition, just as different languages become what they are by refiguring and reinstancing basic patterns of phonemic opposition. Lévi-Strauss notes that his own work does not describe the resolution of oppositions or refer their working and temporal development to some more basic process. He explicitly accepts the thought that "this book on myths is itself a kind of myth,"[34] in being another refiguring and reinstancing of a common pattern of oppositions, and that one might just as well regard the myths of the Bororo in central Brazil as a reading of Lévi-Strauss' text rather than vice versa.

Lévi-Strauss' work on structural opposition in all forms of thought, mythology, and social organization was taken up by Louis Althusser and combined with Marx's attention to the history of the class struggle and the work of Freud (and Lacan) on eternally effective mechanisms of dreamwork and of subject formation. For Marx communist society as "the *definitive* resolution of the antagonism between man and nature, and between man and man"[35] remains possible and even foreordained by human beings' natural development of their productive power. Communism is "the true solution of the conflict between existence and essence, between objectification and self-affirmation, between freedom and necessity, between individual and species. It is the solution of the riddle of history and knows itself to be this solution."[36] For Freud, health, stability in family life and professional life, and commitment to the ways of civilization (despite its discontents) remained a more modest but achievable ideal. For Althusser, in contrast, structural opposition without resolution is omnipresent. "Ideology," he writes, "has no history,"[37] which is to say that there is no ideal, primitive, natural, human prehistory where structural opposition is lacking and no end state where structural opposition might be resolved.

---

[33] Lévi-Strauss, *Raw and the Cooked*, p. 11.   [34] *ibid.*, p. 6.

[35] Karl Marx, "Economico-Philosophic Manuscripts of 1844," in *The Portable Karl Marx*, ed. Eugene Kamenka (Harmondsworth: Penguin, 1983), pp. 131–152 at pp. 149–50.

[36] *ibid.*, p. 150.

[37] Louis Althusser, "Ideology and Ideological State Apparatuses," trans. Ben Brewster, reprinted in *Critical Theory Since 1965*, ed. Adams and Searle, pp. 239–50 at p. 239B.

People dream about the resolution of social antagonisms, and they develop accounts – ideologies – of how this might be done. But these accounts are only standing fantasies, not recipes that can be effectively followed in such a way that all could live freely. Structural oppositions persist, as "the future lasts a long time."[38] Given the manifold agonies of social history, it is difficult to evade this thought.

The consequences of Althusser's views of art and criticism as forms of social practice are, as I have argued, "immediate and powerful."[39] The visions of blending social actuality with the ideal that are put forward by writers, painters, composers, filmmakers, and so on in the form of exemplary gestures are, if they are coherent and well plotted, now readily seen as pieces of ideology that involve repressions of the interest of some disfavored group (atheists, or workers, or women, or the urban underclass, etc., as may be). Less coherent, more circumstantial and fragmentary works (the later films of Godard?) may seem more interesting in being closer to the texture of always unresolved antagonisms in daily life. Critical interpretation turns away from appreciative elucidation and toward the investigation of the use of the work in a social context by a maker seeking a reputation and an audience wishing for reinforcement, all within the terms of one or another form of struggle. It comes to seem hopeless and naïve to try to evaluate works objectively in terms of artistic achievement: all that is left are opposed uses and preferences.[40] Numbers of important theorists and critics of the various disciplines of art have done powerful critical and theoretical work along these generally Althusserian lines: Fredric Jameson on Joseph Conrad, T. J. Clark on Edouard Manet, Marc Weiner on Richard Wagner, Rosalind Krauss on Jackson Pollock, Jerome McGann on the English Romantics, for example, among many, many others.

---

[38] The title of Althusser's 1992 memoir: *L'Avenir dure longtemps*. Althusser, *The Future Lasts Forever: A Memoir*, trans. Richard Veasey (New York: New Press, 1993). For a full account of Althusser's structural Marxism, constrasted with classical, teleological Marxism, see Eldridge, "Althusser and Ideological Criticism of the Arts." Pages 166–82 outline Althusser's views and their relations to the views of Marx, Freud, and Lacan.

[39] Eldridge, "Althusser and Ideological Criticism of the Arts," p. 182. In the remainder of this paragraph I summarize pp. 182–88 of this essay.

[40] See the discussion in chapter 7 above of the views of Herrnstein Smith and Bourdieu.

Foster's postmodern sociocultural criticism

Within the practices of art, especially the visual arts, awareness of the pervasiveness of social antagonisms has resulted in what Hal Foster aptly describes as a "turn [since 1960] from medium-specific elaborations to debate-specific projects."[41] Many artists now take themselves less centrally to make beautiful or well-formed objects or performances in an expressive medium and more centrally to investigate social conflict. Within this turn, Foster notes "three areas of investigation [that are shared by both art and critical theory]: the structure of the sign, the constitution of the subject, and the siting of the institution [including not only the museum, but also the university as the home of the disciplines of art and theory]."[42] That is to say, artists and critics alike now worry, especially in the visual arts, about signs (and work-texts) as caught up in structures of formal, semantic, and social opposition (as sketched by Saussure), about how subjects come to have sectarian social identities and to engage in compensatory fantasy, and about the relations of academies, publishing houses, orchestras, and universities to social and economic powers.

Within this broad style of work we typically are presented with what Foster calls "the return of the real" as "traumatic realism."[43] The work of art either calls attention to suffering that is induced by social antagonisms, as in varieties of art that investigate phenomena as various as homelessness and the bodily self-image of women, or it "screens"[44] the real via repetition (as in Warhol's multiple silk-screen images of Marilyn Monroe): that is, it blocks attention to the real with a decorative image, but this blocking is repeated so insistently that we are made aware of the suffering that underlies it. The "shift in conception...to the real as a thing of trauma...may," Foster argues, "be definitive in contemporary [visual] art, let alone in contemporary theory, fiction, and film."[45] Foster himself reads the work of Cindy Sherman as powerfully advancing this sense of the real as a scene of trauma, as she presents us with images of the manifold things that can be done to her (through her own dependent self-conception) by Hollywood, by society, by disease, by systems of waste disposal, by, in general, "a symbolic order in crisis"[46] in being marked by

---

[41] Hal Foster, *The Return of the Real* (Cambridge, MA: MIT Press, 1996), p. xi.

[42] *ibid.*, p. xiv.   [43] *ibid.*, p. 130.   [44] *ibid.*, p. 132.   [45] *ibid.*, p. 146.

[46] *ibid.*, p. 165.

pervasive violence and antagonisms and in allowing release and freedom to no one.

Work – whether artistic or critical – that begins from and enacts a sense of the real as a scene of trauma can be powerful and acutely insightful, especially against the grain of wishes for widely shared and deep pleasure in either art or social life. As Foster himself notes, however, this kind of work can express and collapse into a "posture of indifference" that expresses both "a fatigue with the politics of difference," since nothing can really be done, and even "a more fundamental fatigue: a strange drive to indistinction, a paradoxical desire to be desireless, to be done with it all, a call of regression beyond the infantile to the inorganic."[47] In German literature this is familiar as *Sehnsucht nach dem Tod*, a longing for death as a release from the inevitable frustration of desire and aspiration for full human meaningfulness by social antagonism, as in Kafka's "The Hunger Artist" or "In the Penal Colony." Or the pursuit of accomplished social identity might simply be given up, as in the disappearance "into the zone" of Tyrone Slothrop at the end of *Gravity's Rainbow*. If artistic and critical work continue to focus on always repeating, unaddressable social antagonisms, then it threatens, as Foster puts it, to restrict "our political imaginary to two camps: the abjectors and the abjected, and [to] the assumption that in order not to be counted among sexists and racists one must become the phobic object of such subjects."[48] It is better to take sides with the relatively powerless than with the powerful, when only side-taking seems possible.

Can artistic beauty still matter? What about fun?

But is taking sides all that is possible? Even if it does take place, does it entirely dominate all acts of artistic making? In reaction against structuralist antihumanism, there has been some recent return to talk of pleasure and beauty. Sometimes this takes the form of insistence on experiences of aesthetic value and pleasure that are provided by traditional works of high art, as in Hilton Kramer's defense of the canon of visual art. "The more minimal the art, the more maximum the explanation," Kramer is supposed to have said. Why not stop worrying about taking sides and open ourselves to the experience of pleasure in art? Alternatively, in exhaustion

---

[47] *ibid.*, p. 164.   [48] *ibid.*, p. 166.

and impatience with critical theory and with politics, both artists and fans are likely often to insist that making and paying attention to art are fun. Such insistence can sometimes seek to turn our attentions to phenomena of "low" art and popular culture, as in the art critic Dave Hickey's enthusiasms for rock music, the neon lights of Las Vegas, the stage shows of Liberace, and the magic shows of Siegfried and Roy: enthusiasms that he sees as of a piece with genuine enthusiasm for high art as well. As Hickey reflects on his experience of Siegfried and Roy,

> You never think, How was it done? You simply take pleasure in seeing the impossible appear possible and the invisible made visible...We are...mortal creatures, who...can appreciate levitating tigers and portraits by Raphael for what they are – songs of mortality sung by the prisoners of time.[49]

That is, since we are all dead in the long run, why not accept the fact that there are some things in which some of us take pleasure "for its own sake" in the meantime? Why not accept "the appearance of images, that by virtue of the pleasure they give, are efficacious in their own right"?[50] Who has to care about either art's cultivation of the human or its reinscription of social antagonisms? Why can't we just have fun? Is there anything wrong with caring about the guitar solos of Eddie Van Halen or the latest television situation comedy?

The trouble with this view – despite its considerable attractiveness in urging us to be faithful to our own felt experience – is that it risks assimilating art to decoration, entertainment, or whatever is successfully marketed, overlooking the significance of more difficult works that interrogate our condition. But if we then return to more difficult works that invite and encourage thought about deep longings in relation to social actuality, then we seem back in Schillerian satiric or elegiac cultivation of the human or in politicized structuralist antihumanism, tendentious or emptily provocative.

---

[49] Dave Hickey, *Air Guitar: Essays on Art and Democracy* (Los Angeles, CA: Distributed Art Publishers, 1997), p. 189, cited in Alexander Nehamas, "The Return of the Beautiful: Morality, Pleasure, and the Value of Uncertainty," *Journal of Aesthetics and Art Criticism* 58, 4 (fall 2000), pp. 392–403 at p. 399A.

[50] Hickey, *The Invisible Dragon: Four Essays on Beauty* (Los Angeles, CA: Distributed Art Publishers, 1993), p. 16, cited in Nehamas, "Return of the Beautiful," p. 399B.

Art and social aspiration

Given our uncertainties about what is possible for us in relation to social actuality, each of these stances remains both reasonable and in some
measure limited. It seems important to keep alive the idea that we have
deep aspirations for meaningfulness that we seek to express in relation to
ever-changing social actuality and to regard the making of works of art as
a model of a process of free meaning-making in which we might all hope
to participate more fully.[51] It is reasonable to hope that artists might, as
Wordsworth put it, "create the taste by which [they are] to be enjoyed"[52]
and in doing so move us toward fuller forms of human community in
significant meaning-making. Yet if we insist that this is the central function of art, we risk missing both how much fun "lower" forms of art can
be and how efforts at artistic meaning-making might also be politically
one-sided. If we insist that art directly confronts our antagonized social
actuality and the traumas that it produces, then we might avoid these
risks, but fall instead into tendentiousness, in the form of either social-
ist realism (boy-meets-tractor stories, or Horatio Alger stories, or voyages
of self-discovery of oneself "as an x") or empty sneering and provocative-
ness. It seems reasonable and important to enjoy the activities of writing,
painting, composing, choreographing, and so on, but if we write, paint,
compose, or choreograph simply to have fun, then we run the risk of failing to think about social actuality and subjective aspiration in the deep
way that the making of art can sometimes embody.

Dewey seconds these thoughts in acknowledging that we live in an
imperfect society and that in an imperfect society artistic making that is
aimed at aesthetic affirmation will inevitably and appropriately be surrounded by escapist entertainment (and, we can add, politicized art and
theory) as its natural penumbrae.

> In an imperfect society – and no society will ever be perfect – fine art
> will be to some extent an escape from, or an adventitious decoration of,
> the main activities of living. But in a better ordered society than that in
> which we live, an infinitely greater happiness than is now the case

---

[51] The best accounts of artistic making as a model for the cultivation of subjectivity
as such *in situ* are Kant's theory of genius (see chapter 5 above) and Charles Altieri's
work on artistic making in his *Subjective Agency* (Oxford: Basil Blackwell, 1994).
[52] Wordsworth, "Essay Supplementary to the Preface (1815)," in *Selected Poems and
Prefaces*, ed. Stillinger, p. 477.

would attend all modes of production. We live in a world in which there is an immense amount of organization, but it is an external organization, not one of the ordering of a growing experience, one that involves, moreover, the whole of the live creature, toward a fulfilling conclusion. Works of art that are not remote from common life, that are widely enjoyed in a community, are signs of a unified collective life. But they are also marvelous aids in the creation of such a life. The reconciling of the material of experience in the act of expression is not an isolated event confined to the artist and to a person here and there who happens to enjoy the work. In the degree in which art exercises its office, it is also a remaking of the experience of the community in the direction of greater order and unity.[53]

This, or something like it, remains true, even if art never exercises its office quite wholly and unambiguously, in the conditions of social actuality under which we live.

Some contemporary practices of art: primitivism, avant-gardism, vernacularism, and constructivism

Both the traditional media of art – architecture, literature, music, painting, sculpture, and dance – and the more recent media of photography and film have been clearly shown to offer exemplary possibilities of aesthetic affirmation. There is no chance that the major works in these media – from the Parthenon and Rouen Cathedral to the photographs of Edward Weston and the films of Jean Renoir and Alfred Hitchcock – will altogether lose their holds on our imaginations and on our sense of how imagination might explore possibilities of meaningfulness (and its inhibition) that are latent in social actuality. As works are produced and put before audiences within each of these media, we are more than likely to continue to receive them as satires (comedies or tragedies) and elegies (idylls and elegies in the narrow sense), and we are more than likely to continue to argue about whether they achieve aesthetic affirmation or whether they are rather tendentious, empty, politicized, merely decorative, entertaining, fun, morbid, witty, moralistic, and so on, as may be.[54] It is worth a moment's reflection, however, to consider just how some newly emerging disciplines of artistic

---

[53] Dewey, *Art as Experience*, pp. 80–81.   [54] See chapter 7 above.

making undertake to achieve aesthetic affirmation and to present a sub-ject matter as a focus for thought and emotional attitude, distinctively fused to the imaginative exploration of material.

A number of varieties of what might be called primitivist (not primi-tive) art have become current in recent years. This work seems to aim at inducing awe and reverence for primeval nature and to remind us of our own transitoriness as a species in the face of it, somewhat in the man-ner of symbolic art (the pyramids of Egypt, say), as Hegel discusses it. The minimalist cyclic musical compositions of Philip Glass and Steve Reich, for example, often seem to aim at producing a felt sense of "primeval time" as opposed to the time of agency, politics, history, and human projects of the cultivation of self and culture. This music has affinities with more cyclic and modal, less aggressively cadenced works in the Indian musical tradition. It can seem to some ears on the one hand empty and merely decorative, but to other ears or the same ears at other times to be an apt reminder of human finitude and the mystery of life.

The environmental art of Robert Smithson and Richard Long seems to aim at a similar effect – massive arrangements of earth, as though carried out by prehuman gods or by time itself, prior to the dawn of historical time. Christo's wrappings of buildings and massive adornments of features of the landscape ("wrapped" islands, the 25-mile nylon cloth "Running Fence") have a similar effect, mixed with a kind of sensuous attraction as the cloth moves with the wind and changes appearance in sun and shadow. All this work seems designed deliberately to resist the thought that works of art are always, only, or centrally made by specific individu-als to human scale and for private ownership. They present themselves as both monumental and transitory, beyond human time. On a smaller scale, Tibetan sand mandalas that have attracted some interest are likewise tran-sitory works meant to be contemplated for their spiritual significance for a time, but owned by no one, and soon erased and scattered.[55] The direc-tor Werner Herzog produces in some of his films, especially in *Aguirre, the Wrath of God* (1972), a sense of the transitoriness of the human by shoot-ing natural phenomena – running water, plays of light and shadow on a landscape – in wide-angle deep focus and incorporating these shots into a

---

[55] See the discussion of sand mandalas in Freeland, *But is it Art?*, pp. 115–16. I was able to see a sand mandala built, displayed, and then removed after a few weeks from McCabe Library at Swarthmore College.

plot of the disappearance of the human. The camera can focus sharply –
as they eye cannot: for it the image on the screen is always blurred somewhere, though in sharp focus everywhere – on an entire wide-angle shot
of change, as though a transaction were taking place between the camera
and the scene itself, leaving any human audience altogether to one side.

A second mode of partial resistance and partial accommodation to
the traditions of "high" fine art has developed in recent attention to folk
arts and crafts. Some serious composers such as Dvorak, Stravinsky, and
Copeland, not to mention Beethoven, Schumann, and Bach, have long
made use of traditional folk melodies and motifs. But with the advent
of recording technologies it has become possible for many people to pay
attention to traditional folk practices of music in their own right. Delta
blues, Scottish Highland reels, the Aissawa music of Morocco, and Sene-
galese Tabala Wolof are all now widely available in recordings, along with
music in hundreds of other styles. These styles of music are objects of
serious attention in their own right. They retain in many cases closer connections with dance and with lived experience than do the traditions of
high art music in the West. Entertainment, fun, and vernacularism seem
to mix easily with one another, at least for certain musicians and audiences, without worrying much about somber self-interrogation or the
cultivation of the human in the forms of satire and elegy.

In the visual arts, attention to quilt making and woodcarving, among
other folk practices, as serious disciplines of art continues to increase.
Tribal masks, traditional pottery, and jewelry all claim places in museums of art as well as of folklore. If there sometimes seems to be a bit
of escapism from the traditions of high art and into hobbyism, there are
nonetheless serious vernacular developments of form, thought, and gesture in these media. It has been a major project of some forms of feminist
thought and practice to reestablish the interest of the kinds of artistic
production – cooking, table-setting, weaving, jewelry making, and knit-
ting, among many other forms of practice – that were traditionally seen
as women's work. Reclaiming these practices as vehicles of art as well as
of domestic use is another way of interrogating and developing the possibilities of meaningful production in relation to social actuality. We are,
rightly, more aware than we used to be of both how central the labors of
women are to social reproduction, how confined within certain spheres
of social reproduction women have often been, and of the interest and
value of what they have managed to produce. This awareness is entirely

compatible with taking an interest also in hitherto neglected works of "high" art produced by women working in traditional disciplines and in contemporary work by women. There is a risk, of course, that a sectarian political interest in advancing the social possibilities of women may lead to overvaluing some works in virtue of their messages and their social histories of production rather than their achievements of aesthetic affirmation, but this risk seems no greater than that of overvaluing some works by men just because they are made within the traditional media of art.

Against the grain of recoveries and continuances of tradition – whether canonical high art traditions or vernacular traditions – avant-gardism remains a strong presence in contemporary art, particularly in the visual arts. Since at least Duchamp and Dada in the early years of the twentieth century, there has developed a continuing practice of antimuseum art. This arises in part out of the practice, as Kendall Walton puts it, of "destroying the illusion"[56] that a painting or a sculpture is a simple reproduction of reality. Perhaps under the pressure of photography, painters in particular began to feel compelled somehow to make it visually evident that a painting is the result of an ideational process or a process of thinking and construction. Representation becomes indistinct, as in John Marin, or bare patches of canvas are left, as in late Cézanne, or collage is introduced and perspective is undone, as in Braque and early Picasso, or at the extreme the canvas is ripped, or slashed, or adorned with feathers or casts or sticks, as in some works of Robert Rauschenberg, Jasper Johns, or late Frank Stella. Or a deliberately puzzling sculptural object is presented, as in Duchamp's *Bicycle Wheel* (1913) – a bicycle wheel mounted inverted on a stool. The references within the modernist texts of Calvino and Barth to acts of authorial production function similarly. The point of these avant-garde strategies is to inhibit the audience's participation in the fiction that all that is going on is the "neutral" presentation of an object or world[57] and to call attention instead to artistic ideation, frequently as commentary on a social context. The experimental films of Stan Brakhage and Andy Warhol, the late work of Samuel Beckett, such as *Breath* (1983), and Berthold Brecht's use of asides and addresses to the

---

[56] Kendall Walton, *Mimesis as Make-Believe*, p. 276, citing Barbara Rose, *American Art Since 1900* (New York: Frederick A. Praeger, 1967), p. 52 on the paintings of John Marin.
[57] See Walton, *Mimesis as Make-Believe*, p. 275.

audience in order to achieve aesthetic distancing or alienation function similarly. A risk of this kind of work is that it will be repetitive, tendentious, and relatively empty, in declining centrally to represent a definite subject matter as a focus for thought through the working of material in a medium. But the formal limits of success in the enterprise of aesthetic affirmation are unclear, and avant-garde work has at least the advantage of taking the semantic and social dimensions of the practice of art making seriously, refusing to indulge in decorativism.

It seems difficult, in the face of the complexities and antagonisms that mark social actuality, to construct a realistic, coherent plot of the achievement of deep meaningfulness. We are now more familiar with and appreciative of explicitly ambiguous resolutions (*The Graduate*), disappearing protagonists (*Gravity's Rainbow*), and sheer overwhelming complexity (*JR*) than audiences perhaps were in the past (though consider *Tristram Shandy* or *Don Quixote*). We are more alert to the presence of complexity and contradiction in works that may once have seemed to offer unambiguous resolutions in happy marriages (*Middlemarch*, *Pride and Prejudice*). Given our awareness of complexity and contradiction in social actuality, we are likewise more uncertain about the value of works that seem to exemplify the resolution of antagonisms in a gesture or visual experience. The beauties of abstract expressionist painting (Morris Louis, Mark Rothko) can sometimes seem hyperbolically self-important and sometimes to afford a guilty pleasure. It is sometimes hard not to wonder, "Who am I to wallow in such color and space?"

Two prominent artistic practices build on our awareness of complexity by offering resistance – but differently from more manic, surrealist influenced avant-garde experimentalism – to immediate sensuous satisfactions in the experiences of reading, listening, or viewing. Minimalist or constructivist art (as in Sol LeWitt's conceptual installation works or the sculptures of Donald Judd and Tony Smith; or in music in some of the works of Elliot Carter; or in the stories of Donald Barthelme) call attention in the first instance to the elements or parts of (prior) works – to lines, curves, beams, short motifs, or words and phrases – rather than offering us immediately the satisfactions of achieved coherent wholeness in which we might linger. They seek to make us aware of what the artist is doing in manipulating parts or elements and of what *we* are doing ourselves in experiencing parts or elements as parts that *we*, the audience, must relate to one another or for which we must find a use. The persona of the artist seems cooler and less sensuous; the elements we are given to experience seem more austere and related to thought; we are invited to respond with self-conscious thinking more immediately than with emotion. Minimalist and constructivist strategies are natural in an age that has grown suspicious of unambiguous pleasure.

Performance art manifests a similar awareness of social complexity and seeks a similar distance from pleasurable experience but in a somewhat different way. Instead of producing either a text (a novel, poem, or play; a sonata, quartet, or symphony) or an object (a painting or sculpture), performance art brings the artist into immediate confrontation with an audience, in the hope of commenting on and changing habits of social life and thought. The English performance artists Gilbert & George, for example, "relinquish familiar human behavior to attain the status of art."[58] In their most famous work, *The Singing Sculpture* (1969, repeated many times thereafter), they cover themselves with bronze powder and stand on a pedestal in a gallery space, as a piece of human sculpture.[59] In other works they have explored drunkenness, excretion, and sexual deviance. When they do produce a visual image, the aim is the provocative criticism of self and society much more than it is visual pleasure. *Eight Shits* (1994) shows Gilbert & George a bit larger than life-size, with underwear below their knees, otherwise unclothed, and surrounded by six large turds (the size of their human figures) protruding into the image from its edges. They remark that "our reason for making pictures is to change people and not to congratulate them on how they are."[60] "We want Our Art to speak across the barriers of knowledge directly to People about their Life and not about their knowledge of art."[61] A great deal of performance art, including the self-mutilations of Chris Burden and Marina Abramovic,[62] the social commentary performances of Karen Finley and Vito Acconci

---

[58] Linda Weintraub, *Art on the Edge and Over: Searching for Art's Meaning in Contemporary Society, 1970s–1990s* (Litchfield, CT: Art Insights, 1996), p. 73.

[59] *ibid.*

[60] Gilbert & George, "What Our Art Means," in *Gilbert & George. The Charcoal and Paper Sculptures, 1970–1974* (Bordeaux: Musée d'Art Contemporain de Bordeaux, 1986); quoted in *ibid*, p. 76.

[61] Gilbert & George, *A Day in the Life of George & Gilbert, the Sculptors* (Gilbert & George, 1971), quoted in Weintraub, *Art on the Edge and Over*, p. 74.

[62] On Abramovic, see Weintraub, *Art on the Edge and Over*, pp. 59–64.

(*Following Piece*, 1969), and the "shopping art" of Haim Steimbach,[63] seems inspired by similar aims. For example, Steimbach remarks that he is trying to show that socially shaped desire can be refigured otherwise. "Everyday objects produced by our society may be turned into objects of desire more than one time. I am trying [in purchasing objects and installing them in a gallery] to demonstrate that an object may be consumed more than one time and desired in more than one way."[64]

All of these varying practices of art – moves "beyond human time," the recovery of suppressed traditions, aesthetic distancing, art as construction, art as performance, and art as social critique – are sometimes taken up not only in interaction with one another and with the traditional media of art, but also in engagement with developments in the technologies of images and texts. Video installations have become staples of the Whitney and Venice biennial exhibitions of new art. Nam June Paik's video installation art was the subject of a major retrospective show at the Guggenheim Museum in New York in 2000. Computer art, investigating the possibilities of the digital manipulation of images, flourishes as both a form of art and a form of commercial practice. The internet Museum of Computer Art sponsors online exhibitions and offers "Donnie Awards" each year in the categories of "open all digital art, fractal and algorithmic art, and enhanced photography."[65] Computer graphic designers produce visually striking web pages and special effects for movies. Artists undertake to document their lives with daily online postings of near stream-of-consciousness narratives of their experiences, or they present large chunks of their lives directly with 24-hour webcams. Music videos combine art direction and set design with fashion, threads of plot, dance, image manipulation, and music. Photocopy art appropriates images, often from the mass media, and recombines them to form new ones, presenting these new images both for visual pleasure and as social commentary.[66]

Surrounding and to some extent permeating all these practices of other than "high" traditional art is popular culture. Images, music, and text for the sakes of entertainment, instruction, provocation, and commerce circulate continuously and widely through print mass media, radio,

---

[63] On Steimbach, see Weintraub, *Art on the Edge and Over*, pp. 135–39.

[64] Haim Steinbach, "Inteview" (by Joshua Decter), *Journal of Contemporary Art* 5 (fall 1992), p. 117, quoted in Weintaub, *Art on the Edge and Over*, p. 137.

[65] See http://www.museumofcomputerart.com

[66] See the history of photocopy art archived at http://www.artfocus.com/copyart.htm

television, and the movies. The experience of images, music, and text in the mass media is an inescapable fact of life for most of today's world. Even if one were not to own a television or radio and to avoid popular magazines, it would be difficult to avoid either billboards or recorded popular music in one's environment, unless one systematically cultivated rural reclusion. Artists of all kinds have responded to this mass circulation of images, music, and text, both working themselves within these media as scriptwriters, directors, musicians, graphic ad designers, set dressers, and so on, and by incorporating into independent work images, music, and text that are in general circulation. In the visual arts, the early 1960s pop works of Andy Warhol and Roy Lichtenstein, among others, were the most prominent and successful responses to popular culture. It is often both frustrating and deeply interesting to think about these works. What are we to make of Warhol's *Brillo Boxes* or images of Marilyn, or of Lichtenstein's giant blowups of comic book images? Are they objects meant for visual pleasure? Are they fun, or witty, or cerebral and meant to provoke thought, or intended as social critique and commentary, or blatantly commercial themselves? Quite probably they are all of these things, just as movies and television shows can also try all at once to be commercially successful, witty, moving, reflective, and fun, and can sometimes succeed. Just what can be done in new media that use new technologies – both of mass art and of the production of "singular objects" – remains to be worked out as these media are explored. For example, what are the artistic possibilities of the electronic sampling and recutting of lines or motifs from rock music, as in rap and hip-hop?[67] Ted Cohen has usefully described a number of important dissimilarities between movies and television. Movies are watched in different locations at different times, typically by an audience that is larger than a few intimates but smaller than the crowd at a high school basketball game. Television programs are watched by millions of people simultaneously, but by people alone or in fairly small groups and

---

[67] Richard Shusterman defends the artistic interest of this work in "The Fine Art of Rap," in R. Shusterman, *Pragmatist Aesthetics: Living Beauty, Rethinking Art* (Oxford: Basil Blackwell, 1992), pp. 201–35 and again in "Art in Action, Art Infraction: Goodman, Rap, Pragmatism (New Reality Mix)," in R. Shusterman, *Practicing Philosophy: Pragmatism and the Philosophical Life* (London: Routledge, 1997), pp. 131–53. This is interesting work, though to my ear he both overrates the formal achievements in these media and suggests that rap is both more serious and less centrally commercial than perhaps even its practitioners suppose.

scattered across millions of different locations. These dissimilarities set up quite different possibilities for artistic representation, expression, and formal achievement in these two media. It seems more natural to expect coherent plot closure from a movie that one may well see only once, just as one expects closure in a traditional play. (Movies, of course, have possibilities of close-ups, tracking and traveling shots, multiple points of view, dissolves, cuts, use of landscape, etc., that are closed to plays, while plays can rely on the bodily presence of actors and on their action "in the moment" on different occasions of performance in ways that movies cannot.) In contrast, both the situation comedy and the ensemble drama have developed on television as natural ways of investigating shifting relations among characters whom we continue as an audience to visit week after week for whatever the natural life of a series (five or more years if very successful) turns out to be.[68]

In all practices of contemporary art, a great deal is a matter of experimentation, contestation, and interaction with other artistic practices and with the wider phenomena of social life. The traditional practices of "high" art either make use of the vernacular or they shun it and turn toward self-enclosure and modernist hermeticism (or both). Practices of mass and popular art are either dominated by commerce or more responsive to the artistic imperative to present a subject matter as a focus for thought and emotional attitude, distinctively fused to the imaginative exploration of material (or both). New technologies invite and enable the continuation of traditional aesthetic affirmation by other means or its transformation into intellectualism, provocation, advertising, or social commentary (or all of this at once).

Throughout all this experimentation, contestation, and interaction both with other art practices and with the wider culture, a central issue remains how to balance and blend some measure of vernacularism with some measure of formal constructivism. Without vernacularism, purely formal, constructive works of art become artificial, intellectual constructions. Without distinctively worked through formal construction that is both innovative and absorbing, vernacular works become in one way or another utilititarian: politicized or commercial or self-aggrandizing, among many other possibilities.

---

[68] See Ted Cohen, "Television: Contemporary Thought," in *Encyclopedia of Aesthetics*, ed. Kelly, vol. IV, pp. 369–70.

In a bleak but prescient book, Leonard Meyer argues that the collapse of "high" art into formalism and constructivism, exemplified by academic coterie serialism in music, is virtually inevitable in modernity, since vernacular life is dominated by industrial routine, and no cultivation of individual selfhood is any longer possible in relation to it. Outside academically formal and constructive works, there are only more or less vulgar entertainments and empty gestures. In music apart from serialism there is only either purely vernacular "tribal music" (rock and pop), "ambient music" (elevator music), and "transcendental particularist music" (John Cage's music as "sounds heard at a bus stop" or any sounds as a focus of Zen attention).[69] "Ours," Meyer concludes, "is and will remain a Brownian-motion culture"[70] with little possibility of significant individual achievements of meaningfulness in relation to social actuality. Social actuality is too divided, contested, fragmented, incoherent, and dominated by commerce for that.

Yet however incoherent and contested social actuality is, it continues also to offer materials of life for clarification and problems for art to address: subject matters to be presented as a focus for thought and emotional attitude, distinctively fused to the imaginative exploration of material. It is hard to imagine that human beings will stop caring about this and hard to believe that success in this enterprise is impossible. Jazz (from Armstrong to Coltrane, and beyond), modern through-composed music that engages with the vernacular (from Stravinsky to Shostakovich and Rorem, and beyond), the modern novel (from Joyce and Faulkner to Morrison, Pynchon, Rushdie, and beyond), dance (from Balanchine to Tharp, Morris, and beyond) and modern movies (from Renoir and Hitchcock to Herzog and Scorsese, and beyond) all testify along with many other practices to the continuing power of art to come to life in relation to social actuality.

---

[69] Leonard B. Meyer, *Music, the Arts, and Ideas: Patterns and Predictions in Twentieth-Century Culture*, new edn (Chicago, IL: University of Chicago Press, 1994). See especially chapter 5, "The End of the Renaissance?," pp. 68–84, and "Postlude," pp. 317–49.

[70] *ibid.*, p. 349.

11   Epilogue: the evidence of things not seen

Throughout these chapters I have repeatedly invoked the formula that works of art present a subject matter as a focus for thought and emotional attitude, distinctively fused to the imaginative exploration of material. This formula proposes that works of art typically have representational, expressive, and formal dimensions, all of which, both independently and in interaction, are normal foci of attention in making and responding to a work. I have attempted to outline debates about how original works might be made and what their interest is, how works of art distinctively call for interpretation, how they engage our emotions, how they explore the exercise of agency, and how they enter into and comment on wider social developments.

What, then, is the status of this formula that undertakes to sum up the dimensions of art and to lend some order to the debates? Is it a definition of art? Does it specify conditions that are individually necessary and jointly sufficient for anything being a work of art?

I do propose this formula as a definition, but not as a specification of necessary and sufficient conditions. Instead this formula is proposed as a specification of *criteria*, in Wittgenstein's sense of that term, for calling something art. Pain-behavior, for example, is a criterion for pain, according to Wittgenstein. It is, first of all, inconceivable that in general pain should have no relation to pain-behavior. Our grip on what pain is arises out of the fact that pain-behaviors such as crying, wincing, withdrawing, and so on are natural expressions of pain. Infants and small children produce a range of pain-behaviors immediately in expression of pain, without intervening conceptualization, and so, sometimes, do adults. That pain-behavior is a natural expression of pain is part of the grammar of the concept *pain*.

But pain-behavior is neither a sufficient nor a necessary condition for pain. Pain-behavior can be feigned or simulated, present when the pain itself is absent. Pain-behavior can be suppressed, absent when the pain itself is present. There are a number of different kinds of pain-behavior, from the most natural and immediate (screaming and withdrawing) to the somewhat more controlled and conventionalized (saying "I have a headache"). Typically some but not all kinds of pain-behavior are present in any single case.

Yet the connection between pain-behavior and pain is neither merely conventional, learned, and artificial, nor is it altogether causal and unrelated to consciousness and human expressiveness. It is a mistake to think of the pain as perfectly inner (in either the private mind or the brain) and the behavior as "merely outer" (either simply caused or merely expressed according to artificial convention). When pain-behavior is present and pain is absent, we require a special story about what is going on ("x is feigning pain in order to solicit sympathy"; or "it's a play"). Likewise when pain is present and pain-behavior is absent ("x is ignoring his pain and focusing on the task at hand"; or "x does not like making a show of himself"). A grasp of the connections between multiple kinds of pain and multiple kinds of pain-behavior, including the behaviors of feigning and suppressing it, is central to knowing what pain is. It is part of the grammar of pain to know that in certain circumstances this kind of wince counts as an expression of this kind of pain, while in other circumstances this tightness of the face expresses another kind of pain and this cry yet another.

The representational, formal, and expressive dimensions of art function similarly as criteria for calling anything art. This is a conceptual claim that is put forward in order to elucidate and organize our linguistic and conceptual practice, in a situation in which we are confused by the varieties of artistic practices, by the varieties of things people say about them, and by the powerful but obscure character of our own responses. In the grip of these confusions, we are likely to emphasize one criterion too much at the expense of the others.[1] In some works one of the criteria may be much less clearly and obviously fulfilled. Purely instrumental music and abstract painting lack conspicuous and obvious representationality, even if it can be argued (as I have argued) that works of these kinds symbolize and explore abstract patterns of human action. Some political art lacks a conspicuous formal dimension (even if it can be argued that varieties of absorbing form may be much more plastic than we had

---

[1] See my discussion, explicating the work of Stanley Cavell, of criterial claims as claims of reason in Eldridge, *Leading a Human Life*, pp. 107–08.

thought). Some conceptual art lacks a conspicuous and obvious expressive dimension (even if it can be argued that wit and austerity of thought are expressive values that are embodied in the work). When all of these three dimensions – the representational, the formal, and the expressive – are either absent or at least not conspicuously present, then we tend to say that the object or action in question is not a work of art but rather a manufactured commodity or a routine action (not a performance) in the service of a more fully preplanned end. If a claim to art is nonetheless made on its behalf, then we require a special story about how this object or act (a thumbtack? a solving of a crossword puzzle?), in all its ordinariness, nonetheless counts. If such claims succeed, as they sometimes can, then that will typically be because it can be made out that the object or act in question possesses more representationality, formal interest, and expressiveness than had first met the eye or ear.

If this definition – a work of art presents a subject matter as a focus for thought and emotional attitude, distinctively fused to the imaginative exploration of material – is right, then it must help us to be clearer about what we are doing in making and attending to art and about why making and attending to art matter to us. It must, in particular, among other things play some role in identifying and evaluating works. It must sum up usefully the general kinds of things we do and might say in arguing the merits of a particular case: it must specify our criteria. Because, however, the criteria are multiple, because they are differently satisfiable in different media and against the backgrounds of different traditions and social contexts, and because special, innovative stories about how they might be satisfied are possible, this definition will not enable us to settle difficult cases of identification and evaluation sharply and unambiguously.[2] We will naturally have different ways as artists of undertaking to satisfy these criteria and different readinesses as members of an audience to respond to different strategies for their satisfaction. We can hope to talk out some different responses in critical conversation and so come to see more of another's point in responding to the work,[3] but it is unlikely that there will be universal agreement in either interpretation or evaluation.

Anne Sheppard has observed that works of literature (and by implication works of art in general) are like metaphors.[4] In representing and expressing, but in a novel way, with a special focus on the materials of

---

[2] See chapter 7 above.   [3] See chapters 6 and 7 above.
[4] Sheppard, *Aesthetics*, pp. 119–31.

a medium (words, line and color, sound as tone, space and volume, etc.), works of art, like metaphors, invite interpretation. Comparisons among different works are possible and useful. Critical elucidation and para-phrase of metaphors and works of art is open-ended, as new aspects of wording or other formal arrangements are noticed; elucidations and paraphrases are sometimes contested among different responders. The metaphor and the work seem to "show" something, in and through their specific materials, as much as to "say" it. We are aware of and alert to the "presence" of an artist in the metaphor and in the work, in having a sense of a governing intentionality trying to mean something distinctive (and not wholly preplanned) by the work and through its formed elements. Though we may be initially puzzled and provoked into interpretation, ad-vances in clarity about the meanings of works and metaphors is possible through critical elucidation and other forms of the understanding of art.

Why do we make metaphors and art? Why do we undertake to mean or represent things expressively and in distinctive formal arrangements, otherwise than as straightforward statements? Monroe Beardsley claims that the successful work of art affords

> a remarkable kind of *clarification*, as though the jumble in our minds were being sorted out...In aesthetic experience we have experience in which means and end are so closely interrelated that we feel no separation between them. One thing leads to the next and finds its place in it; the end is immanent in the beginning, the beginning is carried up into the end. Such experience allows the least emptiness, monstrosity, frustration, lack of fulfillment, and despair – the qualities that cripple much of human life.[5]

The experience of art – both of making art and of following its significant gestures – offers an anticipation of human expressive freedom and full meaningfulness: of mind representing objects and actions, expressing and clarifying attitudes toward them, through the dense, attentive working of the materials of a medium.

Making and attending to art take place, however, under what Dewey calls the condition of "the incoherence of our [modern] civilization,"[6] with its pervasive commodity production, intense and extensive division of labor, and consequent social antagonisms. In this condition it becomes

---

[5] Beardsley, *Aesthetics*, pp. 574, 575.   [6] Dewey, *Art as Experience*, p. 337.

difficult, often, to see the satisfying realization of freely chosen purposes in work and in life. Art, according to Dewey, helps us to catch glimpses of widely endorsable free purposiveness in representation and expression that is embodied in the working of materials, so that it helps us to be not quite altogether dominated by "a babel of tongues"[7] and by pervasive social antagonisms. "Art has been," according to Dewey, "the means of keeping alive the sense of purposes that outrun evidence and of meanings that transcend indurated habit."[8] In presenting a subject matter as a focus for thought and emotional attitude, distinctively fused to the imaginative exploration of material, art provides the evidence of things not seen.

---

[7] *ibid.*, p. 336. Compare also George Steiner's thought that art is what helps us to live during the "long Saturday" between the Friday of crucifixion (pervasive antagonism, envy, felt meaninglessness) and the Sunday of the resurrection (achieved meaningfulness and reciprocity within sensuous human life). See George Steiner, *Real Presences* (Chicago, IL: University of Chicago Press, 1989), pp. 231–32.

[8] Dewey, *Art as Experience*, p. 348.

Bibliography

Abrams, M. H., *Doing Things with Texts: Essays in Criticism and Critical Theory*, ed. Michael Fischer (New York: W. W. Norton, 1989).

Abrams, M. H., *The Mirror and the Lamp* (Oxford: Oxford University Press, 1953).

Abrams, M. H., *Natural Supernaturalism: Tradition and Revolution in Romantic Literature* (New York: W. W. Norton, 1971).

Adams, Hazard, and Searle, Leroy (eds.), *Critical Theory Since 1965* (Tallahassee, FL: Florida State University Press, 1986).

Adorno, Theodor W., *Aesthetic Theory*, ed. and trans. Robert Hullot-Kentor (Minneapolis, MN: University of Minnesota Press, 1997).

Adorno, Theodor W., *Negative Dialectics*, trans. E. B. Ashton (New York: Continuum, 1973).

Adorno, Theodor, "Resignation," *Telos* 35 (spring 1968), pp. 165–68.

Althusser, Louis, "Ideology and Ideological State Apparatuses," trans. Ben Brewster, reprinted in *Critical Theory Since 1965*, ed. Adams and Searle, pp. 239–50.

Altieri, Charles, *Subjective Agency* (Oxford: Basil Blackwell, 1994).

Aristotle, *Poetics*, trans. Richard Janko (Indianapolis, IN: Hackett, 1987).

Aristotle, *Rhetoric*, trans. W. Rhys Roberts, in *The Basic Works of Aristotle*, ed. Richard McKeon (New York: Random House, 1941), pp. 1325–451.

Bahktin, Mikhail M., *The Dialogic Imagination*, ed. Michael Holquist, trans. Caryl Emerson and Michael Holquist (Austin, TX: University of Texas Press, 1981).

Barrell, John, *Poetry, Language and Politics* (Manchester: Manchester University Press, 1988).

Barthes, Roland, "The Death of the Author," (1968); reprinted in *Philosophy of Art*, ed. Neill and Ridley, pp. 386–90.

Battersby, Christine, *Gender and Genius: Towards a Feminist Aesthetics* (London: Women's Press, 1989; reprinted Bloomington, IN: Indiana University Press, 1990).

Baxandall, Michael, *Patterns of Intention: On the Historical Explanation of Pictures* (New Haven, CT: Yale University Press, 1985).

Beardsley, Monroe C., *Aesthetics: Problems in the Philosophy of Criticism*, 2nd edn (Indianapolis, IN: Hackett, 1981).

Beardsley, Monroe C., *Aesthetics from Classical Greece to the Present: A Short History* (University, AL: University of Alabama Press, 1975).

Bell, Clive, *Art* (1914), chapter 1, "The Aesthetic Hypothesis," reprinted in *Philosophy of Art*, ed. Neill and Ridley, pp. 99–110.

Benjamin, Walter, "The Work of Art in the Age of Mechanical Reproduction," in Walter Benjamin, *Illuminations*, trans. Harry Zohn, ed. Hannah Arendt (New York: Harcourt, Brace, & World, 1968), pp. 217–51.

Berger, John, *Ways of Seeing* (Harmondsworth: Penguin, 1972).

Bernstein, J. M., "Aesthetics, Modernism, Literature: Cavell's Transformations of Philosophy," in *Stanley Cavell*, ed. R. Eldridge (Cambridge: Cambridge University Press, 2003), pp. 107–42.

Binkley, Timothy, "Piece: Contra Aesthetics," *Journal of Aesthetics and Art Criticism* 35 (1977), pp. 265–77; reprinted in *Philosophy Looks at the Arts*, ed. Margolis, pp. 25–44.

Bloom, Harold, *The Anxiety of Influence: A Theory of Poetry* (Oxford: Oxford University Press, 1973).

Booth, Wayne C., *The Company we Keep: An Ethics of Fiction* (Berkeley, CA: University of California Press, 1988).

Bourdieu, Pierre, *Distinction: A Social Critique of the Judgement of Taste*, trans. Richard Nice (Cambridge, MA: Harvard University Press, 1984).

Brooks, Cleanth, *The Well Wrought Urn* (New York: Reynal & Hitchcock, 1947).

Carroll, Noël, "Art and Ethical Criticism: An Overview of Recent Directions of Research," *Ethics* 110, 2 (January 2000), pp. 350–87.

Carroll, Noël, "Art, Narrative, and Moral Understanding," in *Aesthetics and Ethics*, ed. Levinson, pp. 126–60.

Carroll, Noël, *Beyond Aesthetics: Philosophical Essays* (Cambridge: Cambridge University Press, 2001).

Carroll, Noël, "Moderate Moralism," *British Journal of Aesthetics* 36, 3 (1996), pp. 223–37.

Carroll, Noël, "Morality and Aesthetics: Historical and Conceptual Overview," in *Encyclopedia of Aesthetics*, ed. Kelly, vol. III, pp. 79–82.

Carroll, Noël, *Philosophy of Art: A Contemporary Introduction* (London: Routledge, 1999).

Carroll, Noël, *The Philosophy of Horror, or Paradoxes of the Heart* (London: Routledge, 1990).

Carroll, Noël, *A Philosophy of Mass Art* (Oxford: Clarendon Press, 1998).

Carroll, Noël, "The Wheel of Virtue: Art, Literature, and Moral Knowledge," *Journal of Aesthetics and Art Criticism* 60, 1 (winter 2002), pp. 3–26.

Cavell, Stanley, "Aesthetic Problems of Modern Philosophy," in Cavell, *Must We Mean What We Say?*, pp. 73–96.

Cavell, Stanley, "Being Odd, Getting Even," in Cavell, *In Quest of the Ordinary*, pp. 105–49.

Cavell, Stanley, *In Quest of the Ordinary: Lines of Skepticism and Romanticism* (Chicago, IL: University of Chicago Press, 1988).

Cavell, Stanley, "Music Discomposed," in Cavell, *Must We Mean What We Say?*, pp. 180–212.

Cavell, Stanley, *Must We Mean What We Say?* (New York: Charles Scribner's Sons, 1969).

Cavell, Stanley, *This New yet Unapproachable America: Lectures after Emerson after Wittgenstein* (Albuquerque, NM: Living Batch Press, 1989).

Chipp, Herschel B. (ed.), *Theories of Modern Art* (Berkeley, CA: University of California Press, 1968).

Chua, Daniel K. L., *Absolute Music and the Construction of Meaning* (Cambridge: Cambridge University Press, 1999).

Cohen, Ted, "Aesthetic/non-Aesthetic and the Concept of Taste: A Critique of Sibley's Position," *Theoria* 29 (1973), pp. 113–52; reprinted in *Aesthetics*, ed. Dickie and Sclafani, pp. 838–66.

Cohen, Ted, "High and Low Thinking About High and Low Art," *Journal of Aesthetics and Art Criticism* 51, 2 (spring 1993), pp. 151–56.

Cohen, Ted, "Identifying with Metaphor: Metaphors of Personal Identification," *Journal of Aesthetics and Art Criticism* 57, 4 (fall 1999), pp. 399–409.

Cohen, Ted, "Television: Contemporary Thought," in *Encyclopedia of Aesthetics*, ed. Kelly, vol. IV, pp. 369–70.

Cohen, Ted, "Three Problems in Kant's Aesthetics," *British Journal of Aesthetics* 42, 1 (January 2002), pp. 1–12.

Cohen, Ted, and Guyer, Paul (eds.), *Essays in Kant's Aesthetics* (Chicago, IL: University of Chicago Press, 1982).

Coleridge, Samuel Taylor, *Biographia Literaria*, ed. George Watson (London: J. M. Dent, 1965).

Collingwood, R. G., *The Principles of Art* (Oxford: Clarendon Press, 1938).

Crisp, Roger, and Slote, Michael (eds.), *Virtue Ethics* (Oxford: Oxford University Press, 1997).

Currie, Gregory, "The Moral Psychology of Fiction," *Australasian Journal of Philosophy* 73 (1995), pp. 250–59.

Currie, Gregory, "Realism of Character and the Value of Fiction," in *Aesthetics and Ethics*, ed. Levinson, pp. 161–81.

Dahlhaus, Carl, *The Idea of Absolute Music*, trans. Roger Lustig (Chicago, IL: University of Chicago Press, 1989).

Danto, Arthur C., *Embodied Meanings: Critical Essays and Aesthetic Meditations* (New York: Farrar, Straus, & Giroux, 1994).

Danto, Arthur C., "Philosophy as/and/of Literature," *Grand Street* 3, 3 (spring 1984), pp. 151–76.

Danto, Arthur C., "The Space of Beauty: Review of *The Power of the Center: A Study of Composition in the Visual Arts* by Rudolf Arnheim," *New Republic* (November 15, 1982), pp. 32B–35B.

Danto, Arthur C., *The Transfiguration of the Commonplace* (Cambridge, MA: Harvard University Press, 1981).

Danto, Arthur C., *The Wake of Art: Criticism, Philosophy, and the Ends of Taste*, ed. Gregg Horowitz and Tom Huhn (Amsterdam: Overseas Publishers Association, 1998).

Davidson, Donald, "The Second Person," in Davidson, *Subjective, Intersubjective, Objective*, pp. 107–21.

Davidson, Donald, *Subjective, Intersubjective, Objective* (Oxford: Clarendon Press, 2001).

Davies, Stephen, *Musical Meaning and Expression* (Ithaca, NY: Cornell University Press, 1994).

Derrida, Jacques, *Of Grammatology*, trans. Gayatri Chakravorty Spivak (Baltimore, MD: Johns Hopkins University Press, 1974).

Derrida, Jacques, "Structure, Sign and Play in the Discourse of the Human Sciences," in *Structuralist Controversy*, ed. Macksey and Donato, pp. 247–65.

Dewey, John, *Art as Experience* (New York: Penguin Putnam, 1934).

Dickie, George, *Art and the Aesthetic* (Ithaca, NY: Cornell University Press, 1974).

Dickie, George, *The Art Circle* (New York: Haven Publications, 1984).

Dickie, George, and Sclafani, Richard J. (eds.), *Aesthetics: A Critical Anthology* (New York: St. Martin's Press, 1977).

Duchamp, Marcel, "Interview with James Johnson Sweeney," in "Eleven Europeans in America," *Bulletin of the Museum of Modern Art* (New York) 12, 4–5 (1946); reprinted in *Theories of Modern Art*, ed. Chipp, pp. 392–95.

Eaton, Marcia, "Morality and Ethics: Contemporary Aesthetics and Ethics," in *The Encyclopedia of Philosophy*, ed. Kelly, vol. III, pp. 282–85.

Eldridge, Richard, "Aesthetics and Ethics," in *Oxford Handbook to Aesthetics*, ed. Levinson, pp. 722–32.

Eldridge, Richard, "Althusser and Ideological Criticism of the Arts," in *Explanation and Value in the Arts*, ed. Ivan Gaskell and Salim Kemal; reprinted in Eldridge, *Persistence of Romanticism*, pp. 165–88.

Eldridge, Richard, "Form and Content: An Aesthetic Theory of Art," *British Journal of Aesthetics* 25, 4 (autumn 1985), pp. 303–16; reprinted in *Philosophy of Art*, ed. Neill and Ridley, pp. 239–53.

Eldridge, Richard, *Leading a Human Life: Wittgenstein, Intentionality, and Romanticism* (Chicago, IL: University of Chicago Press, 1997).

Eldridge, Richard, *On Moral Personhood: Philosophy, Literature, Criticism, and Self-Understanding* (Chicago, IL: University of Chicago Press, 1987).

Eldridge, Richard, *The Persistence of Romanticism: Essays in Philosophy and Literature* (Cambridge: Cambridge University Press, 2001).

Eldridge, Richard, "Problems and Prospects of Wittgensteinian Aesthetics," *Journal of Aesthetics and Art Criticism* 45, 3 (spring 1987), pp. 251–61.

Emerson, Ralph Waldo, "Self-Reliance," in *Selections from Ralph Waldo Emerson*, ed. Stephen E. Whicher (Boston, MA: Houghton Mifflin, 1957), pp. 147–68.

Feagin, Susan L., *Reading with Feeling* (Ithaca, NY: Cornell University Press, 1996).

Fish, Stanley, "Is there a Text in this Class?," in S. Fish, *Is there a Text in this Class* (Cambridge, MA: Harvard University Press, 1980); reprinted in *Critical Theory Since 1965*, ed. Adams and Searle, pp. 525–33.

Foster, Hal, "Postmodernism: A Preface," in *The Anti-Aesthetic: Essays on Post-Modern Culture*, ed. H. Foster (Port Townsend, WA: Bay Press, 1983), pp. ix–xvi.

Foster, Hal, *The Return of the Real* (Cambridge, MA: MIT Press, 1996).

Foucault, Michel, *The Order of Things*, trans. not named (New York: Random House, 1970).

Foucault, Michel, "What is an Author?," in *Critical Theory Since 1965*, ed. Adams and Searle, pp. 138–48.

Freeland, Cynthia, *But is it Art?* (Oxford: Oxford University Press, 2001).

Fried, Michael, *Absorption and Theatricality: Painting and Beholder in the Age of Diderot* (Berkeley, CA: University of California Press, 1980).

Fried, Michael, *Art and Objecthood: Essays and Reviews* (Chicago, IL: University of Chicago Press, 1998).

Frye, Northrop, "The Drunken Boat," in *Romanticism Reconsidered*, ed. N. Frye (New York: Columbia University Press, 1963), pp. 1–25.

Furtak, Rick Anthony, "Poetics of Sentimentality," *Philosophy and Literature* 26, 1 (April 2002), pp. 207–15.

Gallie, W. B., "Is *The Prelude* a Philosophical Poem?," *Philosophy* 22 (1947), pp. 124–38; reprinted in Wordsworth, *Prelude 1799, 1805, 1850*, pp. 663–78.

Gardner, John, *On Moral Fiction* (New York: Harper Collins, 1978).

Gaskell, Ivan, *Vermeer's Wager: Speculations on Art History, Theory, and Museums* (London: Reaktion, 2000).

Gaskell, Ivan, and Kemal, Salim (eds.), *Explanation and Value in the Arts* (Cambridge: Cambridge University Press, 1993).

Gaut, Berys, "The Ethical Criticism of Art," in *Aesthetics and Ethics*, ed. Levinson, pp. 182–203.

Goffen, Rona (ed.), *Titian's Venus of Urbino* (Cambridge: Cambridge University Press, 1997).

Goldman, Alan, "Representation: Conceptual and Historical Overview," in *Encyclopedia of Aesthetics*, ed. Kelly, vol. IV, pp. 137A–139B.

Goodman, Nelson, *The Languages of Art*, 2nd edn (Indianapolis, IN: Hackett, 1976.

Goodman, Nelson, *Ways of Worldmaking* (Indianapolis, IN: Hackett, 1978).

Gould, Timothy, "The Audience of Originality: Kant and Wordsworth on the Reception of Genius," in *Essays in Kant's Aesthetics*, ed. Cohen and Guyer, pp. 179–93.

Gould, Timothy, "Genius: Conceptual and Historical Overview," in *Encyclopedia of Aesthetics*, ed. Kelly, vol. II, pp. 287–92.

Guyer, Paul, *Kant and the Claims of Taste* (Cambridge, MA: Harvard University Press, 1979).

Hagberg, G. L., *Art as Language: Wittgenstein, Meaning, and Aesthetic Theory* (Ithaca, NY: Cornell University Press, 1995).

Hampshire, Stuart, "Logic and Appreciation," *World Review* (October 1952); reprinted in *Art and Philosophy*, ed. Kennick, pp. 651–57.

Hanson, Karen, "How Bad Can Good Art Be?," in *Aesthetics and Ethics*, ed. Levinson, pp. 204–26.

Harrison, Bernard, *Inconvenient Fictions: Literature and the Limits of Theory* (New Haven, CT: Yale University Press, 1991).

Hegel, G. W. F., *Aesthetics: Lectures on Fine Art*, trans. T. M. Knox (Oxford: Clarendon Press, 1975).

Hegel, G. W. F., *Elements of the Philosophy of Right*, ed. Allen W. Wood, trans. H. B. Nisbet (Cambridge: Cambridge University Press, 1991).

Hegel, G. W. F., *Phenomenology of Spirit*, trans. A. V. Miller (Oxford: Clarendon Press, 1977).

Heidegger, Martin, "The Origin of the Work of Art," trans. Albert Hofstadter, in *Poetry, Language, Thought* (New York: Harper & Row, 1971), pp. 17–87.

Hölderlin, Friedrich, *Essays and Letters on Theory*, ed. and trans. Thomas Pfau (Albany, NY: State University of New York Press, 1988).

Horowitz, Gregg, and Huhn, Tom, "The Wake of Art: Criticism, Philosophy, and the Ends of Taste," in Danto, *Wake of Art*, pp. 1–56.

Huhn, Tom, book review, "*The Field of Cultural Production: Essays on Art and Literature* by Pierre Bourdieu," *Journal of Aesthetics and Art Criticism* 54, 7 (winter 1996), pp. 88–90.

Hume, David, *An Enquiry Concerning Human Understanding*, ed. Eric Steinberg (Indianapolis, IL: Hackett, 1977).

Hume, David, "Of the Standard of Taste," in *Philosophy of Art*, ed. Neill and Ridley, pp. 255–68.

Hume, David, "Of Tragedy," in D. Hume, *Essays Moral, Political and Literary* (Oxford: Oxford University Press, 1963), pp. 221–30.

Hutcheson, Francis, *An Inquiry Concerning Beauty, Harmony, and Design*, ed. Peter Kivy (The Hague: Martinus Nijhoff, 1973).

Isenberg, Arnold, "Critical Communication," *Philosophical Review* 57 (July 1949), pp. 330–44; reprinted in *Philosophy of Art*, ed. Neill and Ridley, pp. 363–73.

Kant, Immanuel, *Critique of the Power of Judgment*, trans. Paul Guyer and Eric Matthews (Cambridge: Cambridge University Press, 2000).

Kelly, Michael (ed.), *Encyclopedia of Aesthetics*, 4 vols. (Oxford: Oxford University Press, 1998).

Kemal, Salim, *Kant's Aesthetic Theory: An Introduction* (New York: St. Martin's Press, 1992).

Kennick, W. E., "Does Traditional Aesthetics Rest on a Mistake?," *Mind* 67, 267 (July 1958); reprinted in *Aesthetics Today*, ed. Philipson and Gudel, pp. 459–76.

Kennick, W. E. (ed.), *Art and Philosophy*, 2nd edn (New York: St. Martin's Press, 1979).

Kerman, Joseph, *Contemplating Music* (Cambridge, MA: Harvard University Press, 1985).

Kieran, Matthew, "Art, Imagination, and the Cultivation of Morals," *Journal of Aesthetics and Art Criticism* 54, 4 (fall 1996), pp. 337–51.

Kivy, Peter, *The Chorded Shell: Reflections on Musical Expression* (Princeton, NJ: Princeton University Press, 1980).

Kivy, Peter, "Recent Scholarship and the British Tradition: A Logic of Taste – The First Fifty Years," in *Aesthetics: A Critical Anthology*, ed. Dickie and Sclafani, pp. 626–42.

Kramer, Lawrence, *Classical Music and Postmodern Knowledge* (Berkeley, CA: University of California Press, 1995).

Kristeller, Paul Oskar, "The Modern System of the Arts," *Journal of the History of Ideas* 12 (1951, 1952); reprinted in *Art and Philosophy*, ed. Kennick, pp. 7–33.

Levinson, Jerrold (ed.), *Aesthetics and Ethics: Essays at the Intersection* (Cambridge: Cambridge University Press, 1998).

Levinson, Jerrold, "Defining Art Historically," *British Journal of Aesthetics* 19 (1979); reprinted in *Philosophy of Art*, ed. Neill and Ridley, pp. 223–39.

Levinson, Jerrold, "Music and Negative Emotion," in *Music and Meaning*, ed. Robinson, pp. 215–41.

Levinson, Jerrold (ed.), *The Oxford Handbook to Aesthetics* (Oxford: Oxford University Press, 2003).

Lévi-Strauss, Claude, *The Raw and the Cooked: Introduction to a Science of Mythology*, volume I, trans. John Weightman and Doreen Weightman (New York: Harper & Row, 1969).

Lippard, Lucy, "The Spirit and the Letter," *Art in America* 80, 4 (April 1990), pp. 238–45.

Lopes, Dominic M. McIver, "Representation: Depiction," in *Encyclopedia of Aesthetics*, ed. Kelly, vol. IV, pp. 139B–143B.

Lukács, Georg, "Art and Objective Truth," (1954); reprinted in *Critical Theory Since 1965*, ed. Adams and Searle, pp. 791–807.

Lyas, Colin, *Aesthetics* (Montreal: McGill-Queen's University Press, 1997).

Macksey, Richard, and Donato, Eugenio (eds.), *The Structuralist Controversy: The Languages of Criticism and the Sciences of Man* (Baltimore, MD: Johns Hopkins University Press, 1972).

Mandelbaum, Maurice, "Family Resemblances and Generalization Concerning the Arts," *American Philosophical Quarterly* 2, 3 (1965); reprinted in *Philosophy of Art*, ed. Neill and Ridley, pp. 193–201.

Marcuse, Herbert, *The Aesthetic Dimension: Toward A Critique of Marxist Aesthetics*, trans. Erica Sherover (Boston, MA: Beacon Press, 1977).

Margolis, Joseph (ed.), *Philosophy Looks at the Arts*, revised edn (Philadelphia, PN: Temple University Press, 1978).

Marx, Karl, "Economico-Philosophic Manuscripts of 1844," in *The Portable Karl Marx*, ed. Eugene Kamenka (Harmondsworth: Penguin, 1983), pp. 131–52.

Maus, Fred Everett, "Music as Drama," in *Music and Meaning*, ed. J. Robinson, pp. 105–30.

McClary, Susan, *Feminine Endings: Music, Gender, and Sexuality* (Minneapolis, MN: University of Minnesota Press, 1991).

McLaughlin, Thomas M., "Clive Bell's Aesthetic: Tradition and Significant Form," *Journal of Aesthetics and Art Criticism* 35, 4 (summer 1977), pp. 433–43.

Meltzer, Françoise, "Originality in Literature," in *Encyclopedia of Aesthetics*, ed. Kelly, vol. III, pp. 413–16.

Meyer, Leonard B., *Music, the Arts, and Ideas: Patterns and Predictions in Twentieth-Century Culture*, new edn (Chicago, IL: University of Chicago Press, 1994).

Mill, J. S., "On Liberty," in J. S. Mill, *Utilitarianism; On Liberty; Essay on Bentham*, ed. Mary Warnock (New York: New American Library, 1974), pp. 126–250.

Mothersill, Mary, *Beauty Restored* (Oxford: Clarendon Press, 1984).

Mullin, Amy, "Evaluating Art: Morally Significant Imagining Versus Moral Soundness," *Journal of Aesthetics and Art Criticism* 60, 2 (spring 2002), pp. 137–48.

Murdoch, Iris, *Metaphysics as a Guide to Morals* (Harmondsworth: Penguin, 1991).

Nehamas, Alexander, "Return of the Beautiful: Morality, Pleasure, and the Value of Uncertainty," *Journal of Aesthetics and Art Criticism* 58, 4 (fall 2000), pp. 392–403.

Neill, Alex, "'An Unaccountable Pleasure': Hume on Tragedy and the Passions," *Hume Studies* 24, 2 (November 1998), pp. 335–54.

Neill, Alex, "Fear, Fiction, and Make-Believe," *Journal of Aesthetics and Art Criticism* 49, 1 (winter 1991), pp. 47–56.

Neill, Alex, "Hume's 'Singular Phenomenon,'" *British Journal of Aesthetics* 39, 2 (April 1999), pp. 112–25.

Neill, Alex, and Ridley, Aaron (eds.), *The Philosophy of Art: Readings Ancient and Modern* (New York: McGraw-Hill, 1995).

Newcomb, Anthony, "Action and Agency in Mahler's Ninth Symphony, Second Movement," in *Music and Meaning*, ed. J. Robinson, pp. 131–53.

Nietzsche, Friedrich, *The Birth of Tragedy and the Case of Wagner*, trans. Walter Kaufmann (New York: Random House, 1967).

Nussbaum, Martha C., "Exactly and Responsibly: A Defense of Ethical Criticism," *Philosophy and Literature* 22, 2 (October 1998), pp. 343–65.

Nussbaum, Martha C., *The Fragility of Goodness: Luck and Ethics in Greek Tragedy and Philosophy* (Cambridge: Cambridge University Press, 1986).

Nussbaum, Martha C., "Literature and Ethical Theory: Allies or Adversaries?," *Yale Journal of Ethics* 9 (2000), pp. 5–16.

Nussbaum, Martha C., *Love's Knowledge: Essays on Philosophy and Literature* (Oxford: Oxford University Press, 1990).

Paddison, Max, *Adorno's Aesthetics of Music* (Cambridge: Cambridge University Press, 1993).

Palmer, Frank, *Literature and Moral Understanding* (Oxford: Clarendon Press, 1992).

Pavel, Thomas G., *Fictional Worlds* (Cambridge, MA: Harvard University Press, 1986).

Philipson, M., and Gudel, P. J. (eds.), *Aesthetics Today*, revised edn (New York: New American Library, 1980).

Pillow, Kirk, *Sublime Understanding* (Cambridge, MA: MIT Press, 2001).

Pippin, Robert B., *Henry James and Modern Moral Life* (Cambridge: Cambridge University Press, 2000).

Plato, *Ion*, trans. Lane Cooper, in Plato, *The Collected Dialogues*, ed. Edith Hamilton and Huntingdon Cairns (Princeton, NJ: Princeton University Press, 1961), pp. 215–28.

Plato, *Republic*, trans. G. M. A. Grube, revised C. D. C. Reeve (Indianapolis, IN: Hackett, 1992).

Plato, *Symposium*, trans. Alexander Nehamas and Paul Woodruff (Indianapolis, IN: Hackett, 1989).

Posner, Richard, "Against Ethical Criticism," *Philosophy and Literature* 21, 1 (April 1997), pp. 1–27.

Putnam, Hilary, "Literature, Science, and Reflection," in H. Putnam, *Meaning and the Moral Sciences* (London: Routledge & Kegan Paul, 1978), pp. 83–96.

Robinson, Jenefer (ed.), *Music and Meaning* (Ithaca, NY: Cornell University Press, 1997).

Radford, Colin, "How can We be Moved by the Fate of Anna Karenina?," *Proceedings of the Aristotelian Society*, supplementary vol. 49 (1975), pp. 67–80.

Robinson, Lillian S., "Treason our Text: Feminist Challenges to the Literary Canon," *Tulsa Studies in Women's Literature* (1983); reprinted in *Critical Theory Since 1965*, ed. Adams and Searle, pp. 572–82.

Rorty, Richard, "The Contingency of Selfhood,' in R. Rorty, *Contingency, Irony, and Solidarity* (Cambridge: Cambridge University Press, 1989), pp. 23–43.

Savile, Anthony, *The Test of Time: An Essay in Philosophical Aesthetics* (Oxford: Clarendon Press, 1982).

Schapiro, Meyer, "On the Aesthetic Attitude in Romanesque Art," in M. Schapiro, *Romanesque Art: Selected Papers* (New York: G. Braziller, 1977), pp. 1–28.

Schier, Flint, *Deeper into Pictures: An Essay on Pictorial Representation* (Cambridge: Cambridge University Press, 1986).

Schiller, Friedrich, *Essays*, ed. Walter Hinderer and Daniel O. Dahlstrom (New York: Continuum, 1993).

Schiller, Friedrich, "On Naïve and Sentimental Poetry," trans. Daniel O. Dahlstrom, in Schiller, *Essays*, pp. 179–260.

Schiller, Friedrich, *On the Aesthetic Education of Man, in a Series of Letters*, trans. Reginald Snell (London: Routledge & Kegan Paul, 1954).

Schlegel, Friedrich, *Philosophical Fragments*, trans. Peter Firchow (Minneapolis, MN: University of Minnesota Press, 1991).

Saussure, Fernand de, *Course in General Linguistics*, trans. Wade Baskin (New York: McGraw Hill, 1959).

Scruton, Roger, *The Aesthetics of Music* (Oxford: Oxford University Press, 1997).

Scruton, Roger, *Art and Imagination* (London: Routledge & Kegan Paul, 1982).

Sheppard, Anne, *Aesthetics: An Introduction to the Philosophy of Art* (Oxford: Oxford University Press, 1987).

Shusterman, Richard, "Art as Dramatization," *Journal of Aesthetics and Art Criticism* 59, 4 (fall 2001), pp. 363–72.

Shusterman, Richard, *Practicing Philosophy: Pragmatism and the Philosophical Life* (London: Routledge, 1997).

Shusterman, Richard, *Pragmatist Aesthetics: Living Beauty, Rethinking Art* (Oxford: Basil Blackwell, 1992).

Sircello, Guy, "Arguing About Art," in *Aesthetics Today*, ed. Philipson and Gudel, pp. 477–96.

Sircello, Guy, *Mind and Art: An Essay on the Varieties of Expression* (Princeton, NJ: Princeton University Press, 1972).

Smith, Barbara Herrnstein, *Contingencies of Value: Alternative Perspectives for Critical Theory* (Cambridge, MA: Harvard University Press, 1988).

Steiner, George, *Real Presences* (Chicago, IL: University of Chicago Press, 1989).

Stolnitz, Jerome, "Of the Origins of 'Aesthetic Disinterestedness,'" in *Aesthetics: A Critical Anthology*, ed. Dickie and Sclafani, pp. 606–25.

Subotnik, Rose Rosengard, "How Could Chopin's A-Major Prelude be Deconstructed?," in R. R. Subotnik, *Deconstructive Variations: Music and Reason in Western Society* (Minneapolis, MN: University of Minnesota Press, 1996), pp. 39–147.

Tolstoy, Leo, *What is Art?*, trans. Aylmer Maude (Indianapolis, IN: Bobbs-Merrill, 1960).

Tomasello, Michael, *The Cultural Origins of Human Cognition* (Cambridge, MA: Harvard University Press, 1999).

Tormey, Alan, "Art and Expression: A Critique," in *Philosophy Looks at the Arts*, ed. Margolis, pp. 346–61.

Walton, Kendall, "Categories of Art," *Philosophical Review* 79 (1970), pp. 334–67; reprinted in *Philosophy Looks at the Arts*, ed. Margolis, pp. 88–114.

Walton, Kendall, *Mimesis as Make-Believe: On the Foundations of the Representational Arts* (Cambridge, MA: Harvard University Press, 1990).

Weintraub, Linda, *Art on the Edge and Over: Searching for Art's Meaning in Contemporary Society, 1970s–1990s* (Litchfield, CT: Art Insights, 1996).

Weitz, Morris, "The Role of Theory in Aesthetics," *Journal of Aesthetics and Art Criticism* 15 (1956); reprinted in *Philosophy of Art*, ed. Neill and Ridley, pp. 183–92.

Wilde, Oscar, "Preface," in *The Picture of Dorian Gray*, ed. Peter Ackroyd (Harmondsworth: Penguin, 1982).

Wittgenstein, Ludwig, *The Brown Book*, in Ludwig Wittgenstein, *The Blue and Brown Books* (New York: Harper & Row, 1958).

Wittgenstein, Ludwig, *Philosophical Investigations*, 3rd edn, trans. G. E. M. Anscombe (New York: Macmillan, 1958).

Wolfe, Tom, *The Painted Word* (New York: Farrar, Straus, & Giroux, 1975).

Wollheim, Richard, *Art and its Objects*, 2nd edn (Cambridge: Cambridge University Press, 1980).

Wollheim, Richard, *Painting as an Art* (Princeton, NJ: Princeton University Press, 1987).

Woodmansee, Martha, *The Author, Art, and the Market: Rereading the History of Aesthetics* (New York: Columbia University Press, 1994).

Woodruff, Paul, "Aristotle on Mimesis," in *Essays on Aristotle's Poetics*, ed. A. Rorty (Princeton, NJ: Princeton University Press, 1992), pp. 73–95.

Wordsworth, William, "Essay Supplementary to the Preface (1815)," in *Selected Poems and Prefaces*, ed. Stillinger, pp. 471–81.

Wordsworth, William, "Preface to Lyrical Ballads," in *Selected Poems and Prefaces*, ed. Stillinger, pp. 445–64.

Wordsworth, William, *The Prelude* (1850), in *Selected Poems and Prefaces*, ed. Stillinger, pp. 193–366.

Wordsworth, William, *The Prelude 1799, 1805, 1850*, ed. Jonathan Wordsworth, M. H. Abrams, and Stephen Gill (New York: W. W. Norton, 1979).

Wordsworth, William, *Selected Poems and Prefaces*, ed. Jack Stillinger (Boston, MA: Houghton Mifflin, 1965).

INDEX

✓ Sept 30, 2014 –◦ No Marking –H

LaVergne, TN USA
01 February 2011

214703LV00001B/111-130/P